Twelfth Edition

THE
BLUE BOOK
OF GRAMMAR AND
PUNCTUATION

An Easy-to-Use Guide with Clear Rules,
Real-World Examples, and Reproducible Quizzes

Lester Kaufman
Jane Straus

JB JOSSEY-BASS™
A Wiley Brand

Copyright ©2021 by Lester Kaufman. All rights reserved.

Jossey-Bass
A Wiley Imprint
111 River St, Hoboken, NJ 07030
www.josseybass.com

Jossey-Bass books and products are available through most bookstores. To contact Jossey-Bass directly, call our Customer Care Department within the U.S. at 800–956–7739, outside the U.S. at +1 317 572 3986, or fax +1 317 572 4002.

Wiley also publishes its books in a variety of electronic formats and by print-on-demand. Some material included with standard print versions of this book may not be included in e-books or in print-on-demand. If this book refers to media such as a CD or DVD that is not included in the version you purchased, you may download this material at http://booksupport.wiley.com. For more information about Wiley products, visit www.wiley.com.

Library of Congress Cataloging-in-Publication Data is Available:

ISBN 9781119653028 (paperback)
ISBN 9781119653035 (epdf)
ISBN 9781119652847 (ebook)

Cover design: Wiley

TWELFTH EDITION

SKY10027063_051721

This book is dedicated to my late wife, Jane Straus. She was a brilliant, multitalented woman with boundless energy and a natural gift for clarifying all matters complex. She put her heart and soul into everything she undertook. She was taken from us far too soon.
I am deeply grateful for the love and support of my wife, Ellen Kahn, and my daughter, Zoe, for putting up with the seemingly endless hours in my office improving and refining this new edition.

—LESTER KAUFMAN

CONTENTS

1 GRAMMAR   1

2 PUNCTUATION   31

3 CAPITALIZATION   69

4 WRITING NUMBERS   79

5   CONFUSING WORDS AND HOMONYMS   85

6   QUIZZES   155

7 ANSWERS TO QUIZZES 193

PREFACE AND ACKNOWLEDGMENTS

Jane Straus created her English language instructional materials because she "found no books that conveyed the rules of English in—well—plain English." Over the years of teaching basic English language skills to state and federal government employees as well as to individuals in the private sector and in nonprofit organizations, she refined her materials, eventually creating *The Blue Book of Grammar and Punctuation* and its related website, GrammarBook.com.

In the introduction to the tenth edition, the author spoke of her 2003 brain tumor diagnosis, how it led to her next bold steps in life, and her successful surgery to remove the tumor. Unfortunately, in 2009, she learned she had a new, unrelated brain tumor—this time malignant. Jane Ruth Straus passed away on February 25, 2011.

Due to the outpouring of appreciation for her work, her husband, Lester Kaufman, continued to oversee the GrammarBook.com website so that anyone around the world could still benefit from her life's work. He also collected ideas and suggestions for changes, new material, and improvements to *The Blue Book*. After making the acquaintance of Tom Stern, a Marin County, California, writer and editor, Kaufman recognized that Stern possessed the knowledge, skills, experience, and passion needed to thoroughly re-examine *The Blue Book* and revise it to make it a first-rate grammar resource for everyone.

First and foremost, thanks must go to the late Jane Straus for her vision and persistence in creating a reference guide and workbook that is popular and easy to understand.

We deeply appreciate the late writer and editor Tom Stern for his keen insights and creative additions to both the eleventh and twelfth editions. We also thank talented writer Jonathan

Davis and retired English teacher Patti Clements for their invaluable contributions to this edition's rules and guidance as well as their conscientious work on the quizzes.

We could not have succeeded in updating this book without the assistance of the staff and editors at Jossey-Bass and literary agent Cathy Fowler, who steadfastly believed in the book's value. We also thank the thousands of loyal readers of the GrammarBook.com website who, by offering valuable input daily, have helped shape the rules, examples, and quizzes.

ABOUT THE AUTHORS

Lester Kaufman is the publisher of GrammarBook.com. A lifelong public servant, he first served as a teacher in the Peace Corps, and eventually he completed the final years of his federal career with the U.S. Environmental Protection Agency. He married Jane Straus in 1987.

After his retirement from the Environmental Protection Agency, Kaufman began assisting with the operation of Straus's fledgling website and helped edit previous editions of *The Blue Book of Grammar and Punctuation.*

Following Jane Straus's untimely passing in February 2011, Kaufman assumed management of GrammarBook.com, which features an informative and entertaining weekly newsletter that encourages readers to ask grammar questions and offer their views on the state of twenty-first-century English.

Jane Straus (1954–2011) was an educator, life coach, and best-selling author. To prepare for a job teaching English to employees of the state of California in 1975, Straus scoured the library for materials that conveyed the rules of grammar and punctuation in plain English. Finding no such resources, she wrote the rules her own way, made up exercises, ran off some copies, and hoped for the best.

The class was a hit. More and more state employees demanded that they get an equal opportunity to benefit from Straus's no-nonsense instruction in English grammar and usage. She continued to refine her materials, eventually turning them into *The Blue Book of Grammar and Punctuation.*

When the Internet was born, she launched a website, GrammarBook.com, which has helped millions of people all over the world improve their English grammar. Straus became a sought-after speaker in the fields of grammar, public speaking, and life coaching. Her other book is *Enough Is Enough! Stop Enduring and Start Living Your Extraordinary Life* (Jossey-Bass, 2005).

INTRODUCTION

Now in its twelfth edition, *The Blue Book of Grammar and Punctuation* will help you write and speak with confidence. You don't have to be an English major to understand grammar and punctuation. You just need rules and guidelines that are easy to understand, with real-world examples.

Whether you are an instructor who is teaching students the rules of English, or a student, executive, professional writer, or avid blogger honing your grammar and punctuation skills, this book will help you zip through tests (including the SAT), reports, essays, letters, e-mails, and résumés. It will help you (and your writing) impress your teachers, your bosses, your clients, and other readers.

Every generation of English scholars despairs because the language always seems to be at a crisis point. But it is undeniable that everywhere one looks nowadays, the principles in this book are casually and cavalierly violated.

The Blue Book will prove to be a valuable tool for teachers and students in achieving the goals of the Common Core State Standards Initiative. Studying the chapters and working through the quizzes will provide students of all ages with the skills and knowledge they need to succeed beyond high school—in college and in the workplace. Students will learn how to use formal English in their writing and speaking and how to better express themselves through language. We also recommend reading the works of great writers to experience firsthand the art and beauty of effective communication.

This book is logical, self-paced, and fun to use, with scores of interesting and challenging quizzes that you may photocopy to your heart's content. Best of all, you can look forward to instant gratification, because the answers to the quizzes are included.

Throughout the text, certain terms have been set in boldface type (for instance, at the beginning of Chapter One, **noun, common nouns, proper nouns**). Due to space and other considerations, we could not always explore these linguistic terms as thoroughly as we might have wished. Readers are strongly urged to look further into these terms on their own. We also recommend that those who are serious about improving their English grammar always keep a dictionary close by and use it assiduously.

If you don't have time to research several leading reference books to figure out where the next comma should go or whether to write *who* or *whom*, you will find *The Blue Book* to be a pleasure to use. Dedicated to eliminating unnecessary jargon, it highlights the most important grammar, punctuation, and capitalization rules and guidelines and clarifies some of the language's most confusing and confounding words.

Throughout the book, we use the word *rule* in a liberal sense. The boundary between *rule* and *guideline* can be blurry. The *rule* stated by one writing style guide may differ from the *rule* in another. In many of these cases, we will state the predominant or sensible practice but then illustrate other acceptable methods. The most important *guideline* in such cases is simply to be consistent in your own writing.

In Chapter One, "Grammar," you will learn how to find nouns, verbs, and subjects and make sure they agree with one another. We will talk about the unpredictable behavior of irregular verbs. Next, you will learn about clauses and phrases, the keys to understanding sentence structure. Then, on to pronoun usage, so that you will know whether to write *I* or *me, he* or *him, who* or *whom*, etc. In this twelfth edition, we include pronoun guidance recognizing the value of gender-neutral language, which aims to treat people equally and is inclusive of people whose gender identity is not strictly male or female.

From there, in the "Adjectives and Adverbs" section, you will discover why some words have *-ly* added to them, and why you must say, "I did well on the test," rather than "I did good on the test." After that, you will breeze through prepositions, learning some surprising rules, and we will debunk at least one myth. (*Hint*: Is it safe to ask, "What are you talking about?" or must we ask, "About what are you talking?")

The "Effective Writing" section of Chapter One will give you helpful tips for constructing sentences and paragraphs that flow gracefully, making it easier to write quickly and well.

Chapter Two, "Punctuation," takes on all the usual suspects: proper spacing with punctuation and the proper use of periods, commas, semicolons, colons, quotation marks, question marks, parentheses and brackets, apostrophes, hyphens, dashes, ellipses, exclamation points, and slashes. The best part about this and other chapters is that you will find an abundance of examples that you run across every day.

Then comes Chapter Three, "Capitalization," in which you will get your most vexing questions answered, learning which words to capitalize in a title and when to capitalize job titles, such as *president* or *director*.

In Chapter Four, "Writing Numbers," you will learn the importance of consistency when using numerals or writing out numbers. You will also learn how to write fractions and large numbers.

After that, you will enjoy spending time reading all about *affect* vs. *effect*, *lay* vs. *lie*, *their* vs. *there* vs. *they're*, and *its* vs. *it's* in Chapter Five, "Confusing Words and Homonyms." We have provided hundreds of words and phrases for you in this chapter, so you will never again have to be confused by the differences between *farther* and *further*, *continual* and *continuous*, *flaunt* and *flout*, *tortuous* and *torturous*, and all the rest of the trickiest and most commonly misused words and phrases in the English language.

Promise not to skip the quizzes, pretests, or mastery tests in Chapter Six, "Quizzes." The more you practice, the more confident you will become. Once you get over any fears about test taking, we think you will find the quizzes both enjoyable and challenging. You will find the answers in Chapter Seven, "Answers to Quizzes."

Please visit www.GrammarBook.com, where you will find the quizzes in the book in a multiple-choice, interactive format. If you are a teacher or are really jazzed about improving your English skills, on the website you will also find

- Hundreds of additional downloadable, interactive quizzes in the "Subscription" area
- All the rules and examples you see in the book
- A sign-up box on the home page for our free, weekly e-newsletter with tips and articles
- Our blog containing over 500 articles, including reader questions and our responses, extensively exploring English grammar and punctuation more broadly than possible in the book.
- Dozens of free one-minute videos by Jane Straus on English language usage
- Recommendations for further reading and study

The Blue Book of Grammar and Punctuation and the website represent American English rules and guidelines. Explore the Grammar Blog tab on the website, which includes some exploration of the differences between US and UK English.

The point of grammar proficiency is to be clear and direct and to avoid misunderstanding. We hope you will come away from this book with this mantra: "Think before you write." Be sure every sentence conveys what you mean, with no possibility of ambiguity or inadvertent meaninglessness.

That being said, as George Orwell wrote in 1946, "Break any of these rules sooner than say anything outright barbarous."

We hope you find *The Blue Book* to be both enjoyable and invaluable.

NOTE

The authors researched the leading reference books on American English grammar and punctuation, including *The Chicago Manual of Style, The Associated Press Stylebook*, Fowler's *Modern English Usage*, Bernstein's *The Careful Writer*, and many others. The authors provide rules, guidance, and examples based on areas of general agreement among the authorities. Where the authorities differ, this book provides options to follow based on the reader's purpose in writing, with this general advice: be consistent.

CHAPTER 1

GRAMMAR

FINDING NOUNS, VERBS, AND SUBJECTS

Definitions
- A **noun** is a word or set of words for a person, place, thing, or idea. A noun of more than one word (*tennis court, gas station*) is called a **compound noun**.

There are **common nouns** and **proper nouns**. Common nouns are words for a general class of people, places, things, and ideas (*man, city, award, honesty*). They are not capitalized. Proper nouns are always capitalized. They name specific people, places, and things (*Joe, Chicago, Academy Award*).

- A **verb** is a word or set of words that shows action (*runs, is going, has been painting*); feeling (*loves, envies*); or state of being (*am, are, is, have been, was, seem*).

NOTE
We will use the standard of underlining subjects once and verbs twice.

Examples: He ran around the block.
I like my friend.
They seem friendly.

State-of-being verbs are called **linking verbs**. They include all forms of the verb *to be* (*be, being, been, am, is, are, was, were*), plus such words as *look, feel, appear, act, go,* followed by an adjective. (See the "Adjectives and Adverbs" section later in this chapter.)

Examples: You look happy.
We feel fine.
He went ballistic.

Verbs often consist of more than one word. For instance, *had been breaking down* is a four-word verb. It has a two-word main verb, *breaking down* (also called a **phrasal verb**), and two **helping verbs** (*had* and *been*). Helping verbs are so named because they help clarify the intended meaning.

Many verbs can function as helping verbs, including *is, shall, must, do, has, can, keep, get, start, help,* etc.

You will sometimes hear the word **participle**, which is the form of a verb used with helping verbs to make verb tenses or is used to form adjectives. For instance, *breaking* and *broken* are the present and past participles, respectively, of the verb *break. A broken dish* is an example of a phrase containing a participle as an adjective (see the "Adjectives and Adverbs" section later in this chapter).

Verbs often take **direct objects**, which receive the action of the verb carried out by the subject.

Examples: I like cake. (*cake* receives the action, *like*, done by the subject, *I*)
She lifts weights. (*weights* receives the action, *lifts*, done by the subject, *She*)

Verbs may also take **indirect objects**, which receive the direct object. You can spot an indirect object if it makes sense to place *to* or *from* in front of it.

Examples: I gave Joe the cake. (The indirect object, *Joe*, receives the direct object, *cake*, given by the subject, *I*. Note that you could also say *I gave the cake **to** Joe*.)
She did me a favor. (The indirect object, *me*, is affected by the direct object, *favor*, done by the subject, *She*. Note that you could also say *She did a favor **for** me*.)

Sometimes verbs require prepositions to complete a sentence. (See the "Prepositions" section later in this chapter.) A noun affected by a preposition is called simply the **object of a preposition**.

Examples: *Stop talking about them.* (The object of the preposition *about* is *them*.)
I saw someone inside the house. (The object of the preposition *inside* is *the house*.)

Gerund is another verb-related term we'll mention only briefly. Gerunds are also called verbal nouns, because they are formed when verbs have *-ing* added to them and are used as nouns.

Example: Walking is great exercise. (The *–ing* word, the gerund, is the subject of the sentence.)

- A **subject** is the noun, pronoun (see the "Pronouns" section later in this chapter), or set of words that performs the verb.

Examples: *The woman hurried.*
Woman is the subject.
She was late.
She is the subject.
The Shape of Water *won an Academy Award.*
The Shape of Water is the subject.

Rule 1. To find the subject and verb, always find the verb first. Then ask who or what performed the verb.

Examples: *The jet engine **passed** inspection.*
Passed is the verb. Who or what passed? The engine, so *engine* is the subject. (If you included the word *jet* as the subject, lightning will not strike you. But technically, *jet* is an adjective here and is part of what is known as the complete subject.)
*From the ceiling **hung** the chandelier.*
The verb is *hung*. Now, if you think *ceiling* is the subject, slow down. Ask *who* or *what* hung. The answer is the chandelier, not the ceiling. Therefore, *chandelier* is the subject.

Rule 2. Sentences can have more than one subject and more than one verb.

Examples: *I like cake, and he likes ice cream.* (Two subjects and two verbs)
He and I like cake. (Two subjects and one verb)
She lifts weights and jogs daily. (One subject and two verbs)

Rule 3. If a verb follows *to*, it is called an **infinitive**, and it is not the main verb. You will find the main verb either before or after the infinitive.

> **Examples**:   *He is trying to leave.*
> *To leave* is an infinitive; the main verb is *trying*.
> *To leave was his wish.*
> The main verb is *was*.

NOTE

One of the most stubborn superstitions in English is that it is wrong to insert a word between the *to* and the verb in an infinitive. This is called a **split infinitive** (*to **gladly** pay*, *to **not** go*). There is no English scholar alive who will say a split infinitive is technically wrong. However, split infinitives tend to be clumsy and unnecessary. Experienced writers do not use them without good reason.

Rule 4. Any request or command, such as *Stop!* or *Walk quickly*, has the understood subject *you*, because if we ask who is to stop or walk quickly, the answer must be "you."

> **Example**:   (<u>You</u>) *Please* <u>*bring*</u> *me some coffee.*
> *Bring* is the verb. Who will do the bringing? The subject *you* is understood.

SUBJECT-VERB AGREEMENT

Being able to find the right subject and verb will help you correct errors of subject-verb agreement.

Basic rule. A singular subject (*she, Bill, car*) takes a singular verb (*is, goes, shines*), whereas a plural subject takes a plural verb.

> **Example**:   *The* <u>list</u> *of items* <u>is</u>/<u>are</u> *on the desk.*
> If you know that *list* is the subject, then you will choose *is* for the verb.
> ***Exceptions to the Basic rule:***
> a. The first-person pronoun *I* takes a plural verb (*I go, I drive*).
> b. The basic form of the verb is used after certain main verbs such as *watch, see, hear, feel, help, let,* and *make* (*He watched Ronaldo score the winning goal.*)

Rule 1. A subject will come before a phrase beginning with *of*. This is a key rule for understanding subjects. The word *of* is the culprit in many, perhaps most, subject-verb mistakes.

Hasty writers, speakers, readers, and listeners might miss the all-too-common mistake in the following sentence:

Incorrect: A bouquet of yellow roses lend color and fragrance to the room.
Correct: A <u>bouquet</u> of yellow roses <u>lends</u>. . . (*bouquet lends*, not *roses lend*)

Rule 2. Two singular subjects connected by *or*, *either/or*, or *neither/nor* require a singular verb.

Examples: My <u>aunt</u> or my <u>uncle</u> <u>is arriving</u> by train today.
Neither <u>Juan</u> nor <u>Carmen</u> **is** available.
Either <u>Kiana</u> or <u>Casey</u> <u>is helping</u> today with stage decorations.

Rule 3. The verb in an *or*, *either/or*, or *neither/nor* sentence agrees with the noun or pronoun closest to it.

Examples: Neither the <u>plates</u> nor the serving <u>bowl</u> <u>goes</u> on that shelf.
Neither the serving <u>bowl</u> nor the <u>plates</u> <u>go</u> on that shelf.

This rule can lead to bumps in the road. For example, if *I* is one of two (or more) subjects, it could lead to this odd sentence:

Awkward: Neither she, my friends, nor I am going to the festival.

If possible, it's best to reword such grammatically correct but awkward sentences.

Better: Neither she, I, nor my friends are going to the festival.
OR
She, my friends, and I are not going to the festival.

See the "Pronouns" section, Rules 11a and 11b for more discussion of subject-verb agreement with pronouns.

Rule 4. As a general rule, use a plural verb with two or more subjects when they are connected by *and*.

Example: A <u>car</u> and a <u>bike</u> <u>are</u> my means of transportation.

But note these exceptions:

Exceptions: <u>Breaking and entering</u> <u>is</u> *against the law.*
The <u>bed and breakfast</u> <u>was</u> *charming.*

In those sentences, *breaking and entering* and *bed and breakfast* are compound nouns.

NOTE

Some think it is incorrect to place a personal pronoun first in a multi-subject sentence.

Examples: *I, my dad, and my step-mom are going to the movies.*
She and Orville bought a dog.

While not grammatically incorrect per se, it is a courtesy to place the pronoun last,
except when awkward to do so as shown under **Rule 3** above.

Rule 5a. Sometimes the subject is separated from the verb by such words as *along with*, *as well as*, *besides*, *not*, etc. These words and phrases are not part of the subject. Ignore them and use a singular verb when the subject is singular.

Examples: *The <u>politician</u>, along with the newsmen, <u>is expected</u> shortly.*
<u>Excitement</u>, *as well as nervousness,* <u>is</u> *the cause of her shaking.*

Rule 5b. Parentheses are not part of the subject.

Examples: <u>Joe</u> *(and his trusty mutt)* <u>was</u> *always welcome.*
If this seems awkward, try rewriting the sentence.

Rule 6. In sentences beginning with *here* or *there*, the true subject follows the verb.

Examples: *There <u>are</u> four <u>hurdles</u> to jump.*
There <u>is</u> a high <u>hurdle</u> to jump.
Here <u>are</u> the <u>keys</u>.

NOTE

The word *there's*, a contraction of *there is*, leads to bad habits in informal sentences like *There's a lot of people here today*, because it's easier to say "there's" than "there are." Take care never to use *there's* with a plural subject.

Rule 7. Use a singular verb with distances, periods of time, sums of money, etc., when considered as a unit.

> **Examples:**   *Three miles **is** too far to walk.*
> *Five years **is** the maximum sentence for that offense.*
> *Ten dollars **is** a high price to pay.*
> **BUT**
> *Ten dollars (i.e., dollar bills) **were** scattered on the floor.*

Rule 8a. With words that indicate portions—e.g., *a lot, a majority, percent, some, all*—Rule 1 given earlier in this section is reversed, and we are guided by the noun after *of*. If the noun after *of* is singular, use a singular verb. If it is plural, use a plural verb.

> **Examples:**   *A lot of the **pie** has disappeared.*
> *A lot of the **pies** have disappeared.*
> *Fifty percent of the **pie** has disappeared.*
> *Fifty percent of the **pies** have disappeared.*
> *A third of the **city** is unemployed.*
> *A third of the **people** are unemployed.*
> *All of the **pie** is gone.*
> *All of the **pies** are gone.*
> *Some of the **pie** is missing.*
> *Some of the **pies** are missing.*

NOTE

Some teachers, editors, and the SAT testing service, perhaps for convenience, have considered *none* to be strictly singular. However, authorities agree that *none* has been both singular and plural since Old English and still is. If in context it seems like a singular to you, use a singular verb; if it seems like a plural, use a plural verb. When *none* is clearly intended to mean "not one," it is followed by a singular verb.

Rule 8b. With **collective nouns** such as *group, jury, family, audience, population,* the verb might be either singular or plural, depending on the writer's intent.

> **Examples:**   *All of my **family** has arrived OR have arrived.*
> *Most of the **jury** is here OR are here.*
> *A third of the **population** was not in favor OR were not in favor of the bill.*

NOTE

Anyone who uses a plural verb with a collective noun must take care to be accurate—and also consistent. It must not be done carelessly. The following is the sort of flawed sentence one sees and hears a lot these days:

The staff is deciding how they want to vote.
Careful speakers and writers would avoid assigning the singular *is* and the plural *they* to *staff* in the same sentence.

Consistent: *The staff **are** deciding how **they** want to vote.*

Rewriting such sentences is recommended whenever possible. The preceding sentence would read even better as:

*The staff members **are** deciding how **they** want to vote.*

Rule 9. The word *were* replaces *was* in sentences that express a wish or are contrary to fact:

> **Example:**   *If Joe **were** here, you'd be sorry.*

Shouldn't *Joe* be followed by *was*, not *were*, given that *Joe* is singular? But Joe isn't actually here, so we say *were*, not *was*. The sentence demonstrates the **subjunctive mood**, which is used to express a hypothetical, wishful, imaginary, compulsory, or factually contradictory thought. The subjunctive mood pairs singular subjects with what we usually think of as plural verbs.

> **Examples:**   *I wish it **were** Friday.*
> *She requested that he **raise** his hand.*
> *The foreman demanded that Joe **wear** safety goggles.*

In the first example, a wishful statement, not a fact, is being expressed; therefore, *were*, which we usually think of as a plural verb, is used with the singular subject *it*. (Technically, *it* is the singular subject of the object clause in the subjunctive mood: *it were Friday*.)

Normally, *he raise* would sound terrible to us. However, in the second example, where a request is being expressed, the subjunctive mood is correct.

Note: The subjunctive mood is losing ground in spoken English but should still be used in formal speech and writing.

IRREGULAR VERBS

English verbs are either **regular** or **irregular**. We call a verb regular when we add *ed* (*wanted*, *looked*) or sometimes just *d* (*created*, *loved*) to form what are called the **simple past tense** and the **past participle** (see third and fourth paragraphs below). A regular verb's simple past tense and past participle are always identical.

Not so with irregular verbs. They form the simple past tense and the past participle in any number of unpredictable ways. Some irregular verbs, like *let*, *shut*, and *spread*, never change, whether present or past. Others, like *feel* and *teach*, become modified versions of themselves (*felt*, *taught*) to form both the past tense and the past participle. Still others, like *break* and *sing*, change to form the past tense (*broke*, *sang*) and change again to form the past participle (*broken*, *sung*). And then there are a few really weird ones, like *go*: its past participle (*gone*) is recognizable enough, but its simple past tense is a strange new word (*went*).

Let's get back to the irregular verb *break*. The simple past tense is *broke*, which we use in sentences like *I broke your dish*. We use the past participle, *broken*, to form **compound verbs** in sentences like *I **have broken** your dish*. The compound verb *have broken* is so called because we've added a **helping verb** (*have*) to the main verb's past participle (*broken*). Be careful never to add a helping verb to the simple past form of an irregular verb—*I have broke your dish* is an embarrassing confession in more ways than one.

The past participle of an irregular verb can also function as an adjective: *a **broken** dish*. But the simple past form, if it differs from the participle, cannot function as an adjective: *a **broke** dish* is substandard English.

There are far fewer irregular verbs than regular ones, but we use them all the time. "The ten commonest verbs in English (*be*, *have*, *do*, *say*, *make*, *go*, *take*, *come*, *see*, and *get*) are all irregular," notes Steven Pinker, an American experimental psychologist and linguist, "and about 70% of the time we use a verb, it is an irregular verb." Pinker acknowledges 180 irregular English verbs, but there is an online Extended Irregular Verb Dictionary which contains over 470 irregular verbs, including rare ones such as *bestrew*, *enwind*, and *hagride*.

Proper use of irregular verbs requires old-fashioned memorization—there are no secret formulas or shortcuts. This is why these words can create havoc for conscientious speakers of English.

CLAUSES AND PHRASES

Definitions

- A **clause** is a group of words containing a subject and verb. An **independent clause** is a simple sentence. It can stand on its own.

Examples: *She is hungry.*
               I am feeling well today.

- A **dependent clause** cannot stand on its own. It needs an independent clause to complete a sentence. Dependent clauses often begin with such words as *although*, *since*, *if*, *when*, and *because*.

Examples: *Although she is hungry. . .*
               Whoever is hungry. . .
               Because I am feeling well. . .

Dependent	Independent
Although she is hungry,	*she will give him some of her food.*
Whatever they decide,	*I will agree to.*

- A **phrase** is a group of words without a subject-verb component, used as a single part of speech.

Examples: *Best friend* (this phrase acts as a noun)
               Needing help (this phrase acts as an adjective; see the "Adjectives and
                    Adverbs" section later in this chapter)
               With the blue shirt (this **prepositional phrase** acts as an adjective; see the
                    "Prepositions" section later in this chapter)
               For twenty days (this prepositional phrase acts as an adverb)

PRONOUNS

Definition

- A **pronoun** (*I*, *me*, *he*, *she*, *herself*, *you*, *it*, *that*, *they*, *each*, *few*, *many*, *who*, *whoever*, *whose*, *someone*, *everybody*, etc.) is a word that takes the place of a noun. In the sentence *Joe saw Jill, and he waved at her*, the pronouns *he* and *her* take the place of *Joe* and *Jill*, respectively. There are three types of pronouns: **subject** (for example, *he*); **object** (*him*); or **possessive** (*his*).

Rule 1. Subject pronouns are used when the pronoun is the subject of the sentence. You can remember subject pronouns easily by filling in the blank subject space for a simple sentence.

> *Example*:   ___ *did the job.*

I, he, she, we, they, who, whoever, etc., all qualify and are, therefore, subject pronouns.

Rule 2. Subject pronouns are also used if they rename the subject. They will follow *to be* verbs, such as *is, are, was, were, am, will be, had been*, etc.

> *Examples*:   *It is he.*
> *This is she speaking.*
> *It is we who are responsible for the decision to downsize.*

NOTE

In informal English, most people tend to follow *to be* verbs with object pronouns like *me, her, them*. Many English scholars tolerate this distinction between formal and casual English.

Example:	*It could have been them.*
Technically correct:	*It could have been **they**.*
Example:	*It is just me at the door.*
Technically correct:	*It is just **I** at the door.*

Rule 3. This rule surprises even language watchers: when *who* refers to a personal pronoun (*I, you, he, she, we, they*), it takes the verb that agrees with that pronoun.

> *Correct*:   *It is I who **am** sorry.* (*I **am***)
> *Incorrect*:   *It is I who is sorry.*
> *Correct*:   *It is you who **are** mistaken.* (*you **are***)
> *Incorrect*:   *It is you who's mistaken.*

Rule 4. In addition to subject pronouns, there are also object pronouns, known more specifically as **direct object, indirect object,** and **object of a preposition** (for more detail, see the definition of a **verb** in the Finding Nouns, Verbs, and Subjects section). Object pronouns include *me, him, herself, us, them, themselves*.

Examples: *Jean saw **him**.*
                 Him is the direct object of the verb *saw*.

                 *Give **her** the book.*
                 The direct object of *give* is *book*, and *her* is the indirect object. Indirect
                     objects always have an implied *to* or *for* in front of them: *Give* **[to] her**
                     the book. Do **[for] me** *a favor.*

                 *Are you talking to **me**?*
                 Me is the object of the preposition *to*.

Rule 5. The pronouns *who*, *that*, and *which* become singular or plural depending on the subject.
If the subject is singular, use a singular verb. If it is plural, use a plural verb.

Example: *He is the only one of those men who **is** always on time.*
                 The word *who* refers to *one*. Therefore, use the singular verb *is*.

Sometimes we must look more closely to find a verb's true subject:

Example: *He is one of those men who **are** always on time.*
                 The word *who* refers to *men*. Therefore, use the plural verb *are*.

In sentences like this last example, many would mistakenly insist that *one* is the subject,
requiring **is** *always on time*. But look at it this way: *Of those men who **are** always on time, he is one.*

Rule 6. Pronouns that are singular (*I, he, she, it, everyone, everybody, anyone, anybody, no one,
nobody, someone, somebody, each, either, neither,* etc.) require singular verbs. This rule is frequently overlooked when using the pronouns *each, either,* and *neither,* followed by *of*. Those
three pronouns always take singular verbs. Do not be misled by what follows *of*.

Examples: *Each of the girls sings well.*
                 Either of us is capable of doing the job.
                 Neither of them is available to speak right now.

Exception 1: The singular pronouns *I* and *you* take plural verbs.
Examples: *I sing well.*
                 You sing well.
                 She sings well.

Exception 2: When *each* follows a noun or pronoun in certain sentences, even experienced
writers sometimes get tripped up:

Incorrect:	*The women each gave her approval.*
Correct:	*The women each gave their approval.*
Incorrect:	*The words* are *and* there *each ends with a silent vowel.*
Correct:	*The words* are *and* there *each end with a silent vowel.*

These examples do not contradict Rule 6, because *each* is not the subject, but rather an **adjunct** describing the true subject.

Rule 7. To decide whether to use the subject or object pronoun after the words *than* or *as*, mentally complete the sentence.

Examples:	*Tranh is as smart as she/her.*
	If we mentally complete the sentence, we would say *Tranh is as smart as she is.* Therefore, *she* is the correct answer.
	Zoe is taller than I/me.
	Mentally completing the sentence, we have *Zoe is taller than I am.*
	Daniel would rather talk to her than I/me.
	We can interpret this sentence in two ways: *Daniel would rather talk to her than to me.* **OR** *Daniel would rather talk to her than I would.* A sentence's meaning can change considerably, depending on the pronoun you choose.

Rule 8. The possessive pronouns *yours, his, hers, its, ours, theirs,* and *whose* never need apostrophes. Avoid mistakes like *her's* and *your's*.

Rule 9. The only time *it's* has an apostrophe is when it is a contraction for *it is* or *it has*. The only time *who's* has an apostrophe is when it means *who is* or *who has*. There is no apostrophe in *oneself*. Avoid "one's self," a common error.

Examples:	*It's been a cold morning.*
	The thermometer reached its highest reading.
	He's the one who's always on time.
	He's the one whose wife is always on time.
	Keeping oneself ready is important.

Rule 10. Pronouns that end in *-self* or *-selves* are called **reflexive pronouns**. There are nine reflexive pronouns: *myself, yourself, himself, herself, itself, oneself, ourselves, yourselves,* and *themselves*.

Reflexive pronouns are used when both the subject and the object of a verb are the same person or thing.

Example: *Joe helped* **himself**.

If the object of a preposition refers to a previous noun or pronoun, use a reflexive pronoun:

Example: *Joe bought it for himself.*

Reflexive pronouns help avoid confusion and nonsense. Without them, we might be stuck with sentences like *Joe helped Joe.*

Correct: *I worked myself to the bone.*
                The object *myself* is the same person as the subject *I*, performing the act of working.
Incorrect: *My brother and myself did it.*
Correct: *My brother and I did it.*
                Don't use *myself* unless the pronoun *I* or *me* precedes it in the sentence.
Incorrect: *Please give it to John or myself.*
Correct: *Please give it to John or me.*
Correct: *You saw me being myself.*
                Myself refers back to *me* in the act of being.

A sentence like *Help yourself* looks like an exception to the rule until we realize it's shorthand for **You** *may help yourself.*

In certain cases, a reflexive pronoun may come first.

Example: *Doubting himself, the man proceeded cautiously.*

Reflexive pronouns are also used for emphasis.

Example: *He himself finished the whole job.*

Rule 11a. The use of *they* and *their* with singular pronouns is frowned upon by many traditionalists. To be consistent, it is a good practice to try to avoid *they* and its variants (e.g., *them*, *their*, *themselves*) with previously singular nouns or pronouns.

Not consistent: *Someone has to do it, and they have to do it well.*

The problem is that *someone* is singular, but *they* is plural. If we change *they* to *he or she*, we get a rather clumsy sentence, even if it is technically correct.

> **Technically correct:**   *Someone has to do it, and he or she has to do it well.*

Replacing an inconsistent sentence with a poorly written one is a bad bargain. The better option is to rewrite.

> **Rewritten:**   *Someone has to do it, and has to do it well.*

Many writers abhor the *he or she* solution. Following are more examples of why rewriting is a better idea than using *he or she* or *him or her* to keep sentences consistent.

Inconsistent:	*No one realizes when their time is up.*
Awkward:	*No one realizes when his or her time is up.*
Rewritten:	*None realize when their time is up.*
Inconsistent:	*If you see anyone on the trail, tell them to be careful.*
Awkward:	*If you see anyone on the trail, tell him or her to be careful.*
Rewritten:	*Tell anyone you see on the trail to be careful.*

Rule 11b. When rewriting is not practical and gender-neutrality is desired, use *they, them, their, themself, or themselves* with singular nouns, proper nouns, and pronouns. (This is sometimes referred to as the *singular they*, which has a long history in the English language.)

> **Example**:   *If you see Charlie on the trail, tell them to be careful.*

Rule 12 When a pronoun is linked with a noun by *and*, mentally remove the *and* + noun phrase to avoid trouble.

Incorrect:	*Her and her friend came over.*
	If we remove *and her friend*, we're left with the ungrammatical *Her came over.*
Correct:	**She** *and her friend came over.*
Incorrect:	*I invited he and his wife.*
	If we remove *and his wife*, we're left with the ungrammatical *I invited he.*
Correct:	*I invited* **him** *and his wife.*
Incorrect:	*Bill asked my sister and I.*
	If we remove *my sister and*, we're left with the ungrammatical *Bill asked I.*
Correct:	*Bill asked my sister and* **me**.

> **NOTE**
>
> Do not combine a subject pronoun and an object pronoun in phrases like *her and I* or *he and me*. Whenever *and* or *or* links an object pronoun (*her, me*) and a subject pronoun (*he, I*), one of those pronouns will always be wrong.
>
> **Incorrect:**   *Her and I went home.*
> **Correct:**   *She and I went home.* (She went and I went.)

Rule 13. If two people possess the same item, and one of the joint owners is written as a pronoun, use the possessive form for both.

Incorrect:	*Maribel and my home*
Incorrect:	*mine and Maribel's home*
Correct:	*Maribel's and my home*
Incorrect:	*he and Maribel's home*
Incorrect:	*him and Maribel's home*
Correct:	*his and Maribel's home*
Incorrect:	*you and Maribel's home*
Incorrect:	*yours and Maribel's home*
Correct:	*Maribel's and your home*

Note: As the above examples demonstrate, when one of the co-owners is written as a pronoun, use **possessive adjectives** (*my, your, her, our, their*). Avoid **possessive pronouns** (*mine, yours, hers, ours, theirs*) in such constructions.

WHO VS. WHOM

The pronoun *who* is always subjective. Use *who* wherever you would use the subjective pronouns *I, he, she, we,* or *they*. It is correct to say **Who** *wants to go?* because we would say **I** *want to go* or **We** *want to go.*

The pronoun *whom* is always an object. Use *whom* wherever you would use the objective pronouns *me, him, her, us,* or *them*. It is not correct to say *Who did you choose?* We would say **Whom** because you choose **me** or **them.**

Handy memory aid: Use this *they* or *them* method to decide whether *who* or *whom* is correct:

they = who
them = whom

Examples: **Who**/*Whom wrote the letter?*
They wrote the letter. Therefore, *who* is correct.
Who/**Whom** *should I vote for?*
Should I vote for *them*? Therefore, *whom* is correct.
We all know **who**/*whom pulled that prank.*
This sentence contains two clauses: *we all know* and *who/whom pulled that prank.* We are interested in the second clause because it contains the *who/whom. They* pulled that prank. Therefore, *who* is correct.
*We wondered who/***whom** *the book was about.*
This sentence contains two clauses: *we wondered* and *who/whom the book was about.* Again, we are interested in the second clause because it contains the *who/whom.* The book was about *them.* Therefore, *whom* is correct.

Note: This rule is compromised by an odd infatuation people have with *whom*—and not for good reasons. At its worst, the use of *whom* becomes a form of one-upmanship some employ to appear sophisticated. The following is an example of the pseudo-sophisticated *whom.*

Incorrect: *a woman whom I think is a genius*
In this case *whom* is not the object of *I think.* Put *I think* at the end and the mistake becomes obvious: *a woman whom is a genius, I think.*
Correct: *a woman* **who** *I think is a genius*

Learn to spot and avoid this too-common pitfall.

WHOEVER VS. WHOMEVER

To determine whether to use *whoever* or *whomever*, the *they/them* rule in the previous section applies:

they = whoever
them = whomever

Rule 1. The presence of *whoever* or *whomever* generally indicates a dependent clause. Use *whoever* or *whomever* to agree with the verb in that dependent clause, regardless of the rest of the sentence.

Examples: *Give it to* **whoever**/*whomever asks for it first.*
They ask for it first. Therefore, *whoever* is correct.
*We will hire whoever/***whomever** *you recommend.*

You recommend them. Therefore, *whomever* is correct.
We will hire **whoever**/*whomever is most qualified.*
They are most qualified. Therefore, *whoever* is correct.

Rule 2. When the entire *whoever/whomever* clause is the subject of the verb that follows the clause, analyze the clause to determine whether to use *whoever* or *whomever*.

Examples: *Whoever is elected will serve a four-year term.*
Whoever is the subject of *is elected*. The clause *whoever is elected* is the
    subject of *will serve.*
Whomever you elect will serve a four-year term.
Whomever is the object of *elect*. *Whomever you elect* is the subject of
    will serve.

A word to the wise: *Whomever* is even more of a vogue word than *whom*. Many use it indiscriminately to sound cultured, figuring that no one will know any better.

WHO, THAT, WHICH

Rule 1. *Who* and sometimes *that* refer to people. *That* and *which* refer to groups or things.

Examples: *Anya is the one* **who** *rescued the bird.*
"The Man **That** *Got Away" is a great song with a grammatical title.*
Lokua is on the team **that** *won first place.*
She belongs to a great organization, **which** *specializes in saving*
    endangered species.

Rule 2a. *That* introduces what is called an **essential clause** (also known as a **restrictive** or **defining clause**). Essential clauses add information that is vital to the point of the sentence.

Example: *I do not trust products* **that** *claim "all natural ingredients" because this phrase*
    can mean almost anything.
We would not know the type of products being discussed without the
    that clause.

Rule 2b. *Which* introduces a **nonessential clause** (also known as a **nonrestrictive** or **nondefining clause**), which adds supplementary information.

Example: *The product claiming "all natural ingredients,"* **which** *appeared in the Sunday newspaper, is on sale.*

The product is already identified. Therefore, *which appeared in the Sunday newspaper* is a nonessential clause containing additional, but not essential, information.

NOTE

Essential clauses do not have commas introducing or surrounding them, whereas nonessential clauses are introduced or surrounded by commas.

Rule 3. If *that* has already appeared in a sentence, writers sometimes use *which* to introduce the next clause, whether it is essential or nonessential. This is done to avoid awkward formations.

Example: *That which doesn't kill you makes you stronger.*

This sentence is far preferable to the ungainly but technically correct *That that doesn't kill you makes you stronger.*

NOTE

The distinction between *that* and *which*, though a useful guideline, is not universally accepted as a hard-and-fast rule. For many centuries and up to the present, *which* has been routinely used by great writers and journalists to introduce essential clauses.

ADJECTIVES AND ADVERBS

Definitions

- An **adjective** is a word or set of words that **modifies** (i.e., describes) a noun or pronoun. Adjectives may come before the word they modify.

Examples: *That is a* **cute** *puppy.*
She likes a **high school** *senior.*

Adjectives may also follow the word they modify:

Examples: *That puppy looks **cute**.*
                  *The technology is **state-of-the-art**.*

- An **adverb** is a word or set of words that modifies verbs, adjectives, or other adverbs. Adverbs answer *how, when, where,* or *to what extent—how often* or *how much* (e.g., *daily, completely*).

Examples: *He speaks **slowly** (tells how).*
                  *He speaks **very** slowly (the adverb **very** tells how slowly).*
                  *They arrived **today** (tells when).*
                  *They will arrive **in an hour** (this adverb phrase tells when).*
                  *Let's go **outside** (tells where).*
                  *We looked **in the basement** (this adverb phrase tells where).*
                  *Bernie left **to avoid trouble** (this adverb phrase tells why).*
                  *Jorge works out **strenuously** (tells to what extent).*
                  *Jorge works out **whenever possible** (this adverb phrase tells to what extent).*

Rule 1. Many adverbs end in *-ly*, but many do not. Generally, if a word can have *-ly* added to its adjective form, place it there to form an adverb.

Examples: *She thinks quick/**quickly**.*
                  How does she think? *Quickly.*
                  *She is a **quick**/quickly thinker.*
                  Quick is an adjective describing *thinker*, so no *-ly* is attached.
                  *She thinks **fast**/fastly.*
                  Fast answers the question *how*, so it is an adverb. But *fast* never has *-ly* attached to it.
                  *We performed bad/**badly**.*
                  Badly describes *how* we performed, so *-ly* is added.

Rule 2. Adverbs that answer the question *how* sometimes cause grammatical problems. It can be a challenge to determine if *-ly* should be attached. Avoid the trap of *-ly* with linking verbs such as *taste, smell, look, feel*, which pertain to the senses. Adverbs are often misplaced in such sentences, which require adjectives instead.

Examples: *Pat's roses smell **sweet**/sweetly.*
                  Do the roses actively smell with noses? No; in this case, *smell* is a linking verb—which requires an adjective to modify *roses*—so no *-ly*.
                  *The painter looked **angry**/angrily to us.*

Did the painter look with eyes, or are we describing the painter's appearance? We are describing appearance (the painter appeared angry), so no -ly.

*The painter looked angry/**angrily** at the paint splotches.*

Here the painter actively looked (using eyes), so the -ly is added.

Avoid this common mistake:

Incorrect: *Ingrid feels badly about the news.*

Ingrid is not feeling with fingers, so no -ly.

Correct: *Ingrid feels **bad** about the news.*

Rule 3. The word *good* is an adjective, whose adverb equivalent is *well*.

Examples: *You did a good job.*
Good describes the job.
You did the job well.
Well answers *how*.
You smell good today.
Good describes your fragrance, not how you smell with your nose, so using the adjective is correct.
You smell well for someone with a cold.
You are actively smelling with your nose here, so use the adverb.

Rule 4. The word *well* can be an adjective, too. When referring to health, we often use *well* rather than *good*.

Examples: *You do not look well today.*
I don't feel well, either.

Rule 5. Adjectives come in three forms, also called **degrees**. An adjective in its normal or usual form is called a **positive degree adjective**. There are also the **comparative** and **superlative** degrees, which are used for comparison, as in the following examples:

Positive	Comparative	Superlative
sweet	*sweeter*	*sweetest*
bad	*worse*	*worst*
efficient	*more efficient*	*most efficient*

A common error in using adjectives and adverbs arises from using the wrong form of comparison. To compare two things, always use a **comparative** adjective:

Example: *She is the **cleverer** of the two women* (never *cleverest*)

The word *cleverest* is what is called the **superlative** form of *clever*. Use it only when comparing three or more things:

Example: *She is the **cleverest** of them all.*
Incorrect: *Chocolate or vanilla: which do you like best?*
Correct: *Chocolate or vanilla: which do you like **better**?*

Rule 6. **There are also three degrees of adverbs**. In formal usage, do not drop the *-ly* from an adverb when using the comparative form.

Incorrect: *Terry spoke quicker than Nguyen did.*
Correct: *Terry spoke **more quickly** than Nguyen did.*
Incorrect: *Talk quieter.*
Correct: *Talk **more quietly**.*

Incorrect: *Alfredo is the more efficient assembly worker in the unit.*
Correct: *Alfredo is the **most efficient** assembly worker in the unit.*

Rule 7. When *this, that, these,* and *those* are followed by a noun, they are adjectives. When they appear without a noun following them, they are pronouns.

Examples: *This house is for sale.*
This is an adjective.

This is for sale.
This is a pronoun.

PREPOSITIONS

Definition

- A **preposition** is a word or set of words that indicates location (*in, near, beside, on top of*) or some other relationship between a noun or pronoun and other parts of the sentence (*about, after, besides, instead of, in accordance with*). A preposition isn't a preposition unless it goes with a related noun or pronoun, called the **object of the preposition**.

Examples: *Let's meet before noon.*
Before is a preposition; *noon* is its object.
We've never met before.
There is no object; *before* is an adverb modifying *met*.

Rule 1. A preposition generally, but not always, goes before its noun or pronoun. One of the undying myths of English grammar is that you may not end a sentence with a preposition. But look at the first example that follows. No one should feel compelled to say, or even write, *That is something with which I cannot agree*. Just do not use extra prepositions when the meaning is clear without them.

Correct: *That is something I cannot agree **with**.*
Correct: *Where did you get this?*
Incorrect: *Where did you get this **at**?*
Correct: *How many of you can I depend **on**?*
Correct: *Where did he go?*
Incorrect: *Where did he go **to**?*

Rule 2a. The preposition *like* means "similar to" or "similarly to." It should be followed by an object of the preposition (noun, pronoun, noun phrase), not by a subject and verb. Rule of thumb: Avoid *like* when a verb is involved.

Correct: *You look like your mother.*
That is, you look *similar to* her. (*Mother* is the object of the preposition *like*.)
Incorrect: *You look like your mother does.*
(Avoid *like* with noun + verb.)

Rule 2b. Instead of *like*, use *as, as if, as though*, or *the way* when following a comparison with a subject and verb.

Correct: *You look **the way** your mother does.*
Incorrect: *Do like I ask.* (No one would say *Do similarly to I ask.*)
Correct: *Do **as** I ask.*
Incorrect: *You look like you're angry.*
Correct: *You look **as if** you're angry.* (**OR as though**)

Some speakers and writers, to avoid embarrassment, use *as* when they mean *like*. The following incorrect sentence came from a grammar guide:

Incorrect: *They are considered as any other English words.*
Correct: *They are considered as any other English words would be.*
Correct: *They are considered to be like any other English words.*

Remember: *like* means "similar to" or "similarly to"; *as* means "in the same manner that." Rule of thumb: Do not use *as* unless there is a verb involved.

Incorrect: *I, as most people, try to use good grammar.*
Correct: *I, **like** most people, try to use good grammar.*
Correct: *I, **as** most people **do**, try to use good grammar.*

NOTE

The rule distinguishing *like* from *as, as if, as though*, and *the way* is increasingly ignored, but English purists still insist upon it.

Rule 3. The preposition *of* should never be used in place of the helping verb *have*.

Correct: *I should have done it.*
Incorrect: *I should of done it.*

See also **COUPLE OF; OFF OF; OUT OF; OUTSIDE OF** in Chapter 5, "Confusing Words and Homonyms."

Rule 4. It is a good practice to follow *different* with the preposition *from*. Most traditionalists avoid *different than*. Although it is an overstatement to call *different than* incorrect, it remains polarizing: *A is different than B* comes across as sloppy to a lot of literate readers. If you can replace *different than* with *different from* without having to rewrite the rest of the sentence, why not do so?

Polarizing: *You're different than I am.*
Unchallengeable: *You're different from me.*

See also **DIFFERENT FROM, DIFFERENT THAN** in Chapter 5, "Confusing Words and Homonyms."

Rule 5. Use *into* rather than *in* to express motion toward something. Use *in* to tell the location.

Correct:	*I swam in the pool.*
Correct:	*I walked into the house.*
Correct:	*I looked into the matter.*
Incorrect:	*I dived in the water.*
Correct:	*I dived into the water.*
Incorrect:	*Throw it in the trash.*
Correct:	*Throw it into the trash.*

EFFECTIVE WRITING

Rule 1. Use concrete rather than vague language.

Vague:	*The weather was of an extreme nature on the West Coast.*
	This sentence raises frustrating questions: When did this extreme weather occur? What does "of an extreme nature" mean? Where on the West Coast did this take place?
Concrete:	*California had unusually cold weather last week.*

Rule 2. Use **active voice** whenever possible. Active voice means the subject is performing the verb. **Passive voice** means the subject receives the action.

Active:	*Barry hit the ball.*
Passive:	*The ball was hit.*

Notice that the party responsible for the action—in the previous example, whoever hit the ball—may not even appear when using passive voice. So passive voice is a useful option when the responsible party is not known.

Example:	*My watch was stolen.*

NOTE

The passive voice has often been criticized as something employed by people in power to avoid responsibility:

Example:	*Mistakes were made.*
Translation:	*I made mistakes.*

Rule 3. Avoid overusing *there is, there are, it is, it was*, etc.

Example: *There is a case of meningitis that was reported in the newspaper.*
Revision: *A case of meningitis was reported in the newspaper.*
Even better: *The newspaper reported a case of meningitis.* (Active voice)
Example: *It is important to signal before making a left turn.*
Revision: *Signaling before making a left turn is important.*
              OR
              Signaling before a left turn is important.
              OR
              You should signal before making a left turn.
Example: *There are some revisions that must be made.*
Revision: *Some revisions must be made.* (Passive voice)
Even better: *Please make some revisions.* (Active voice)

Rule 4. To avoid confusion (and pompousness), don't use two negatives to make a positive without good reason.

Unnecessary: *They are not unwilling to help.*
Better: *They are willing to help.*

Sometimes a *not un-* construction may be desirable, perhaps even necessary:

Example: *The book is uneven but not uninteresting.*

However, the novelist-essayist George Orwell warned of its abuse with this deliberately silly sentence: "A not unblack dog was chasing a not unsmall rabbit across a not ungreen field."

Rule 5. Use consistent grammatical form when offering several ideas. This is called **parallel construction**.

Correct: *I admire people who are honest, reliable, and sincere.*
              Note that *are* applies to and makes sense with each of the three adjectives at the end.
Incorrect: *I admire people who are honest, reliable, and have sincerity.*
              In this version, *are* does not make sense with *have sincerity*, and *have sincerity* doesn't belong with the two adjectives *honest* and *reliable*.
Correct: *You should check your spelling, grammar, and punctuation.*
              Note that *check your* applies to and makes sense with each of the three nouns at the end.

Incorrect: *You should check your spelling, grammar, and punctuate properly.*

Here, *check your* does not make sense with *punctuate properly*, and *punctuate properly* doesn't belong with the two nouns *spelling* and *grammar*. The result is a jarringly inept sentence.

Rule 6. Word order can make or ruin a sentence. If you start a sentence with an incomplete phrase or clause, such as *While crossing the street* or *Forgotten by history*, it must be followed closely by the person or thing it describes. Furthermore, that person or thing is always the main subject of the sentence. Breaking this rule results in the dreaded, all-too-common **dangling modifier**, or **dangler**.

Dangler: *Forgotten by history, his autograph was worthless.*

The problem: *his autograph* shouldn't come right after *history*, because *he* was forgotten, not his autograph.

Correct: *He was forgotten by history, and his autograph was worthless.*

Dangler: *Born in Chicago, my first book was about the 1871 fire.*

The problem: the sentence wants to say *I* was born in Chicago, but to a careful reader, it says that *my first book* was born there.

Correct: *I was born in Chicago, and my first book was about the 1871 fire.*

Adding *-ing* to a verb (as in *crossing* in the example that follows) results in a versatile word called a **participle**, which can be a noun, adjective, or adverb. Rule 6 applies to all sentences with a participle in the beginning. Participles require placing the actor immediately after the opening phrase or clause.

Dangler: *While crossing the street, the bus hit her.* (Wrong: the bus was not crossing.)

Correct: *While crossing the street, she was hit by a bus.*

OR

She was hit by a bus while crossing the street.

Rule 7. Place descriptive words and phrases as close as is practical to the words they modify.

Ill-advised: *I have a cake that Mollie baked in my lunch bag.*

Cake is too far from *lunch bag*, making the sentence ambiguous and silly.

Better: *In my lunch bag is a cake that Mollie baked.*

Rule 8. A sentence fragment is usually an oversight, or a bad idea. It occurs when you have only a phrase or dependent clause but are missing an independent clause.

Sentence fragment: *After the show ended.*

Full sentence: *After the show ended, we had coffee.*

Rule 9a. When writing dialogue, indent each new line, enclose it in quotation marks, and attribute it to the speaker. Once the speakers are established, their attributions may be dropped until needed again for clarity. Each change in speaker also begins a new line.

Example: "I want to know where the coins are," Bartholomew said.
"I have no idea," Jacoby replied.
Bartholomew stared at him.
"You do know," he said.
"I do not."
Jacoby gazed back at him blankly.
"Then explain why I found the red dirt on your shoes," Bartholomew said.

If a speaker's dialogue continues beyond one paragraph, an opening quotation mark is placed at the start of each new line. The closing quotation mark appears at the end of the dialogue.

Example: "Then explain why I found the red dirt on your shoes. You and I both know there is only one place it could have come from.
"You must tell me where the coins are, and you will tell me.
"And after you tell me, you will deal with Ricardo yourself."

Rule 9b. A writer can apply many different attributive verbs in describing dialogue. Just a few examples are *added*, *declared*, *muttered*, *responded*, and *yelled*.

Examples: "You will deal with Ricardo yourself as to why the coins were removed," Bartholomew added.
"I will not," Jacoby responded.

While such verbs help to color dialogue and keep it moving, good dialogue will establish context and mood without over-relying on them. The right words and intonation will convey the spirit of a conversation. In some cases, an attributive verb can be redundant.

Example: "You will deal with Ricardo, and you will bear the consequences," Bartholomew insisted. (*The dialogue contains the insistence; the attributive verb can simply be* said.)

CHAPTER 2

PUNCTUATION

SPACING WITH PUNCTUATION

Rule 1. With a computer, use only one space following periods, commas, semicolons, colons, exclamation points, question marks, and quotation marks. The space needed after these punctuation marks is proportioned automatically.

Rule 2. Use no spaces on either side of a hyphen.

(For more rules about hyphens, see the Hyphens section later in this chapter.)

Example: *We borrowed twenty-three sheets of paper.*

Note: For spacing with dashes, see the Dashes section later in this chapter.

PERIODS

Rule 1. Use a period at the end of a complete sentence that is a statement.

Example: *I know him well.*

Rule 2. If the last item in the sentence is an abbreviation that ends in a period, do not follow it with another period.

Incorrect: *This is Alice Smith, M.D..*
Correct: *This is Alice Smith, M.D.*
Correct: *Please shop, cook, etc. We will do the laundry.*

Rule 3. Question marks and exclamation points replace and eliminate periods at the end of a sentence.

COMMAS

Commas and **periods** are the most frequently used punctuation marks. Commas customarily indicate a brief pause; they're not as final as periods.

Rule 1. Use commas to separate words and word groups in a simple series of three or more items.

>   *Example*:   *My estate goes to my husband, son, daughter-in-law, and nephew.*

Note: When the last comma in a series comes before *and* or *or* (after *daughter-in-law* in the above example), it is known as the **Oxford comma**. Most newspapers and magazines drop the Oxford comma in a simple series, apparently feeling it's unnecessary. However, omission of the Oxford comma can sometimes lead to misunderstandings.

>   *Example*:   *We had coffee, cheese and crackers and grapes.*

Adding a comma after *crackers* makes it clear that *cheese and crackers* represents one dish. In cases like this, clarity demands the Oxford comma.

>   *We had coffee, cheese and crackers, and grapes.*

Fiction and nonfiction books generally prefer the Oxford comma. Writers must decide Oxford or no Oxford and not switch back and forth, except when omitting the Oxford comma could cause confusion as in the *cheese and crackers* example.

Rule 2. Use a comma to separate two adjectives when the order of the adjectives is interchangeable.

>   *Example*:   *He is a strong, healthy man.*
>   We could also say *healthy, strong man.*
>   *Example*:   *We stayed at an expensive summer resort.*
>   We would not say *summer expensive resort*, so no comma.

Another way to determine if a comma is needed is to mentally put *and* between the two adjectives. If the result still makes sense, add the comma. In the examples above, *a strong **and** healthy man* makes sense, but *an expensive **and** summer resort* does not.

Rule 3a. Many inexperienced writers run two independent clauses together by using a comma instead of a period. This results in the dreaded **run-on sentence** or, more technically, a **comma splice**.

Incorrect: *He walked all the way home, he shut the door.*

There are several simple remedies:

Correct: *He walked all the way home. He shut the door.*
Correct: *After he walked all the way home, he shut the door.*
Correct: *He walked all the way home, and he shut the door.*

Rule 3b. In sentences where two independent clauses are joined by connectors such as *and*, *or*, *but*, etc., put a comma at the end of the first clause.

Incorrect: *He walked all the way home and he shut the door.*
Correct: *He walked all the way home, and he shut the door.*
Incorrect: *Did he walk all the way home or did he take a bus?*
Correct: *Did he walk all the way home, or did he take a bus?*

Some writers omit the comma if the clauses are both quite short:

Example: *I paint and he writes.*

Rule 3c. If the subject does not appear in front of the second verb, a comma is generally unnecessary.

Example: <u>Morty</u> <u>thought</u> *quickly but still* <u>did</u> *not* <u>answer</u> *correctly.*

But sometimes a comma in this situation is necessary to avoid confusion.

Confusing: *I saw that she was busy and prepared to leave.*
Clearer with comma: *I saw that she was busy, and prepared to leave.*

Without a comma, the reader is liable to think that "she" was the one who was prepared to leave.

Rule 3d. A comma is placed before the word *because* only if needed for clarity.

Example: *The twins attended Tulane because their parents went there.*

This sentence clearly conveys that the main reason the twins went to Tulane was because their parents attended Tulane.

The twins didn't attend Tulane because their parents went there.

This sentence is ambiguous. We're not sure whether they didn't go to Tulane because they wanted to go somewhere other than where their parents went to college, or whether the twins did go to Tulane but for reasons other than that their parents went there.

The twins didn't attend Tulane, because their parents went there.

With the comma before *because*, the sentence more clearly conveys that the twins desired a college other than the one their parents attended.

Rule 4a. When starting a sentence with a dependent clause, use a comma after it.

Example: *If you are not sure about this, let me know now.*

Follow the same policy with introductory phrases.

Example: *Having finally arrived in town, we went shopping.*

However, if the introductory phrase is clear and brief (three or four words), the comma is optional.

Example: *When in town we go shopping.*

But always add a comma if it would avoid confusion.

Example: *Last Sunday, evening classes were canceled.* (The comma prevents a misreading.)

When an introductory phrase begins with a preposition, a comma may not be necessary even if the phrase contains more than three or four words.

Example: *Into the sparkling crystal ball he gazed.*

If such a phrase contains more than one preposition, a comma may be used **unless** a verb immediately follows the phrase.

Examples:
Between your house on Main Street and my house on Grand Avenue, the mayor's mansion stands proudly.
Between your house on Main Street and my house on Grand Avenue is the mayor's mansion.

Rule 4b. But often a comma is unnecessary when the sentence starts with an independent clause followed by a dependent clause.

Example: *Let me know now if you are not sure about this.*

Rule 5a. Use commas to set off nonessential words, clauses, and phrases (see the "Who, That, Which" section in Chapter One, Rule 2b).

Incorrect: *Jill who is my sister shut the door.*
Correct: *Jill, who is my sister, shut the door.*
Incorrect: *The actor knowing it was late hurried home.*
Correct: *The actor, knowing it was late, hurried home.*

In the preceding examples, note the comma after *sister* and *late*. Nonessential words, clauses, and phrases that occur midsentence must be enclosed by commas. The closing comma is called an **appositive comma**. Many writers forget to add this important comma. Following are two instances of the need for an appositive comma with one or more nouns.

Incorrect: *My best friend, Joe arrived.*
Correct: *My best friend, Joe, arrived.*
Incorrect: *The three items, a book, a pen, and paper were on the table.*
Correct: *The three items, a book, a pen, and paper, were on the table.*

Rule 5b. If something or someone is sufficiently identified, the description that follows is considered nonessential and should be surrounded by commas.

Examples: *Freddy, who has a limp, was in an auto accident.*
If we already know which Freddy is meant, the description is not
essential.
The boy who has a limp was in an auto accident.
We do not know which boy is meant without further description; there-
fore, no commas are used.

This leads to a persistent problem. Look at the following sentence:

Example: *My brother Bill is here.*

Now, see how adding two commas changes that sentence's meaning:

Example: *My brother, Bill, is here.*

Careful writers and readers understand that the first sentence means I have more than one brother. The commas in the second sentence mean that Bill is my only brother.

Why? In the first sentence, *Bill* is essential information: it identifies which of my two (or more) brothers I'm speaking of. This is why no commas enclose *Bill*.

In the second sentence, *Bill* is nonessential information—whom else but Bill could I mean?—hence the commas.

Comma misuse is nothing to take lightly. It can lead to a train wreck like this:

Example: *Mark Twain's book*, Tom Sawyer, *is a delight*.

Because of the commas, that sentence states that Twain wrote only one book. In fact, he wrote more than two dozen of them.

Rule 6a. Use a comma after certain words that introduce a sentence, such as *well, yes, why, hello, hey*, etc.

Examples: *Why, I can't believe this!*
No, you can't have a dollar.

Rule 6b. Use commas to set off expressions that interrupt the sentence flow (*nevertheless, after all, by the way, on the other hand, however*, etc.).

Example: *I am, by the way, very nervous about this.*

Rule 6c. In general, use commas to set off the word *too* midsentence. However, it is usually not necessary to precede *too* with a comma at the end of a sentence.

Examples: *My sister, too, loves artichokes.*
My sister loves artichokes too.

Rule 7. Use commas to set off the name, nickname, term of endearment, or title of a person directly addressed.

Examples: *Will you, Aisha, do that assignment for me?*
Yes, old friend, I will.
Good day, Captain.

Rule 8. Use a comma to separate the day of the month from the year, and—what most people forget!—always put one after the year, also.

Example: *It was in the Sun's June 5, 2013, edition.*

No comma is necessary for just the month and year.

Example: *It was in a June 2013 article.*

A comma may be advisable with other incomplete dates.

Examples: *Our planning meetings will take place on Friday, November 13 and Thursday, December 10.*
Our planning meetings will take place on November 13 and December 10.

Rule 9. Use a comma to separate a city from its state, and remember to put one after the state, also.

Example: *I'm from the Akron, Ohio, area.*

Rule 10. Traditionally, if a person's name is followed by *Sr.* or *Jr.*, a comma follows the last name: *Martin Luther King, Jr.* This comma is no longer considered mandatory. However, if a comma does precede *Sr.* or *Jr.*, another comma must follow the entire name when it appears midsentence.

Correct: *Al Mooney Sr. is here.*
Correct: *Al Mooney, Sr., is here.*
Incorrect: *Al Mooney, Sr. is here.*

Rule 11. Similarly, use commas to enclose degrees or titles used with names.

Example: *Al Mooney, M.D., is here.*

Rule 12a. Use commas to introduce or interrupt direct quotations of dialogue or text.

Examples: *He said, "I don't care."*
"Why," I asked, "don't you care?"
Toni Morrison wrote, "If there's a book that you want to read, but it hasn't been written yet, then you must write it."

This rule is optional with one-word quotations.

Example: He said "Stop."

If a quotation is preceded by introductory words such as *that*, *whether*, *if*, a comma is normally not needed.

Example: Was it James Baldwin who wrote that "nothing can be changed until it is faced"?

A comma is not necessary to introduce titles of articles, chapters, songs, etc. (see Quotation Marks, Rule 6).

Example: I recently read an interesting article titled "A Poor Woman's Journey."

Rule 12b. If the quotation comes before *he said*, *she wrote*, *they reported*, *Dana insisted*, or a similar attribution, end the quoted material with a comma, even if it is only one word.

Examples: "I don't care," he said.
"Stop," he said.

Rule 12c. If a quotation functions as a subject or object in a sentence, it might not need a comma.

Examples: Is "I don't care" all you can say to me?
Saying "Stop the car" was a mistake.

Rule 12d. If a quoted question ends in midsentence, the question mark replaces a comma.

Example: "Will you still be my friend?" LaDonna asked.

Rule 13. Use a comma to separate a statement from a question.

Example: I can go, can't I?

Rule 14. Use a comma to separate contrasting parts of a sentence.

Example: That is my money, not yours.

Rule 15a. Use a comma before and after certain introductory words or terms, such as *namely*, *that is*, *i.e.*, *e.g.*, *including*, and *for instance*, when they are followed by a series of items.

Example: *You may be required to bring many items, e.g., sleeping bags, pans, and warm clothing.*

Rule 15b. Commas should precede the term *etc.* and enclose it if it is placed midsentence.

Example: *Sleeping bags, pans, warm clothing, etc., are in the tent.*

NOTE
The abbreviation *i.e.* means "that is"; *e.g.* means "for example."

SEMICOLONS

It's no accident that a **semicolon** is a period atop a comma. Like commas, semicolons indicate an audible pause—slightly longer than a comma's, but short of a period's full stop.

Semicolons have other functions, too. But first, a caveat: avoid the common mistake of using a semicolon to replace a colon (see the "Colons" section).

Incorrect: *I have one goal; to find her.*
Correct: *I have one goal: to find her.*

Rule 1a. A semicolon can replace a period if the writer wishes to narrow the gap between two closely linked sentences (independent clauses).

Examples: *Call me tomorrow; you can give me an answer then.*
                      We have paid our dues; we expect all the privileges listed in the contract.

Rule 1b. Avoid a semicolon when a dependent clause comes before an independent clause.

Incorrect: *Although they tried; they failed.*
Correct: *Although they tried, they failed.*

Rule 2. Use a semicolon before such words and terms as *namely, however, therefore, that is, i.e., for example, e.g., for instance,* etc., when they introduce a complete sentence. It is also preferable to use a comma after these words and terms.

Example: *Bring any two items; however, sleeping bags and tents are in short supply.*

Rule 3. Use a semicolon to separate units of a series when one or more of the units contain commas.

Incorrect: *The conference has people who have come from Moscow, Idaho, Springfield, California, Alamo, Tennessee, and other places as well.*
Note that with only commas, that sentence is hopeless.

Correct: *The conference has people who have come from Moscow, Idaho; Springfield, California; Alamo, Tennessee; and other places as well.*
Note that a semicolon, rather than a comma, after *Tennessee* is correct because *and other places as well* also constitutes a unit of the series.

Correct: *Dante Martinez, a registered nurse; Susan Brooks, a dietician; and Chien-Ling Ko, a physical therapist, attended the meeting.*

In this case, *attended the meeting* is not a unit of the series and therefore is preceded only by a comma.

Rule 4. A semicolon may be used between independent clauses joined by a connector, such as *and, but, or, nor,* etc., when one or more commas appear in the first clause.

Example: *When I finish here, and I will soon, I'll be glad to help you; and that is a promise I will keep.*

Rule 5. Do not capitalize ordinary words after a semicolon.

Incorrect: *I am here; You are over there.*
Correct: *I am here; you are over there.*

COLONS

A **colon** means "that is to say" or "here's what I mean." Colons and semicolons should never be used interchangeably.

Rule 1a. Use a colon to introduce an item or a series of items. Do not capitalize the first item after the colon (unless it's a proper noun).

> **Examples:** *You know what to do: practice.*
>
> *You may be required to bring many things: sleeping bags, pans, utensils, and warm clothing.*
>
> *I want the following items: butter, sugar, and flour.*
>
> *I need an assistant who can do the following: input data, write reports, and complete tax forms.*

Rule 1b. A capital letter generally does not introduce a word, phrase, or incomplete sentence following a colon.

> **Examples:** *He got what he worked for: a promotion.*
>
> *He got what he worked for: a promotion that paid a higher wage.*

Rule 2. Avoid using a colon before a list when it directly follows a verb or preposition that would ordinarily need no punctuation in that sentence.

> **Not recommended:** *I want: butter, sugar, and flour.*
> **Recommended:** *I want butter, sugar, and flour.*
>
> **OR**
>
> *Here is what I want: butter, sugar, and flour.*
>
> **Not recommended:** *I've seen the greats, including: Barrymore, Guinness, and Streep.*
> **Recommended:** *I've seen the greats, including Barrymore, Guinness, and Streep.*

Rule 3. When listing items one by one, one per line, following a colon, capitalization and ending punctuation are optional when using single words or phrases preceded by letters, numbers, or bullet points. If each point is a complete sentence, capitalize the first word and end the sentence with appropriate ending punctuation. Otherwise, there are no hard and fast rules, except to be consistent.

Examples: I want an assistant who can do the following:

a. input data

b. write reports

c. complete tax forms

The following are requested:

- Wool sweaters for possible cold weather.
- Wet suits for snorkeling.
- Introductions to the local dignitaries.

These are the pool rules:

1. Do not run.

2. If you see unsafe behavior, report it to the lifeguard.

3. Did you remember your towel?

4. Have fun!

Rule 4. A colon instead of a semicolon may be used between independent clauses when the second sentence explains, illustrates, paraphrases, or expands on the first sentence.

Example: *He got what he worked for: he really earned that promotion.*

If a complete sentence follows a colon, as in the previous example, authorities are divided over whether to capitalize the first word. Some writers and editors feel that capitalizing a complete sentence after a colon is always advisable. Others advise against it. Still others regard it as a judgment call: If what follows the colon is closely related to what precedes it, there is no need for a capital. But if what follows is a general or formal statement, many writers and editors capitalize the first word.

Example: *Remember the old saying: Be careful what you wish for.*

Rule 5. Capitalize the first word of a complete or full-sentence quotation that follows a colon.

Example: *The host made an announcement: "You are all staying for dinner."*

Rule 6. Capitalize the first word after a colon if the information following the colon requires two or more complete sentences.

Example: *Dad gave us these rules to live by: Work hard. Be honest. Always show up on time.*

Rule 7. If a quotation contains two or more sentences, many writers and editors introduce it with a colon rather than a comma.

    Example: *Dad often said to me: "Work hard. Be honest. Always show up on time."*

Rule 8. For extended quotations introduced by a colon, some style manuals say to indent one-half inch on both the left and right margins; others say to indent only on the left margin. Quotation marks are not used.

    Example: *The author of* Touched, *Jane Straus, wrote in the first chapter*:

        Georgia went back to her bed and stared at the intricate patterns of burned moth wings in the translucent glass of the overhead light. Her father was in "hyper mode" again where nothing could calm him down.

Rule 9. Use a colon rather than a comma to follow the salutation in a business letter, even when addressing someone by his or her first name. (Never use a semicolon after a salutation.) A comma is used after the salutation in more informal correspondence.

    Formal: *Dear Ms. Rodriguez*:
    Informal: *Dear Dave*,

QUOTATION MARKS

The rules set forth in this section are customary in the United States. Great Britain and other countries in the Commonwealth of Nations are governed by quite different conventions. Nowhere is this more apparent than in Rule 4 in this section, a rule that has the advantage of being far simpler than Britain's and the disadvantage of being far less logical.

Rule 1. Use double quotation marks to set off a direct (word-for-word) quotation.

    Correct: *"I hope you will be here," he said.*
    Incorrect: *He said that he "hoped I would be there."* (The quotation marks are incorrect because *hoped I would be there* does not state the speaker's exact words.)

Rule 2a. Always capitalize the first word in a complete quotation, even midsentence.

    Example: *Lamarr said, "The case is far from over, and we will win."*

Rule 2b. Do not capitalize quoted material that continues a sentence.

>   ***Example:***   *Lamarr said that the case was "far from over" and that "we will win."*

Rule 3a. Use commas to introduce or interrupt direct quotations of dialogue or text.

>   ***Examples:***   *He said, "I don't care."*
>   *"Why," I asked, "don't you care?"*
>   *Toni Morrison wrote, "If there's a book that you want to read, but it hasn't been written yet, then you must write it."*

This rule is optional with one-word quotations.

>   ***Example:***   *He said "Stop."*

Rule 3b. If the quotation comes before *he said, she wrote, they reported, Dana insisted,* or a similar attribution, end the quoted material with a comma, even if it is only one word.

>   ***Examples:***   *"I don't care," he said.*
>   *"Stop," he said.*

Rule 3c. If a quotation functions as a subject or object in a sentence, it might not need a comma.

>   ***Examples:***   *Is "I don't care" all you can say to me?*
>   *Saying "Stop the car" was a mistake.*

Rule 4. Periods and commas ALWAYS go inside quotation marks.

>   ***Examples:***   *The sign read, "Walk." Then it read, "Don't Walk," then, "Walk," all within thirty seconds.*
>   *He yelled, "Hurry up."*

Rule 5a. The placement of question marks with quotation marks follows logic. If a question is within the quoted material, a question mark should be placed inside the quotation marks. The same method is used for exclamation marks.

Examples: *Alberta asked, "Will you still be my friend?"*
The question *"Will you still be my friend?"* is part of the quotation.
Alberta yelled in frustration, "I cannot be your friend!"
The exclamation *"I cannot be your friend!"* is part of the quotation.
Do you agree with the saying "All's fair in love and war"?
The question *Do you agree with the saying?* is outside the quotation.
I hate when you say, "All's fair in love and war"!
The exclamation *I hate when you say!* is outside the quotation.

Rule 5b. If a quoted question ends in midsentence, the question mark replaces a comma.

Example: *"Will you still be my friend?" Alberta asked.*

Rule 6. Quotation marks are used for components, such as chapter titles in a book, individual episodes of a TV series, songs from a Broadway show or a music album, titles of articles or essays in print or online, and shorter works such as short stories and poems.

It is customary in American publishing to put the title of an entire composition in italics. Put the title of a short work—one that is or could be part of a larger undertaking—in quotation marks. (If you do not have italics capability, quotation marks will do.)

A "composition" is a creative, journalistic, or scholarly enterprise that is whole, complex, a thing unto itself. This includes books, movies, plays, TV shows, newspapers, magazines, websites, music albums, operas, musical theater, paintings, sculptures, and other works of art.

Example: Richard Burton performed the song "Camelot" in the 1960 Broadway musical *Camelot*.

Although the word is the same, "Camelot" the song takes quotation marks because it's part of a larger work—namely, a full-length show called *Camelot*.

Rule 7. Use single quotation marks for quotations within quotations.

Examples: *Dan said, "In a town outside Brisbane, I saw 'Tourists go home' written on a wall. But then someone told me, 'Pay it no mind, lad.' "*
Byung-hoon warned, "Mother will be angry. 'Wait until your father gets home,' she'll say."

Note that the periods and commas go inside both the single and double quotation marks. Also note that, as a courtesy, there is visible space between adjacent single and double quotation marks.

While American style has periods and commas going inside single and double quotation marks, question marks follow logic. Question marks in a quotation within a quotation can get tricky.

> **Example**:   *"Why do you keep saying, 'This doesn't make sense'?"*

Rule 8a. Quotation marks are often used with technical terms, terms used in an unusual way, or other expressions that vary from standard usage.

> **Examples**:   *It's an oil-extraction method known as "fracking."*
> *He did some "experimenting" in his college days.*
> *I had a visit from my "friend" the tax man.*

Rule 8b. Never use single quotation marks in sentences like the previous three.

> **Incorrect**:   *I had a visit from my 'friend' the tax man.*

The single quotation marks in the above sentence are intended to send a message to the reader that *friend* is being used in a special way: in this case, sarcastically. Avoid this invalid usage. Single quotation marks are valid only within a quotation, as per Rule 7, above.

Rule 9. When quoted material runs more than one paragraph, start each new paragraph with opening quotation marks, but do not use closing quotation marks until the end of the passage.

> **Example**:   *Francis wrote: "I don't paint anymore. For a while I thought it was just a phase*
> *that I'd get over.*
> *"Now, I don't even try."*

Note: For extended quotations, see Rule 8 of Colons for an option that does not use quotation marks.

QUESTION MARKS

Rule 1. Use a question mark only after a direct question.

> **Correct**:   *Will you go with me?*
> **Incorrect**:   *I'm asking if you will go with me?*

Rule 2a. A question mark replaces a period at the end of a sentence.

> **Incorrect**:   *Will you go with me?.*

Rule 2b. Because of Rule 2a, capitalize the word that follows a question mark. Some writers choose to overlook this rule in special cases.

Example: *Will you go with me? with Joe? with anyone?*

Rule 3a. Avoid the common trap of using question marks with **indirect questions**, which are statements that contain questions. Use a period after an indirect question.

Incorrect: *I wonder if he will go with me?*
Correct: *I wonder if he will go with me.*

OR

I wonder: Will he go with me?

Rule 3b. Some sentences are statements—or demands—in the form of a question. They are called **rhetorical questions** because they don't require or expect an answer. Many should be written without question marks.

Examples: *Why don't you take a break.*
Would you kids knock it off.
What wouldn't I do for you!

Rule 4. Use a question mark when a sentence is half statement and half question.

Example: *You do care, don't you?*

Rule 5. The placement of question marks with quotation marks follows logic. If a question is within the quoted material, a question mark should be placed inside the quotation marks.

Examples: *Alberta asked, "Will you still be my friend?"*
The question "Will you still be my friend?" is part of the quotation.
Do you agree with the saying "All's fair in love and war"?
The question *Do you agree with the saying?* is outside the quotation.

PARENTHESES AND BRACKETS

Parentheses and **brackets** must never be used interchangeably.

Parentheses

Rule 1. Use parentheses to enclose information that clarifies or is used as an aside.

    Example: *He finally answered (after taking five minutes to think) that he did not understand the question.*

If material in parentheses ends a sentence, the period goes after the parentheses.

    Example: *He gave me a nice bonus ($500).*

Commas could have been used in the first example; a colon could have been used in the second example. The use of parentheses indicates that the writer considered the information less important—almost an afterthought.

Rule 2a. Periods go inside parentheses only if an entire sentence is inside the parentheses.

    Example: *Please read the analysis. (You'll be amazed.)*

This is a rule with a lot of wiggle room. An entire sentence in parentheses is often acceptable without an enclosed period:

    Example: *Please read the analysis (you'll be amazed).*

Rule 2b. Take care to punctuate correctly when punctuation is required both inside and outside parentheses.

    Example: *You are late (aren't you?).*
                    Note the question mark within the parentheses. The period after the parentheses is necessary to bring the entire sentence to a close.

Rule 3. Parentheses, despite appearances, are not part of the subject.

    Example: *Joe (and his trusty mutt)* **was** *always welcome.*

If this seems awkward, try rewriting the sentence:

Example: *Joe (accompanied by his trusty mutt)* **was** *always welcome.*

Rule 4. Commas are more likely to follow parentheses than precede them.

Incorrect: *When he got home, (it was already dark outside) he fixed dinner.*
Correct: *When he got home (it was already dark outside), he fixed dinner.*

Brackets

Brackets are far less common than parentheses, and they are only used in special cases. Brackets (like single quotation marks) are used exclusively within quoted material.

Rule 1. Brackets are interruptions. When we see them, we know they've been added by someone else. They are used to explain or comment on the quotation.

Examples: *"Four score and seven [today we'd say eighty-seven] years ago…"*
                   "Bill shook hands with [his son] Al."

Rule 2. When quoting something that has a spelling or grammar mistake or presents material in a confusing way, insert the term *sic* in italics and enclose it in nonitalic (unless the surrounding text is italic) brackets.
     Sic ("thus" in Latin) is shorthand for, "This is exactly what the original material says."

Example: *She wrote, "I would rather die then [sic] be seen wearing the same outfit as*
                  my sister."
                  The [*sic*] indicates that *then* was mistakenly used instead of *than*.

Rule 3. In formal writing, brackets are often used to maintain the integrity of both a quotation and the sentences others use it in.

Example: *"[T]he better angels of our nature" gave a powerful ending to Lincoln's first*
                  inaugural address.
                  President Abraham Lincoln's memorable phrase came midsentence, so the
                  word *the* was not originally capitalized.

APOSTROPHES

Rule 1. Using an **apostrophe** to show **singular possession**

Rule 1a. To show possession with a singular noun, add an apostrophe plus the letter *s*.

> *Examples*:   *a woman's hat*
> *the boss's wife*
> *Mrs. Chang's house*

Rule 1b. Many common nouns end in the letter *s* (*lens, cactus, bus*, etc.). So do a lot of proper nouns (*Mr. Jones, Texas, Christmas*). There are conflicting policies and theories about how to show possession when writing such nouns. There is no right answer; the best advice is to choose a formula and stay consistent.

Rule 1c. Some writers and editors add only an apostrophe to all nouns ending in *s*. And some add an apostrophe + *s* to every proper noun, be it *Hastings's* or *Jones's*.

One method, common in newspapers and magazines, is to add an apostrophe + *s* (*'s*) to common nouns ending in *s*, but only a stand-alone apostrophe to proper nouns ending in *s*.

> *Examples*:   *the class's hours*
> *Mr. Jones' golf clubs*
> *the canvas's size*
> *Texas' weather*

Note: We sometimes hear that an inanimate object cannot possess, e.g., *the canvas's size* should be written *the size of the canvas*. However, this idea is routinely ignored by good writers (*the rocket's red glare*).

Care must be taken to place the apostrophe outside the word in question. For instance, if talking about a pen belonging to Mr. Hastings, many people would wrongly write *Mr. Hasting's pen* (his name is not Mr. Hasting).

> *Correct*:   *Mr. Hastings' pen*

A widely used technique favored for its simplicity is to write the word as we would speak it. For example, since most people saying "Mr. Hastings' pen" would not pronounce an added *s*, we would write *Mr. Hastings' pen* with no added *s*. But most people would pronounce an added *s* in "Jones's," so we'd write it as we say it: *Mr. Jones's golf clubs*. This method explains the punctuation of *for goodness' sake*.

This method works well with names ending in a silent *s*.

> *Correct:*   *René Descartes' life*

Rule 2. Using an **apostrophe** to show **plural possession**

Rule 2a. **Regular nouns** are nouns that form their plurals by adding either the letter *s* or *es* (*guy, guys; letter, letters; actress, actresses;* etc.). To show plural possession, simply put an apostrophe after the *s*.

> *Correct:*   *guys' night out* (*guy* + *s* + apostrophe)
> *Incorrect:*   *guy's night out* (implies only one guy)
>
> *Correct:*   *two actresses' roles* (*actress* + *es* + apostrophe)
> *Incorrect:*   *two actress's roles*

Rule 2b. Do not use an apostrophe + *s* to make a regular noun plural.

> *Incorrect:*   *Apostrophe's are confusing.*
> *Correct:*   *Apostrophes are confusing.*
>
> *Incorrect:*   *We've had many happy Christmas's.*
> *Correct:*   *We've had many happy Christmases.*

In special cases, such as when forming a plural of a word that is not normally a noun, some writers add an apostrophe for clarity.

> *Example:*   *Here are some do's and don'ts.*

In that sentence, the verb *do* is used as a plural noun, and the apostrophe was added because the writer felt that *dos* was confusing. Not all writers agree; some see no problem with *dos and don'ts.*

However, with single lowercase letters, it is advisable to use apostrophes.

> *Example:*   *My a's look like u's.*

Imagine the confusion if you wrote that sentence without apostrophes. Readers would see *as* and *us*, and feel lost.

Rule 2c. English also has many **irregular nouns** (*child, nucleus, tooth*, etc.). These nouns become plural by changing their spelling, sometimes becoming quite different words. You may find it helpful to write out the entire irregular plural noun before adding an apostrophe or an apostrophe + *s*.

Incorrect:	two childrens' hats
	The plural is *children*, not *childrens*.
Correct:	two children's hats (*children* + apostrophe + *s*)

| Incorrect: | the teeths' roots |
| Correct: | the teeth's roots |

Rule 2d. Things can get really confusing with the possessive plurals of proper names ending in *s*, *ch*, or *z*, such as *Hastings*, *Jones*, *Birch*, and *Sanchez*.

If you're the guest of the Ford family—the *Fords*—you're the *Fords'* guest (*Ford* + *s* + apostrophe). But what if it's the Hastings family?

Most would call them the "Hastings." But that would refer to a family named "Hasting." If someone's name ends in *s*, *ch*, or *z*, we must add *es* for the plural. The plural of *Hastings* is *Hastingses*. The members of the Birch family are the *Birches*.

To show possession, add an apostrophe.

| Incorrect: | the Hastings' dog |
| Correct: | the Hastingses' dog (*Hastings* + *es* + apostrophe) |

| Incorrect: | the Jones' car |
| Correct: | the Joneses' car |

| Incorrect: | the Birchs' home |
| Correct: | the Birches' home |

| Incorrect: | the Sanchez' new baby, the Sanchezs' new baby |
| Correct: | the Sanchezes' new baby |

In serious writing, this rule must be followed no matter how strange or awkward the results.

Rule 2e. Never use an apostrophe to make a name plural.

| Incorrect: | The Wilson's are here. |
| Correct: | The Wilsons are here. |

| Incorrect: | We visited the Sanchez's. |
| Correct: | We visited the Sanchezes. |

Rule 3. With a singular compound noun (for example, *mother-in-law*), show possession with an apostrophe + *s* at the end of the word.

| Example: | my mother-in-law's hat |

If the compound noun (e.g., *brother-in-law*) is to be made plural, form the plural first (*brothers-in-law*), and then use the apostrophe + *s*.

Example: *my two brothers-in-law's hats*

Rule 4a. If two people possess the same item, put the apostrophe + *s* after the second name only.

Example: *Cesar and Maribel's home is constructed of redwood.*

However, if one of the joint owners is written as a pronoun, use the possessive form for both.

Incorrect:	*Maribel and my home*
Incorrect:	*mine and Maribel's home*
Correct:	*Maribel's and my home.*
Incorrect:	*he and Maribel's home*
Incorrect:	*him and Maribel's home*
Correct:	*his and Maribel's home*
Incorrect:	*you and Maribel's home*
Incorrect:	*yours and Maribel's home*
Correct:	*Maribel's and your home*

Note: As the above examples demonstrate, when one of the co-owners is written as a pronoun, use **possessive adjectives** (*my, your, her, our, their*). Avoid **possessive pronouns** (*mine, yours, hers, ours, theirs*) in such constructions.

It should be mentioned that compound possessives are often clunky as well as confusing. For instance, *a picture of her and Cesar's house* could refer to a photo of "her" in front of the house that Cesar owns or a photo of the house that she and Cesar co-own. Big difference. Such ambiguous sentences should just be rewritten.

Rule 4b. In cases of separate rather than joint possession, use the possessive form for both.

Examples: *Cesar's and Maribel's homes are both lovely.*
                  They don't own the homes jointly.

                  Cesar and Maribel's homes are both lovely.
                  The homes belong to both of them.

Rule 5. Use an apostrophe with **contractions**. The apostrophe is placed where a letter or letters have been removed.

> **Examples:** *Doesn't, it's, 'tis, can't, you'd, should've, rock 'n' roll, etc.*
> **Incorrect:** *Does'nt*

Rule 6. There are various approaches to plurals for abbreviations, single letters, and numerals.
Many writers and editors prefer an apostrophe after single capitalized letters. (See *Rule 2b.* in regard to single lowercase letters.)

> **Example:** *I made straight A's.*

With groups of two or more capital letters, apostrophes seem less necessary.

> **Examples:** *There are two new MPs on the base.*
> *He learned his ABCs.*
>
> *She consulted with three M.D.s.*
> *Some write M.D.'s to give the s separation from the second period.*

There are different schools of thought about years and decades. The following examples are all in widespread use:

> **Examples:** *the 1990s*
> *the 1990's*
> *the '90s*
> *the 90's*
> **Awkward:** *the '90's*

Rule 7. Amounts of time or money are sometimes used as possessive adjectives that require apostrophes.

> **Incorrect:** *three days leave*
> **Correct:** *three days' leave*
>
> **Incorrect:** *my two cents worth*
> **Correct:** *my two cents' worth*

Rule 8. The personal pronouns *hers*, *ours*, *yours*, *theirs*, *its*, *whose*, and the pronoun *oneself* never take an apostrophe.

Example:	*Feed a horse grain. It's better for its health.*
Incorrect:	*Who's glasses are these?*
Correct:	*Whose glasses are these?*
Incorrect:	*Talking to one's self in public is odd.*
Correct:	*Talking to oneself in public is odd.*

Rule 9. When an apostrophe comes before a word or number, take care that it's truly an apostrophe (') rather than a single quotation mark (').

Incorrect:	*'Twas the night before Christmas.*
Correct:	*'Twas the night before Christmas.*
Incorrect:	*I voted in '08.*
Correct:	*I voted in '08.*

NOTE

Serious writers avoid the word *'til* as an alternative to *until*. The correct word is *till*, which is many centuries older than *until*.

Rule 10. Beware of **false possessives**, which often occur with nouns ending in *s*. Don't add apostrophes to noun-derived adjectives ending in *s*. Close analysis is the best guide.

Incorrect:	*We enjoyed the New Orleans' cuisine.*

In the preceding sentence, the word *the* makes no sense unless *New Orleans* is being used as an adjective to describe *cuisine*. In English, nouns frequently become adjectives. Adjectives rarely if ever take apostrophes.

Incorrect:	*I like that Beatles' song.*
Correct:	*I like that Beatles song.*

Again, *Beatles* is an adjective, modifying *song*.

Incorrect:	*He's a United States' citizen.*
Correct:	*He's a United States citizen.*

Rule 11. Beware of nouns ending in *y*; do not show possession by changing the *y* to *-ies*.

    Correct: *the company's policy*
    Incorrect: *the companies policy*

To show possession when a noun ending in *y* becomes plural, write *ies'* Do not write *y's*.

    Correct: *three companies' policies*
    Incorrect: *three company's policies*

Exception: Names and other proper nouns ending in *y* become plural simply by adding an *s*. They do not form their plurals with an apostrophe, or by changing the *y* to *ies*.

    Correct: *The Flannerys are coming over.*
    Incorrect: *The Flannery's are coming over.*
    Incorrect: *The Flanneries are coming over.*

    Correct: *The Flannerys' house was robbed.*
    Incorrect: *The Flanneries' house was robbed.*

HYPHENS

There are two things to keep in mind about this misunderstood punctuation mark. First, there should not be spaces around hyphens. Second, **hyphens** should not be used interchangeably with dashes (with the exception of Rule 6 below), which are noticeably longer.

Hyphens' main purpose is to glue words together. They notify the reader that two or more elements in a sentence are linked. Although there are rules and customs governing hyphens, there are also situations when writers must decide whether to add them for clarity.

Hyphens Between Words

Rule 1a. Generally, hyphenate two or more words when they come before a noun they modify and act as a single idea. This is called a **compound adjective**.

    Examples: *an off-campus apartment*
                      state-of-the-art design

When a compound adjective follows a noun, a hyphen is usually not necessary.

    Example: *The apartment is off campus.*

However, some established compound adjectives are always hyphenated. Double-check with a dictionary or online.

Example: *The design is state-of-the-art.*

Rule 1b. Use **suspended hyphens** when two or more compound adjectives come before the noun they modify.

Example: *We offer the finest protective equipment, including latex- and phthalate-*
free gloves.

Incorrect: *You can expect a three-four-week delay in processing.*
Correct: *You can expect a three- to four-week delay in processing.*

This is equivalent to writing You can expect a three-week to four-week delay in processing.

Rule 2a. A hyphen is frequently required when forming original compound verbs for vivid writing, humor, or special situations.

Examples: *The slacker video-gamed his way through life.*
Queen Victoria throne-sat for six decades.

Rule 2b. When writing out new, original, or unusual compound nouns, writers should hyphenate whenever doing so avoids confusion.

Examples: *I changed my diet and became a no-meater.*
No-meater is too confusing without the hyphen.

The slacker was a video gamer.
Video gamer is clear without a hyphen, although some writers might
prefer to hyphenate it.

Writers using familiar compound verbs and nouns should consult a dictionary or look online to decide if these verbs and nouns should be hyphenated.

Rule 3. An often overlooked rule for hyphens: The adverb *very* and adverbs ending in *ly* are not hyphenated.

Incorrect: *the very-elegant watch*
Incorrect: *the finely-tuned watch*

This rule applies only to adverbs. The following two examples are correct because the *ly* words are not adverbs:

Correct: *the friendly-looking dog*
Correct: *a family-owned cafe*

Rule 4. Hyphens are often used to tell the ages of people and things. A handy rule, whether writing about years, months, or any other period of time, is to use hyphens unless the period of time (years, months, weeks, days) is written in plural form:

With hyphens: *We have a two-year-old child.*
                   We have a two-year-old.
No hyphens: *The child is two years old.* (Because *years* is plural.)
Exception: *The child is one year old.* (Or *day, week, month,* etc.)

Note that when hyphens are involved in expressing ages, two hyphens are required. Many writers forget the second hyphen:

Incorrect: *We have a two-year old child.*
                Without the second hyphen, the sentence is about an "old child."

Rule 5. Never hesitate to add a hyphen if it solves a possible problem. Following are two examples of well-advised hyphens:

Confusing: *Springfield has little town charm.*
With hyphen: *Springfield has little-town charm.*
                 Without the hyphen, the sentence seems to say that Springfield is a dreary place. With the hyphen, *little-town* becomes a compound adjective, making the writer's intention clear: Springfield is a charming small town.
Confusing: *She had a concealed weapons permit.*
With hyphen: *She had a concealed-weapons permit.*
                 With no hyphen, we can only guess: Was the *weapons permit* hidden from sight, or was it a permit for concealed weapons? The hyphen makes *concealed-weapons* a compound adjective, so the reader knows that the writer meant *a permit for concealed weapons.*

Rule 6. When using numbers, hyphenate spans or estimates of time, distance, or other quantities. Remember not to use spaces around hyphens.

     Examples: *3:15-3:45 p.m.*
                       1999-2016
                       300-325 people

Note: Most publishers use the slightly longer **en dash** (see the "Dashes" section) instead of a hyphen in this situation.

     Examples: *3:15–3:45 p.m.*
                       1999–2016
                       300–325 people

Rule 7a. In general, with physical quantities, use a hyphen when the unit, abbreviation, or symbol is spelled out.

     Examples: *80-pound bag*
                       six-centimeter caterpillar (**Note:** the number is spelled out here because it's less than ten and not used with a symbol or abbreviation.)
                       100-meter dash

Rule 7b. In general, hyphens are not used between the numeral and the abbreviation or symbol, even when they are in adjectival form.

     Examples: *80 lb. bag*
                       6 cm caterpillar
                       100 m dash (**Note:** use a period when abbreviating English units but not when abbreviating metric units.)

NOTE
Rules 7a. and 7b. are based on standard usages in mathematical, statistical, technical, and scientific texts. However, specialized fields such as healthcare, education, and science often adhere to their own specific stylebook. In those cases, the stylebook should serve as the writer's guiding authority.

Rule 8. Hyphenate all compound numbers from *twenty-one* through *ninety-nine*.

Examples: *thirty-two children*
one thousand two hundred twenty-one dollars

Rule 9a. Hyphenate all spelled-out fractions. But do not hyphenate fractions introduced with *a* or *an*.

Examples: *More than one-third of registered voters oppose the measure.*
More than a third of registered voters oppose the measure.

Rule 9b. When writing out numbers with fractions, hyphenate only the fractions *unless* the construction is a compound adjective.

Correct: *The sign is five and one-half feet long.*
Correct: *A five-and-one-half-foot-long sign.*
Incorrect: *The sign is five-and-one-half feet long.*

See also *Rule 2b* in Chapter 4, "Writing Numbers."

Rule 10a. Do not hyphenate proper nouns of more than one word when they are used as compound adjectives.

Incorrect: *She is an Academy-Award nominee.*
Correct: *She is an Academy Award nominee.*

Rule 10b. However, hyphenate most double last names.

Example: *Sir Winthrop Heinz-Eakins will attend.*

Rule 11. Many editors do not hyphenate certain well-known expressions. They believe that set phrases, because of their familiarity (e.g., *high school*, *twentieth century*), can go before a noun without risk of confusing the reader.

Examples: *a high school senior*
an ice cream cone
a twentieth century throwback

However, other editors prefer hyphenating all compound modifiers, even those with low risk of ambiguity.

Examples: *a high-school senior*
an ice-cream cone
a twentieth-century throwback

Rule 12. When in doubt, look it up. Some familiar phrases may require hyphens. For instance, is a book *up to date* or *up-to-date*? Don't guess; have a dictionary close by, or look it up online.

Hyphens with Prefixes and Suffixes

A **prefix** (*a*, *un*, *de*, *ab*, *sub*, *post*, *anti*, etc.) is a letter or set of letters placed before a **root** word. The word *prefix* itself contains the prefix *pre*. Prefixes expand or change a word's meaning, sometimes radically: the prefixes *a*, *un*, *ir*, and *dis*, for example, change words into their opposites (e.g., *political*, **a**political; *friendly*, **un**friendly; *regular*, **ir**regular, *honor*, **dis**honor).

Rule 1. Hyphenate prefixes when they come before proper nouns or proper adjectives.

Examples: *trans-American*
mid-July

Rule 2. In describing family relations, *great* requires a hyphen, but *grand* becomes part of the word without a hyphen.

Examples: *My grandson and my granduncle never met.*
My great-great-grandfather fought in the Civil War.

Do not hyphenate *half brother* or *half sister*.

Rule 3. For clarity, many writers hyphenate prefixes ending in a vowel when the root word begins with the same letter.

Examples: *ultra-ambitious*
semi-invalid

However, in recognition of the modern trend toward spare hyphenation, do not hyphenate after *pre* and *re* prefixes when the root word begins with *e*.

Rule 4. Hyphenate all words beginning with the prefixes *self-*, *ex-* (i.e., *former*), and *all-*.

Examples: *self-assured*
                    ex-mayor
                    all-knowing

Rule 5. Use a hyphen with the prefix *re* when omitting the hyphen would cause confusion with another word.

Examples: *Will she recover from her illness?*
                    I have re-covered the sofa twice.
                    Omitting the hyphen would cause confusion with *recover*.

                    I must re-press the shirt.
                    Omitting the hyphen would cause confusion with *repress*.

                    The stamps have been reissued.
                    A hyphen after *re-* is not needed because there is no confusion with
                        another word.

Rule 6. Writers often hyphenate prefixes when they feel a word might be distracting or confusing without the hyphen.

Examples: *de-ice*
                    With no hyphen we get *deice*, which might stump readers.

                    co-worker
                    With no hyphen we get *coworker*, which could be distracting because it
                        starts with *cow*.

A **suffix** (*y*, *er*, *ism*, *able*, etc.) is a letter or set of letters that follows a root word. Suffixes form new words or alter the original word to perform a different task. For example, the noun *scandal* can be made into the adjective *scandalous* by adding the suffix *ous*. It becomes the verb *scandalize* by adding the suffix *ize*.

Rule 1. Suffixes are not usually hyphenated. Some exceptions:
-style, *-elect*, *-free*, *-based*.

Examples: *Modernist-style paintings*
                    Mayor-elect Smith
                    sugar-free soda
                    oil-based sludge

Rule 2. For clarity, writers often hyphenate when the last letter in the root word is the same as the first letter in the suffix.

> *Examples*:   *graffiti-ism*
> *wiretap-proof*

Rule 3. Use discretion—and sometimes a dictionary—before deciding to place a hyphen before a suffix. But do not hesitate to hyphenate a rare usage if it avoids confusion.

> *Examples*:   *the annual dance-athon*
> *an eel-esque sea creature*

Although the preceding hyphens help clarify unusual terms, they are optional and might not be every writer's choice. Still, many readers would scratch their heads for a moment over *danceathon* and *eelesque*.

DASHES

Dashes can be a complex topic with many subtle uses. The various types include the en dash, em dash, 2-em dash, and 3-em dash. We will limit our discussion to the most common uses of the en and em dashes as they will fulfill the bulk of the needs of most writers.

Em dashes, like commas, semicolons, colons, ellipses, and parentheses, indicate added emphasis, an interruption, or an abrupt change of thought. Experienced writers know that these marks are not interchangeable. Note how dashes subtly change the tone of the following sentences:

> *Examples*:   *You are the friend, the only friend, who offered to help me.*
> *You are the friend—the only friend—who offered to help me.*
>
> *I pay the bills; she has all the fun.*
> *I pay the bills—she has all the fun.*
>
> *I wish you would … oh, never mind.*
> *I wish you would—oh, never mind.*

Rule 1. Words and phrases between dashes are not generally part of the subject.

> *Example*:   *Joe—and his trusty mutt—**was** always welcome.*

Rule 2. Dashes replace otherwise mandatory punctuation, such as the commas after *Iowa* and *2013* in the following examples:

Without dash:	*The man from Ames, Iowa, arrived.*
With dash:	*The man—he was from Ames, Iowa—arrived.*
Without dash:	*The May 1, 2013, edition of the* Ames Sentinel *arrived in June.*
With dash:	*The* Ames Sentinel—*dated May 1, 2013*—*arrived in June.*

Rule 3. Some writers and publishers prefer spaces around dashes.

Example: *Joe — and his trusty mutt — was always welcome.*

En dashes are shorter than em dashes and longer than hyphens. Like hyphens, they can be used for number ranges (see Rule 6 of "Hyphens Between Words").

Examples: *The student council will meet Thursday, 3:15–3:45 p.m.*
During the years 1999–2016, Joshua lived in Fargo, North Dakota.
We expect 300–325 people at the reception.

En dashes also can be used to punctuate **open compound** adjectives like *New York based artist* or *Charles Dickens inspired writer*. *New York* and *Charles Dickens* are called open compounds in these cases because we would not normally hyphenate them. Some writers and publishers prefer using an en dash for these situations, but a hyphen would work as well.

Examples: *New York–based artist*
Charles Dickens–inspired writer

However, consider the open compound expression *apple orchard scented candle*. Using an en dash for this phrase may better clarify the intent for readers over using a hyphen.

Example: *apple orchard–scented candle*

Some methods for forming these punctuation marks on a PC:

En dash—hold down the Alt key and type **0150** on the numeric keypad
Em dash—hold down the Alt key and type **0151** on the numeric keypad

On a Mac:

En dash—press option+hyphen key
Em dash—press option+shift+hyphen key

ELLIPSES

Definition
- An **ellipsis** (plural: *ellipses*) is a punctuation mark consisting of three dots.

Use an ellipsis when omitting a word, phrase, line, paragraph, or more from a quoted passage. Ellipses save space or remove material that is less relevant. They are useful in getting right to the point without delay or distraction:

Full quotation: "*Today, after hours of careful thought, the governor vetoed the bill.*"
With ellipsis: "*Today … the governor vetoed the bill.*"

Although ellipses are used in many ways, the three-dot method is the simplest. Newspapers, magazines, and books of fiction and nonfiction use various approaches that they find suitable. Some writers and editors feel that no spaces are necessary.

Example: *I don't know …I'm not sure.*

A commonly used method we favor is to enclose the ellipsis with a space on each side.

Example: *I don't know … I'm not sure.*

A four-dot method may be used to indicate the period at the end of a sentence, then the ellipsis to indicate omitted material.

Example: *I don't know.… I'm not sure.*

Even more rigorous methods used by some publishers and in legal works require fuller explanations that can be found in other reference books.

Rule 1. Many writers use an ellipsis whether the omission occurs at the beginning of a sentence, in the middle of a sentence, or between sentences.

A common way to delete the beginning of a sentence is to follow the opening quotation mark with an ellipsis, plus a bracketed capital letter:

Example: "*…[A]fter hours of careful thought, the governor vetoed the bill.*"

Other writers omit the ellipsis in such cases, feeling the bracketed capital letter gets the point across.

For more on brackets, see "Parentheses and Brackets," earlier in this chapter.

Rule 2. Ellipses can express hesitation, changes of mood, suspense, or thoughts trailing off. Writers also use ellipses to indicate a pause or wavering in an otherwise straightforward sentence.

> **Examples:**   *I don't know ... I'm not sure.*
> *Pride is one thing, but what happens if she ...?*
> *He said, "I ... really don't ... understand this."*

EXCLAMATION POINTS

Rule 1. Use an exclamation point to show emotion, emphasis, or surprise.

> **Examples:**   *I'm truly shocked by your behavior!*
> *Yay! We won!*

Rule 2. An exclamation point replaces a period at the end of a sentence. It also replaces a mid-sentence comma.

> **Incorrect:**   *I'm truly shocked by your behavior!.*
> **Correct:**   *I'm truly shocked by your behavior!*
>
> **Incorrect:**   *"I'm truly shocked by your behavior!," I told her.*
> **Correct:**   *"I'm truly shocked by your behavior!" I told her.*

Rule 3. Avoid using an exclamation point in formal business writing.

Rule 4. Overuse of exclamation points is a sign of undisciplined writing. The writer F. Scott Fitzgerald once said, "An exclamation point is like laughing at your own joke." Do not use even one of these marks unless you're convinced it is justified.

SLASHES

Despite its popularity, the slash (/), technically known as a *virgule*, is frowned upon by purists. Other than to indicate dates (*9/11/2001*) or to separate lines of poetry ("Celery, raw / Develops the jaw"), it has few defensible uses.

Usually a hyphen, or in some cases the word *or*, will suffice. Instead of writing *the novelist/ poet Eve Jones*, make it *the novelist-poet Eve Jones*. Rather than *available to any man/woman who is qualified*, make it *any man or woman*.

The slash has always been a handy tool for taking notes and writing rough outlines. Substituting *w/o* for *without*, *y/o* for *years old*, and *b/c* for *because* can save valuable time and space.

However, most slashes can—and should—be removed from a final draft. Writers should replace a construction like *any man/woman* with *any man or woman* in their finished work.

"The virgule is a mark that doesn't appear much in first-rate writing," says Bryan A. Garner in *A Dictionary of Modern American Usage*. "Use it as a last resort."

CHAPTER 3

CAPITALIZATION

Capitalization is the writing of a word with its first letter in uppercase and the remaining letters in lowercase. Experienced writers are stingy with capitals. It is best not to use them if there is any doubt.

Rule 1. Capitalize the first word of a document and the first word after a period.

Rule 2. Capitalize proper nouns—and adjectives derived from proper nouns.

> *Examples*: *the Golden Gate Bridge*
> *the Grand Canyon*
> *a Russian song*
> *a Shakespearean sonnet*
> *a Freudian slip*

With the passage of time, some words originally derived from proper nouns have taken on a life, and authority, of their own and no longer require capitalization.

> *Examples*: *herculean* (from the mythological hero Hercules)
> *quixotic* (from the hero of the classic novel *Don Quixote*)
> *draconian* (from ancient-Athenian lawgiver Draco)

The main function of capitals is to focus attention on particular elements within any group of people, places, or things. We can speak of *a lake in the middle of the country*, or we can be more specific and say *Lake Michigan*, which distinguishes it from every other lake on earth.

Capitalization Reference List

- Brand names
- Companies
- Days of the week and months of the year
- Governmental matters

  Congress (but *congressional*), *the U.S. Constitution* (but *constitutional*), *the Electoral College, Department of Agriculture.* **Note**: Many authorities do not capitalize *federal* or *state* unless it is part of the official title: *State Water Resources Control Board*, but *state water board; Federal Communications Commission*, but *federal regulations.*

- Historical episodes and eras

  the Inquisition, the American Revolutionary War, the Great Depression

- Holidays
- Institutions

  Oxford College, the Juilliard School of Music

- Manmade structures

  the Empire State Building, the Eiffel Tower, the Titanic

- Manmade territories

  Berlin, Montana, Cook County

- Natural and manmade landmarks

  Mount Everest, the Hoover Dam

- Nicknames and epithets

  Andrew "Old Hickory" Jackson; Babe Ruth, the Sultan of Swat

- Organizations

  American Center for Law and Justice, Norwegian Ministry of the Environment

- Planets

  Mercury, Venus, Mars, Jupiter, Saturn, Uranus, Neptune, but policies vary on capitalizing *earth*, and it is usually not capitalized unless it is being discussed specifically as a planet: *We learned that Earth travels through space at 66,700 miles per hour.*

- Races, nationalities, and tribes

  Eskimo, Navajo, East Indian, Caucasian, African American

- Religions and names of deities

  Note: Capitalize *the Bible* (but *biblical*). Do not capitalize *heaven, hell, the devil, satanic.*

- Special occasions

  the Olympic Games, the Cannes Film Festival

- Streets and roads

Lowercase Reference List

Here is a list of categories *not* capitalized unless an item contains a proper noun or proper adjective (or, sometimes, a trademark). In such cases, only the proper noun or adjective is capitalized.

- Animals
  antelope, black bear, Bengal tiger, yellow-bellied sapsucker, German shepherd
- Elements
  Always lowercase, even when the name is derived from a proper noun: *einsteinium, nobelium, californium*
- Foods
  Lowercase except for brand names, proper nouns and adjectives, or custom-named recipes: *Tabasco sauce, Russian dressing, pepper crusted bluefin tuna, Mandy's Bluefin Surprise*
- Heavenly bodies besides planets
  Never capitalize the *moon* or the *sun.*
- Medical conditions
  Epstein-Barr syndrome, tuberculosis, Parkinson's disease
- Minerals
- Plants, vegetables, and fruits
  poinsettia, Douglas fir, Jerusalem artichoke, organic celery, Golden Delicious apples
- Seasons and seasonal data
  spring, summertime, the winter solstice, the autumnal equinox, daylight saving time

Rule 3. A thorny aspect of capitalization: where does it stop? When does the *Iraq war* become the *Iraq War*? Why is the legendary *Hope Diamond* not the *Hope diamond?* Everyone writes *New York City*, so why does the *Associated Press Stylebook* recommend *New York state*? There aren't always easy formulas or logical explanations. Research with reference books and search engines is the best strategy.

In the case of brand names, companies are of little help, because they capitalize any word that applies to their merchandise. *Domino's Pizza* or *Domino's pizza*? Is it *Ivory Soap* or *Ivory soap*, a *Hilton Hotel* or a *Hilton hotel*? Most writers don't capitalize common nouns that simply describe the products (*pizza, soap, hotel*), but it's not always easy to determine where a brand name ends. There is *Time* magazine but also the *New York Times Magazine*. No one would argue with *Coca-Cola* or *Pepsi Cola*, but a case could be made for *Royal Crown cola*.

If a trademark starts with a lowercase word or letter (e.g., *eBay, iPhone*), many authorities advise capitalizing it to begin a sentence.

Example: *EBay opened strong in trading today.*

Rule 4. Capitalize titles when they are used before names, unless the title is followed by a comma. Do not capitalize the title if it is used after a name or instead of a name.

Examples: *The president will address Congress.*
Chairman of the Board William Bly will preside at the conference.
The chairman of the board, William Bly, will preside.
The senators from Iowa and Ohio are expected to attend.
Also expected to attend are Senators Buzz James and Eddie Twain.
The governors, lieutenant governors, and attorneys general called for a special task force.
Governor Fortinbrass, Lieutenant Governor Poppins, and Attorney General Dalloway will attend.

NOTE

Out of respect, some writers and publishers choose to capitalize the highest ranks in government, royalty, religion, etc.

Examples: *The President arrived.*
The Queen spoke.
The Pope decreed.

Many American writers believe this to be a wrongheaded policy in a country where, theoretically, all humans are perceived as equal.

Rule 5. Titles are not the same as occupations. Do not capitalize occupations before full names.

Examples: *director Steven Spielberg*
owner Helen Smith
coach Biff Sykes

Sometimes the line between title and occupation gets blurred. One example is *general manager*: is it a title or an occupation? Opinions differ. Same with *professor*: The *Associated Press Stylebook* considers *professor* a job description rather than a title and recommends using lowercase even before the full name: *professor Robert Ames*.

However, titles replacing someone's first name are generally capitalized.

Example: *Here comes Professor Ames.*

Rule 6a. Capitalize a formal title when it is used as a direct address. The more formal the title, the more likely it is to be capitalized.

Examples:
> *Will you take my temperature, Doctor?*
> *We're sorry to report, Captain, that we're headed for choppy waters.*
> *That's what you say, mister.*
> *Good afternoon, sweetheart.*

Rule 6b. Capitalize relatives' family names (kinship names) when they immediately precede a personal name or when they are used alone in place of a personal name.

Examples:
> *I found out that Mom is here.*
> *You look good, Grandpa.*
> *Andy and Opie loved Aunt Bee's apple pies.*

However, these monikers are not capitalized when they are used with possessive nouns or pronouns; when preceded by articles such as *a*, *an*, or *the*; when they follow the personal name; or when they do not refer to a specific person.

Examples:
> *I found out that my mom is here.*
> *Joe's grandpa looks good.*
> *He's the father of her first child.*
> *The James brothers were notorious robbers.*
> *There's not one mother I know who would allow that.*

Rule 6c. Capitalize nicknames in all cases.

Examples:
> *Meet my brothers, Junior and Scooter.*
> *I just met two guys named Junior and Scooter.*

Rule 7. Capitalize specific geographical regions. Do not capitalize points of the compass.

Examples:
> *We had three relatives visit from the West.*
> *Go west three blocks and then turn left.*
> *We left Florida and drove north.*
> *We live in the Southeast.*
> *We live in the southeast section of town.*
> *Most of the West Coast is rainy this time of year.* (referring to the
>   United States)
> *The west coast of Scotland is rainy this time of year.*

Some areas have come to be capitalized for their fame or notoriety:

Examples: *I'm from New York's Upper West Side.*
                   I'm from the South Side of Chicago.
                   You live in Northern California; he lives in Southern California.

Rule 8. In general, do not capitalize the word *the* before proper nouns.

Examples: *We visited the Grand Canyon.*
                   They're fans of the Grateful Dead.

In special cases, if the word *the* is an inseparable part of something's official title, it may be capitalized.

Example: *We visited The Hague.*

Rule 9. It is not necessary to capitalize *city*, *town*, *county*, etc., if it comes before the proper name.

Examples: *the city of New York*
                   New York City
                   the county of Marin
                   Marin County

Rule 10a. Always capitalize the first word in a complete quotation, even midsentence.

Example: *Lamarr said, "The case is far from over, and we will win."*

Rule 10b. Do not capitalize quoted material that continues a sentence.

Example: *Lamarr said that the case was "far from over" and that "we will win."*

Rule 11. For emphasis, writers sometimes capitalize a midsentence independent clause or question.

Examples: *One of her cardinal rules was, Never betray a friend.*
                   It made me wonder, What is mankind's destiny?

Rule 12. Capitalize the names of specific course titles, but not general academic subjects.

Examples: *I must take history and Algebra 101.*
He has a double major in European economics and philosophy.

Rule 13. Capitalize art movements.

Example: *I like Surrealism, but I never understood Abstract Expressionism.*

Rule 14. Do not capitalize the first item in a list that follows a colon.

Example: *Bring the following: paper, a pencil, and a snack.*

For more on capitalization after a colon, go to "Colons," Rules 1, 3, and 4, in Chapter Two.

Rule 15. Do not capitalize "*the national anthem.*"

Rule 16a. Composition titles: which words should be capitalized in titles of books, plays, films, songs, poems, essays, chapters, etc.? This is a vexing matter, and policies vary. The usual advice is to capitalize only the "important" words. But this isn't really very helpful. Aren't all words in a title important?

The following rules for capitalizing composition titles are virtually universal.

- Capitalize the title's first and last word.
- Capitalize all adjectives, adverbs, and nouns.
- Capitalize all pronouns (including *it*).
- Capitalize all verbs, including all forms of the state of being verbs (*am, is, are, was, will be*, etc.).
- Capitalize *no, not*, and the interjection *O* (e.g., *How Long Must I Wait, O Lord?*).
- Do not capitalize an article (*a, an, the*) unless it is first or last in the title.
- Do not capitalize a **coordinating conjunction** (*and, or, nor, but, for, yet, so*) unless it is first or last in the title.
- Do not capitalize the word *to*, with or without an infinitive, unless it is first or last in the title.

Otherwise, styles, methods, and opinions vary; for instance. certain short conjunctions (e.g., *as, if, how, that*) are capped by some, lowercased by others.

A major bone of contention is prepositions. The *Associated Press Stylebook* recommends capitalizing all prepositions of more than three letters (e.g., *with, about, across*). Other authorities advise lowercase until a preposition reaches five or more letters. Still others say not to capitalize any preposition, even big words like *regarding* or *underneath*.

Hyphenated words in a title also present problems. There are no set rules except to always capitalize the first element, even if it would not otherwise be capitalized, such as *to* in *My To-go Order* (some would write *My To-Go Order*). Some writers, editors, and publishers choose not to capitalize words following hyphens unless they are proper nouns or proper adjectives (*Ex-Marine* but *ex-husband*). Others capitalize any word that would otherwise be capped in titles (*Prize-Winning, Up-to-Date*).

Rule. 16b. Many books have subtitles. When including these, put a colon after the work's title and follow the same rules of composition capitalization for the subtitle.

Example: *The King's English: A Guide to Modern Usage*

Note that *A* is capitalized because it is the first word of the subtitle.

Suppose you are reviewing a book whose title on the cover is in capital letters: *THE STUFF OF THOUGHT*. Beneath, in smaller capital letters, is the subtitle, *LANGUAGE AS A WINDOW INTO HUMAN NATURE*. All sides would agree that the main title should be written, *The Stuff of Thought*. But depending on which capitalization policy you choose, the subtitle might be any of the following:

*Language **As** a Window **Into** Human Nature*
*Language **as** a Window **Into** Human Nature*
*Language **As** a Window **into** Human Nature*
*Language **as** a Window **into** Human Nature*

Any title of more than two words can be a challenge. How would you capitalize a title such as *not yet rich*? Since the first and last word in any title are always capitalized, the only question is whether to cap *yet*. In this case, *yet* is an adverb, and adverbs are always capped. So make it *Not Yet Rich*.

Now suppose the title is *rich yet miserable*. This time *yet* is one of the seven coordinating conjunctions (the others are *and, or, nor, but, for,* and *so*). Since coordinating conjunctions are not capitalized in titles, the right answer is *Rich yet Miserable*.

Here are two correctly capitalized titles: *Going up the Road* and *Going Up in a Balloon*. In the first title, *up* is a preposition, and short prepositions are not capitalized. In the second title, *Up* is an adverb and should be capped.

Along the same lines, compare the following three sentences: *I Got It off the Internet, Please Put It Off for Today,* and *I Hit the Off Switch*. In the first example, the preposition *off* is lowercase. But the word must be capped in the second example because *put off*, meaning "to postpone," is a two-word phrasal verb (a verb of two or more words). One-word verbs, helping verbs (see Chapter 1, "Finding Nouns, Verbs, and Subjects"), and phrasal verbs are always capitalized. *Off* is also capped in the third sentence because the word functions as an adjective in that title, and adjectives are always capitalized.

Although the seven coordinating conjunctions are not capitalized, you may have noticed there are many more than seven conjunctions in English. Most of these are called **subordinating conjunctions**, because they join a subordinate clause to a main clause. Familiar examples include *as*, *although*, *before*, *since*, *until*, *when*.

There are three approaches to capping subordinating conjunctions: capitalize them all, lowercase them all, or capitalize them if they are words of four letters or more. Take your pick.

Capitalizing composition titles is fraught with gray areas. Pick a policy and be consistent.

CHAPTER 4

WRITING NUMBERS

Except for a few basic rules, spelling out numbers versus using figures (also called numerals) is largely a matter of writers' preference. Again, consistency is the key.

Policies and philosophies vary from medium to medium. America's two most influential style and usage guides have different approaches: *The Associated Press Stylebook* recommends spelling out the numbers zero through nine and using numerals thereafter—until one million is reached. Here are four examples of how to write numbers above 999,999 in AP style: *1 million*; *20 million*; *20,040,086*; *2.7 trillion*.

The Chicago Manual of Style recommends spelling out the numbers zero through one hundred and using figures thereafter—except for whole numbers used in combination with *hundred, thousand, hundred thousand, million, billion,* and beyond (e.g., *two hundred*; *twenty-eight thousand*; *three hundred thousand*; *one million*). In Chicago style, as opposed to AP style, we would write *four hundred, eight thousand,* and *twenty million* with no numerals—but like AP, Chicago style would require numerals for *401*; *8,012*; and *20,040,086*.

This is a complex topic, with many exceptions, and there is no consistency we can rely on among blogs, books, newspapers, and magazines. This chapter will confine itself to rules that all media seem to agree on.

Rule 1. Spell out all numbers beginning a sentence.

> ***Examples:*** *Twenty-three hundred sixty-one victims were hospitalized.*
> *Twenty twenty was quite a year.*

Note: The *Associated Press Stylebook* makes an exception for years.

> ***Example:*** *2020 was quite a year.*

Rule 2a. Hyphenate all compound numbers from twenty-one through ninety-nine.

Examples: *Forty-three people were injured in the train wreck.*
             Twenty-seven of them were hospitalized.

Rule 2b. Hyphenate all written-out fractions.

Examples: *We recovered about two-thirds of the stolen cash.*
             One-half is slightly less than five-eighths.

However, do not hyphenate terms like *a third* or *a half*.

Rule 3a. With figures of four or more digits, use commas. Count three spaces to the left to place the first comma. Continue placing commas after every three digits. *Important*: Do not include decimal points when doing the counting.

Examples: *1,054 people*
             $2,417,592.21

Note: Some choose not to use commas with four-digit numbers, but this practice is not recommended.

Rule 3b. It is not necessary to use a decimal point or a dollar sign when writing out sums of less than a dollar.

Not advised: *He had only $0.60.*
Better: *He had only sixty cents.*
                OR
                He had only 60 cents.

Rule 3c. Do not add the word "dollars" to figures preceded by a dollar sign.

Incorrect: *I have $1,250 dollars in my checking account.*
Correct: *I have $1,250 in my checking account.*

Rule 4a. For clarity, use *noon* and *midnight* rather than *12:00 PM* and *12:00 AM*.

NOTE

AM and *PM* are also written *A.M.* and *P.M.*, *a.m.* and *p.m.*, and *am* and *pm*. Some put a space between the time and *AM* or *PM*.

Examples: 8 AM
3:09 P.M.
11:20 P.M.

Others write times using no space before *AM* or *PM*.

Examples: 8AM
3:09P.M.
11:20p.m.

For the top of the hour, some write *9:00 PM*, whereas others drop the *:00* and write *9 PM* (or *9 p.m.*, *9pm*, etc.).

Rule 4b. Using numerals for the time of day has become widely accepted.

Examples: *The flight leaves at 6:22 a.m.*
Please arrive by 12:30 sharp.

However, some writers prefer to spell out the time, particularly when using *o'clock*.

Examples: *She takes the four thirty-five train.*
The baby wakes up at five o'clock in the morning.

Rule 5. Mixed fractions are often expressed in figures unless they begin a sentence.

Examples: *We expect a 5½ percent wage increase.*
Five and one-half percent was the expected wage increase.

Rule 6. The simplest way to express large numbers is usually best.

Example: *twenty-three hundred* (simpler than *two thousand three hundred*)

Large round numbers are often spelled out, but be consistent within a sentence.

Consistent: *You can earn from one million to five million dollars.*
Inconsistent: *You can earn from one million dollars to 5 million dollars.*
Inconsistent: *You can earn from $1 million to five million dollars.*

Rule 7. Write decimals using figures.

Example: *A meter is about 1.1 times longer than a yard.*

As a courtesy to readers, many writers put a zero in front of the decimal point with numbers less than one.

Examples: *The plant grew 0.79 inches last year.*
The plant grew only 0.07 inches this year.

(**Note:** For clarity, when needing the symbols for inches or feet, we recommend using the double-prime [″] or the prime [′], respectively, rather than double or single quotation marks.)

Rule 8a. When writing out a number of three or more digits, the word *and* is not necessary. However, use the word *and* to express any decimal points that may accompany these numbers.

Examples: *five thousand two hundred eighty feet*
one thousand one hundred fifty-four dollars
one thousand one hundred fifty-four dollars and sixty-one cents
Simpler: *eleven hundred fifty-four dollars and sixty-one cents*

Rule 8b. When writing out numbers above 999, do not use commas.

Incorrect: *one thousand, one hundred fifty-four dollars, and sixty-one cents.*
Correct: *one thousand one hundred fifty-four dollars and sixty-one cents.*

Rule 9. When it's important to ensure a number is not misinterpreted, some writers will indicate the number in both numerals and written out. The number in parentheses comes second.

Incorrect: *Add (73) seventy-three grams of sodium chloride to the beaker.*
Incorrect: *Add (seventy-three) 73 grams of sodium chloride to the beaker.*
Correct: *Add 73 (seventy-three) grams of sodium chloride to the beaker.*
Correct: *Add seventy-three (73) grams of sodium chloride to the beaker.*

Rule 10. The following examples are typical when using figures to express dates.

Examples: *the 30th of June, 1934*
              June 30, 1934 (no *-th* necessary)

Rule 11a. When spelling out decades, do not capitalize them.

Example: *During the eighties and nineties, the U.S. economy grew.*

Rule 11b. When expressing decades using figures, it is simpler to put an apostrophe before the incomplete numeral and no apostrophe between the number and the *s*.

Preferred: *During the '80s and '90s, the U.S. economy grew.*
Awkward: *During the 80s and 90s, the U.S. economy grew.*

Though not as common, some writers place an apostrophe after the number:

Example: *During the 80's and 90's, the U.S. economy grew.*
Awkward: *During the '80's and '90's, the U.S. economy grew.*

Rule 11c. You may also express decades in complete numerals. Again, it is cleaner to avoid an apostrophe between the year and the *s*.

Example: *During the 1980s and 1990s, the U.S. economy grew.*

Rule 12. Single-digit numbers are usually spelled out, but when they aren't, you are just as likely to see *2s and 3s* as *2's and 3's*. With double digits and above, many (but not everyone) regard the apostrophe as superfluous: *I scored in the high 90s.*

CHAPTER 5

CONFUSING WORDS AND HOMONYMS

Many words in English sound or look alike, causing confusion and not a few headaches. This chapter lists some of these words, and other troublemakers.

A

A, AN

Use *a* when the first letter of the word following has the sound of a consonant. Keep in mind that some vowels can sound like consonants, such as when they're sounded out as individual letters. Also, some letters, notably *h* and *u*, sometimes act as consonants (*home*, *usual*), other times as vowels (*honest*, *unusual*).

Examples: *a yearning*
     a hotel
     a U-turn (pronounced "yoo")
     a NASA study

Use *an* when the first letter of the word following has the sound of a vowel.

Examples: *an unfair charge*
     an honor (the *h* is silent)
     an HMO plan (*H* is pronounced "aitch")
     an NAACP convention (the *N* is pronounced "en")

ABACK

See **taken aback, taken back**

ABBREVIATION, ACRONYM, INITIALISM

There is a fine distinction between these words that some consider nitpicking. *Abbreviation* is the umbrella term for any shortened or contracted form of a word or phrase, such as *Dr.* for *Doctor* or *lb.* for *pound*. Terms such as *FBI, HMO,* and *NAACP*, although widely called acronyms, are actually initialisms. The difference is in how they are spoken. An *initialism* is pronounced letter by letter. An *acronym* is pronounced as if it were a word. The abbreviation *FBI* is pronounced "eff-bee-eye." The acronym *NASA* is pronounced "nassa."

ACCEPT, EXCEPT

Accept means "to acknowledge" or "to agree to."

Except is usually a preposition used to specify what isn't included: *I like all fruits except apples.*

AD, ADD

Ad: short for "advertisement."

Add: to include; to perform addition.

ADAPT, ADOPT

To *adapt* is to take something and change it for a special purpose. A screenwriter adapts a book to make it work as a movie. An organism adapts (itself) to a new environment.

To *adopt* is to take something and use it or make it your own. A government adopts a different policy. A family adopts an orphan.

ADVERSE, AVERSE

Adverse: unfavorable: *an adverse reaction to the medication.*

Averse: not fond of; seeking to avoid: *averse to risk.*

ADVICE, ADVISE

Advice: guidance.

Advise: to suggest; to recommend.

ADVISER, ADVISOR

Both words are acceptable for a person who gives advice. The more common spelling is *adviser*, although *advisor* is often used in formal job titles in the United States and Canada.

AFFECT, EFFECT

Affect as a verb means "to influence": *It affected me strangely.* As a noun, it is a technical term used in psychology to describe someone's emotional state.

Effect as a noun means "result": *It had a strange effect on me.* As a verb, it means "to bring about" or "to cause": *He's trying to effect change in government.*

AFFINITY

Some seven hundred years ago, *affinity* meant "relation by marriage." By extension, the proper use of *affinity* involves mutuality. But that sense of mutual attraction is often absent in contemporary uses of *affinity*, such as these: "She always had an affinity for growing fruit." "I have an affinity for vintage chairs." "My friend has an affinity for making things out of cardboard." In these examples, "growing fruit," "vintage chairs," and "making things out of cardboard" are passive elements, not active components in a relationship. Better to say "a *talent* for growing fruit," "a *fondness* for vintage chairs," "a *flair* for making things out of cardboard."

In the examples above, *affinity* is followed by the preposition *for*. But in formal English, the phrase *affinity for* should be avoided. The editor Theodore M. Bernstein advised writers to "discard *for*" and instead "use *between*, *with*, or sometimes *to*."

Here are three sentences that use *affinity* correctly: "There is a close affinity *between* Khan's music and that of the Brecker Brothers." "Some people have a natural affinity *with* children." "Two vaccines containing native proteins with affinity *to* porcine transferrin were tested."

There is no affinity unless it is shared by both parties.

AGGRAVATE

This word is not a synonym for *annoy* or *irritate*. To *aggravate* is to make something worse: *He started running too soon and aggravated his sprained ankle.*

AHOLD

You can get *hold* of something, and you can get *a hold* of it. But in formal writing, *ahold* is not considered a valid word.

AID, AIDE

An *aid* is a thing that helps.

An *aide* is a living helper or assistant: *His aide brought first aid.*

AIL, ALE

Ail: to be ill.

Ale: an alcoholic beverage.

AISLE, ISLE

Aisle: a corridor.

Isle: an island.

ALIBI

Be careful when you use *alibi*, originally a Latin word meaning "somewhere else." If you have an alibi, you can prove you were elsewhere when the crime occurred. H.W. Fowler, the dean of language scholars, said of *alibi*: "That it should have come to be used as a pretentious synonym for *excuse* is a striking example of the harm that can be done by SLIPSHOD EXTENSION."

ALL BUT ONE

See more than one.

ALL READY, ALREADY

All ready means that everything or everyone is now ready.

Already refers to something accomplished earlier: *We already ate.*

ALL RIGHT

Two words. Someday, *alright* may finally prevail, but it hasn't yet.

ALL-TIME RECORD

The team set an all-time record for consecutive games won. Delete *all-time*. All records are "all-time" records.

Similarly, avoid "new record." The team set a record, not a new record.

ALL TOGETHER, ALTOGETHER

All together: in a group: *We're all together in this.*

Altogether: entirely: *It is not altogether his fault.*

ALLUDE, ELUDE, REFER

Allude means "to mention indirectly." Do not confuse *allude* with *refer*. If we say, "Good old Joe is here," we *refer* to Joe. If we say, "That man with the ready laugh is here," we *allude* to Joe, but we never mention his name.

Allude is also sometimes confused with *elude*, which means "to escape" or "avoid capture."

ALLUSION, ILLUSION

Allusion, the noun form of *allude*, is an indirect, sometimes sly, way of talking about something or someone.

An *illusion* is a false perception.

ALLOWED, ALOUD

Allowed: permitted.

Aloud: said out loud.

ALTAR, ALTER

Altar: a pedestal, usually religious.

Alter: to modify; to change.

ALTHOUGH, THOUGH

These words are interchangeable as conjunctions meaning "in spite of the fact that," "even though."

Though also may be an adverb meaning "however," "nevertheless."

ALUMNA, ALUMNUS; ALUMNAE, ALUMNI

An *alumnus* is a male graduate or former student of a particular school. An *alumna* is a female graduate or former student of a particular school. The plural of *alumnus* is *alumni*; the plural of *alumna* is *alumnae*. But unlike *alumnae*, which refers to a group of women only, *alumni* can be gender neutral.

AMBIGUOUS, AMBIVALENT

Something is *ambiguous* if it is unclear or has more than one meaning.

Ambivalent describes a mixed or undecided state of mind: *Her ambiguous remark left him feeling ambivalent about her.*

AMIABLE, AMICABLE

Both words mean "friendly," but *amiable* generally describes a pleasant person; *amicable* generally describes a cordial situation: *The amiable couple had an amicable divorce.*

AMID, AMIDST

Either is acceptable, but many writers prefer the more concise *amid*.

AMONG, BETWEEN

Among involves three or more items that are part of a larger group or not individually named: *Who among us has not lied? Corina is able to choose from among the finest universities for her future studies.*

Between involves two items as well as more than two when they are specific, individual items: *She couldn't decide between Chinese and Thai food. Corina is able to choose between Stanford, Harvard, McGill, and Oxford for her future studies.*

AMOUNT, NUMBER

Use *amount* for things that cannot be counted and *number* for things that can be counted: *This amount of water is enough to fill a number of bottles.*

The culprit is *amount*. Some might incorrectly say "a large amount of bottles," but no one would say "a large number of water."

a.m., p.m.

The abbreviation *a.m.* refers to the hours from midnight to noon, and *p.m.* refers to the hours from noon to midnight. Careful writers avoid such redundancies as *three a.m. in the morning* (delete *in the morning*) or *eight p.m. this evening* (make it *eight o'clock this evening*).

To avoid confusion, use *midnight* instead of *twelve a.m.* and *noon* instead of *twelve p.m.*

The terms also are frequently written as *am, pm*; AM, PM; and A.M., P.M.

AN

See **a, an**.

AND/OR

"Objectionable to many, who regard it as a legalism," says Roy H. Copperud in *A Dictionary of Usage and Style*. Either say *and* or say *or*.

Occasionally, this solution does not work, as in: "You could be fined and/or put in jail." In such cases, try *x* or *y* or *both*: "You could be fined or put in jail or both."

ANECDOTE, ANTIDOTE

An *anecdote* is a brief, amusing tale.

An *antidote* counteracts or reduces the effects of something unpleasant or even lethal. There are antidotes for snakebites, but there is no known antidote for boring anecdotes.

AN HISTORIC

Some speakers and writers use *an* with certain words starting with an audible *h*—the word *historic* heads the list. But why do those who say *an historic occasion* say *a hotel, a hospital, a happy home*? There is no valid reason to ever say *an historic, an heroic, an horrific*, etc., and anyone who does so is flirting with pomposity.

ANXIOUS, EAGER

The words are different: *anxious*, like *anxiety*, denotes uneasiness.

In casual usage, *anxious* might mean either "enthusiastic" or "worried." But as Bryan A. Garner notes in *A Dictionary of Modern American Usage*, "to use the word merely as a synonym for *eager* is to give in to SLIPSHOD EXTENSION."

ANY MORE, ANYMORE

Use the two-word form to mean "any additional": *I don't need any more help.*

Use *anymore* to mean "any longer": *I don't need help anymore.*

ANY TIME, ANYTIME

Traditionalists do not accept the one-word form, *anytime*. But it is everywhere, and there's no turning back.

There does seem to be a difference between *You may call anytime* and *Do you have any time?* Always use the two-word form with a preposition: *You may call at any time.*

APPRAISE, APPRISE

A school district official was quoted as saying, "We have been appraised of all the relevant issues." Bad choice. The word *appraise* means "to decide the value of." The gentleman clearly meant *apprised*, which means "informed."

ASCENT, ASSENT

Ascent: a climb; movement upward.

Assent: an agreement (noun); to agree (verb).

AS REGARDS

See **in regard(s) to, with regard(s) to**.

ASSUME, PRESUME

Assume: to take for granted without evidence.

Presume: to believe based on evidence.

ASSURE, ENSURE, INSURE

To *assure* is to promise or say with confidence. It is more about saying than doing: *I assure you that you'll be warm enough.*

To *ensure* is to do or have what is necessary for success: *These blankets ensure that you'll be warm enough.*

To *insure* is to cover with an insurance policy.

What you *insure* you entrust to a business. What you *ensure* results from your personal efforts.

ATTAIN, OBTAIN

To *attain* is to achieve; accomplish; reach a certain level or goal: *The knowledge attained in such disciplines will be useful for the rest of your life.*

To *obtain* is to get possession of something—often something material: *A lease with an option to buy is not hard to obtain.*

AURAL, ORAL

Since the two words are pronounced the same, be careful not to write *oral* (having to do with the mouth) if you mean *aural* (having to do with hearing).

AVERSE

See **adverse, averse**.

A WHILE, AWHILE

The two-word phrase *a while* is getting pushed aside by *awhile*. But *awhile* should only be used to mean "for a while." It's a distinction worth preserving: *It took a while, but I was convinced after thinking it over awhile.*

Always use *a while* with prepositions: *After a while, she arrived.*

B

BACKWARD, BACKWARDS

Both forms are acceptable, although the *Associated Press Stylebook* instructs journalists to always use *backward*.

BACTERIA

Staphylococcus is a virulent form of bacteria. No problem there, but with *Staphylococcus is a virulent bacteria*, well, now we have a problem. Avoid "a bacteria." *Bacteria* is plural; the singular is *bacterium*. So a sentence like *The bacteria in the cut was infecting it* is flawed—the bacteria *were* infecting it.

BAIL, BALE

Both words do double duty as noun and verb. As a noun, *bail* commonly refers to money deposited to gain a prisoner's freedom, or *bail* that prisoner *out*.

A *bale* is a large, bound or wrapped package of unprocessed material. To *bale* is to make into a bale.

BAITED BREATH, BATED BREATH

Don't write "baited breath." The word *bated*, a variant of *abated*, means "lessened in intensity," "restrained."

BALL, BAWL

Ball: a round object; a gala event.
Bawl: to cry; howl.

BARBECUE

Note the spelling. People want to put a *q* where the *c* should be. The popular abbreviation, *BBQ*, doesn't help matters.

BARE, BEAR

Bare as an adjective means "unconcealed": *bare arms*. As a verb it means "expose": *to bare one's feelings.*

Bear as a noun refers to a wild animal. As a verb it has many meanings, from "carry" (*bear arms*) to "tolerate" (*I can't bear it*) to "steer" (*bear right at the corner*) to "give birth" (*bear a child*).

BASED OFF (OF)

There's really no excuse for *based off* (*Their favorite classic movies are based off old fairy tales*) or its alternate form, *based off of* (*Dr. House is based off of Sherlock Holmes*). Whoever coined *based off* was just fooling around or talking too fast. It subsequently caught on, and now there are those who defend its legitimacy.

Everyone knows the correct phrase, *based on*, which has been around forever. But somehow, *on* became *off*, or worse, *off of*—a compound preposition that all English authorities reject as substandard (see **off of**). The logical conclusion is that anyone who says "based off" doesn't know what *based* means. As a verb, *to base* means "to form a foundation for." The noun *base* refers to the underlying part that something rests *on*, not *off*.

BASICALLY

This word, especially when it starts a sentence, is probably unnecessary.

BEACH, BEECH

The *beech* tree was close to the windy *beach*.

BEAT, BEET

You can't *beat* my recipe for *beets*.

BECAUSE, SINCE

Because and *since* can be used just about interchangeably to explain the reason for something. But *since* can also refer to a time in the past: *I have waited since yesterday*.

BEG THE QUESTION

Here are three of the countless examples of *beg the question* one can find online: "It begs the question of who Fluke really is." "Exports' clout begs the question: Was NAFTA good or bad?" "He did stand-up comedy once, which begs the question, What can't this guy do?"

In each case, the writer should have said "raises the question" or "suggests the question" or "demands the question."

A succinct definition of *beg the question* is found in H.W. Fowler's *Modern English Usage*: "The fallacy of founding a conclusion on a basis that as much needs to be proved as the conclusion itself." Fowler offers this example: "Capital punishment is necessary because without it murders would increase." There are two unproven assertions in that sentence, and yet the second one is supposed to prove the first.

Here's another kind of question-begging: "Good grammar matters because proper speech or writing makes a difference." In this instance of begging the question, the "proof" is merely the premise restated in different words. That's like saying, "Good grammar matters because I just said so."

BELL, BELLE

Bell: a chime or alarm.
Belle: a lovely woman.

BEMUSE, AMUSE

Do not confuse *bemuse* with *amuse*. They are far from synonymous. To be *bemused* is to be bewildered, confused. It can also mean "distracted."

BENIGHTED

He was a benighted soul in an enlightened time. Many people associate it with *knighted* and think *benighted* is a good thing to be. Far from it. Note the lack of a *k*; don't think *knight*, think *night*. To be *benighted* is to be "in a state of moral or intellectual darkness."

BERTH, BIRTH

Berth: a built-in bed on a train or boat; a space for a boat to dock.
Birth: being born; a beginning.

BESIDE, BESIDES

Besides as an adverb means "in addition" or "moreover": *It's Albert's birthday, and besides, you promised. Besides* is also a preposition meaning "other than" or "except": *Who besides me is hungry?*

Compare that with *The person beside me is hungry. Beside* is a preposition that means "next to," "near," "alongside."

A lot of people say something is "besides the point." They mean *beside* the point. When a statement is beside the point, it misses the mark and settles nothing.

BETTER, BETTOR

Better: of higher quality.
Bettor: a gambler.

BETWEEN

See *among, between*

BIANNUAL, BIENNIAL, SEMIANNUAL

These words do not all mean the same thing. *Biannual* means "twice a year," as does *semiannual*, whereas *biennial* means "occurring every two years."

BITE, BYTE

Don't confuse what your teeth do with *byte*, a computer term for eight bits of information. Adding to the confusion, *sound bite*—a brief excerpt from a longer work—is sometimes mistakenly written "sound byte."

BLOC, BLOCK

The more familiar word is *block*, which can refer to many things: a toy, a cube-shaped object, a city street. Not as versatile is *bloc*: a group united for a particular purpose.

BLOG, POST

A *blog* is a website that regularly adds new material. An entry written for a *blog* is called a *blog post* or just a *post*. Do not call a blog post a "blog."

BLOND, BLONDE

A blonde is a woman with blond hair.

BOAR, BOOR, BORE

Boar: a wild pig.
Boor: a vulgar brute.
Bore: a compulsive chatterbox.

BOARD, BORED

When the *board* called the roll, he was too *bored* to speak up.

BOLDER, BOULDER

Bolder: more daring.
Boulder: a large rock.

BORN, BORNE

To be *born* is to be given birth to, as babies are born. Or it can mean "to be created": ideas are born the moment we think of them. It also means "to arise from": *Timmy's stomachache was born of wolfing his food.*

Borne is the past tense of *bear*, in the sense of "carry." To be *borne* is to be carried: *a mosquito-borne disease*; or to be endured: *Timmy's stomachache had to be borne until it finally went away.*

BRAKE, BREAK

Use your *brake* before you *break* something.

BRIDAL, BRIDLE

Bridal: relating to brides and weddings.

A *bridle* is a head harness, usually for a horse. Not surprisingly, the verb *bridle* means "to control" or "to restrain." But it also means "to pull back the head quickly in anger."

BRING, TAKE

They're not interchangeable. You *bring* something here; you *take* something there. The locations of "here" and "there" are from the perspective of the speaker or writer. Your friend asks you to *bring* her a book, so you *take* the book to her home.

BROACH, BROOCH

To *broach* a topic is to bring it up for discussion: *Now is the time to broach the subject.* As a verb, *broach* also means "to open or enlarge a hole." The noun *broach* refers to a pointed tool which performs that operation.

A *brooch*, a decorative pin or clip, is nothing like a *broach*. But since they're often pronounced alike, and because ignorance never rests, some dictionaries accept *broach* as an alternative spelling of *brooch*.

BURGLARY, ROBBERY

Burglary and *robbery* are not synonyms. *Burglary* is illegal entry of a structure or dwelling with the intent to commit a crime, usually theft. *Robbery* is the act of taking someone else's property by force or the threat of force.

BYTE

See **bite, byte**.

C

CACHE, CACHET, CASH

As a noun, *cache* refers to a hidden supply of valuables, such as food, jewels, and *cash*. But it can also refer to the hiding place where you keep those items. The verb *cache* means "to hide treasure in a secret place": *He cached all of his cash in a cache.*

The noun *cachet* means "prestige; distinction." *Few cities can match the cachet of Paris.*

CALVARY, CAVALRY

Calvary: a depiction of the Crucifixion.
Cavalry: a mobile army unit.

CAN, MAY

I can go means I have the ability and freedom to go.
I may go means I have either an option or permission to go.

CANNON, CANON

Cannon: a large, mounted gun.

Canon: a body of writings; a principle or set of principles.

CANNOT

One word; avoid "can not."

CANVAS, CANVASS

Canvas is a durable fabric.

Canvass as a noun or a verb refers to the door-to-door gathering of votes or opinions.

CAPITAL, CAPITOL

Just remember: the *o* means it's a building. A *capitol* is a government building where a state legislature meets, and the *Capitol* is the building where the U.S. Congress meets.

A *capital* is a city that serves as the seat of government. *We got a tour of the capitol when we went to the capital.*

CARAT, CARET, KARAT

Most of the confusion is caused by *carat* and *karat* because both are associated with jewelry. The purity of gold is measured in *karats*. *Twenty-four-karat gold is 99.9 percent pure, but so soft that it is considered impractical for most jewelry.*

A *carat* is a weight measurement for gemstones: *a two-carat diamond set in an eighteen-karat gold ring.*

A *caret* has nothing to do with any of this. It is a mark an editor makes in a document to show where additional material should be inserted.

CAREEN, CAREER

Grammar sticklers are a stubborn lot. They use *career* the way everyone else uses *careen*. It is *career*, not *careen*, that means "to veer out of control": *The car careered wildly across three lanes. Careen* means "to lean or tip over," and strictly speaking, it's more suitable for describing boats than cars.

CAST, CASTE

Cast: a group of actors or individuals.

Caste: a social class; a rigid system of social distinctions.

CAVALRY

See **calvary, cavalry**.

CEMENT, CONCRETE

People constantly refer to "cement" sidewalks, driveways, walls, etc. However, *cement* is a powder that, when mixed with sand or gravel and water, becomes *concrete*.

CENSOR, CENSURE

They sound similar, and both words deal with negative criticism. *Censor* as a verb means "to remove unacceptable material." As a noun, it means "someone who censors."

Censure as a verb means "to disapprove of" or "to criticize strongly." As a noun, it means "disapproval," even "scorn."

CENTER AROUND

The lecture will center around the economy. Make it "center on." The language scholar Wilson Follett calls *center around* a "geometrically senseless expression." This nonsensical turn of phrase results from scrambling *center on* and *revolve around*. Because those idioms are roughly synonymous, if you use them both enough, they merge in the mind.

CEREAL, SERIAL

Cereal: a breakfast food.

Serial: a story told in regular installments (noun); ongoing, in a series (adjectives).

CHAISE LOUNGE

This example of cultural dyslexia should be avoided at all costs. The correct term is *chaise longue*, meaning "long chair" in French.

CHILDISH, CHILDLIKE

Both are comparisons with children. The difference is that *childish* is unflattering; it's equivalent to *infantile* and only a small improvement on *babyish*. Someone is childish when acting unreasonable or bratty.

Not so with *childlike*, a word that extols youthful virtues, such as sweetness, purity, and innocence.

CHILE, CHILI

If life were fair, *Chile* with an *e* would refer only to a country in South America, and *chili* with a second *i* would refer to a type of pepper, and also to a spicy stew. These spellings are recommended, but with the caveat that not everyone agrees. In New Mexico, the stew they eat is *chile*, not *chili*. The *Associated Press Stylebook* says the dish is *chili*, but the pepper is a *chile*. And there are even some who spell the pepper or the dish *chilli*.

CHOMPING AT THE BIT

It started out as *champing at the bit*, which is still preferred by most dictionaries.

CHORAL, CORAL

Choral: relating to or sung by a choir.

Coral: an underwater organism that makes up reefs; a shade of orange.

CHORALE, CORRAL

A *chorale* can be both a piece of music and a singing group.

A *corral* is an enclosure for horses or other livestock.

CHORD, CORD

When two or more musical tones are sounded simultaneously, the result is a *chord*.

A *cord* is a rope or strand of flexible material.

CITE, SIGHT, SITE

Cite: to quote; to praise; to mention; to order to appear in court.

Sight: the ability to see; a scene or view.

Site: a location or position.

CLASSIC, CLASSICAL

Classic, adjective or noun, is a term of high praise: "of the finest quality" or "a prime example of": *a classic play, a classic pizza.*

The adjective *classical* applies to traditions going back to the ancient Greeks and Romans: *The house featured an array of classical influences.*

Classical music is marked by formal, sophisticated, extended compositions.

CLICHÉ

It's a noun, not an adjective. Yet more and more you see or hear things like *I know it sounds cliché, but…*Make it *I know it sounds **like a** cliché.*

CLICK, CLIQUE

A *click* is a brief percussive noise, but some mistakenly write it when they mean *clique*, a close, exclusive group of people.

CLIMACTIC, CLIMATIC

Climactic—note that middle *c*—means "exciting" or "decisive." It is often confused with *climatic*, which means "resulting from or influenced by climate."

CLOSE PROXIMITY

This phrase is a pompous and redundant way of saying "near." *Proximity* does not mean "distance"; it means "nearness," so *close proximity* means "close nearness."

COARSE, COURSE

Coarse means "rough, lacking in fineness of texture" or "crude, lacking in sensitivity."

Course is usually a noun and has several meanings, mostly having to do with movement or progress, whether it be a *course* taken in school or the *course* of a river.

COHORT

Your friend is a crony, confidant, or collaborator, but not a cohort. In ancient Rome, a *cohort* was a division of three hundred to six hundred soldiers. So careful speakers and writers avoid *cohort* when referring to one person. Your *cohort* is not your comrade, ally, teammate, or assistant. It's a whole group, gang, team, posse: *A cohort of laborers went on strike.*

COIN A PHRASE

To *coin a phrase* is to make one up. But many misuse it when citing or quoting familiar expressions: *His bright idea was, to coin a phrase, dead on arrival.* Since *dead on arrival* is a well-known idiom, the writer didn't "coin" it; he merely repeated it.

COINCIDENCE

See **irony.**

COLLECTABLE, COLLECTIBLE

Both are acceptable, but *collectible* has a slight edge in popularity, especially as a noun.

COLLIDE, CRASH

A *collision* involves two moving objects. A car does not *collide* with a lamppost; it *crashes* into a lamppost.

COMPARE TO, COMPARE WITH

When we compare something *to* something else, we are placing two things—sometimes very different things—in the same category and commenting on connections we perceive. We are expressing an opinion or making an observation. Others might not have noticed these similarities; still others might disagree with them. Some examples: *I'd compare the view from your living room to a painting by Bierstadt. Ruben compared Giorgio's spaghetti to dog food.* Note that these are subjective statements—they are not verifiable.

When we compare something *with* something else, we are not expressing opinions or making personal statements. We are placing two things side by side and noting empirical similarities and differences. Our purpose is to be fair and impartial. The accuracy or inaccuracy of our findings can be verified. For instance, if we compare apples *with* oranges, we find that neither fruit contains fat, cholesterol, or sodium; that oranges contain more than twice as much potassium as apples; that a cup of oranges contains twenty more calories than a cup of apples.

In the writer's guide *Simple and Direct* Jacques Barzun issues this caveat: "Any writer can *compare himself with* Shakespeare and discover how far he falls short; if he *compares himself to* Shakespeare (i.e., puts himself on the same level), then he had better think again."

COMPEL, IMPEL

To *compel* is to force or drive someone to take action by making that person fear the consequences of not doing so.

To *impel* is to persuade someone to take action on moral or ethical grounds.

When you are *compelled* you are coerced, regardless of your wishes. When you are *impelled* you are made to realize that although the choice may be difficult, it is the right thing to do.

COMPLEMENT, COMPLIMENT

As both noun and verb, *complement* refers to an added element that enhances, rounds out, or puts a final touch on something.

Compliment, noun and verb, is about nice words or gestures. *Try this perfect complement to your order, with our compliments.*

COMPLETE, COMPLETELY

These words are often unnecessary. What is the difference between *a complete meltdown* and *a meltdown*? How is *completely exhausted* different from *exhausted*?

COMPRISE

Possibly the most abused two-syllable word in English. It means "contain," "consist of," "be composed of." Most problems could be avoided by remembering this mantra: *The whole comprises its parts.*

Consider this misuse: *Vegetables comprise 80 percent of my diet.* The correct sentence is *Eighty percent of my diet comprises vegetables.* My diet *consists of* vegetables; vegetables do not consist of my diet.

This sentence looks right to most people: *Joe, John, and Bob comprise the committee.* But it's the other way around: *The committee comprises Joe, John, and Bob.*

Another common misuse is the phrase *comprised of*, which is never correct. Most people use *comprised of* as an elegant-seeming alternative to *composed of*. An ad for a cleaning service states, "Our team is comprised of skilled housekeepers." Make it "Our team comprises skilled housekeepers," "Our team is composed of skilled housekeepers," or, perhaps the best choice, "Our team consists of skilled housekeepers."

Since *comprise* already means "composed of," anyone using *comprised of* is actually saying "composed of of."

CONCERTED

One person cannot make a *concerted* effort. A concert implies an orchestra. As Paul Brians points out in his *Common Errors in English Usage*, "To work 'in concert' is to work together with others. One can, however, make a *concentrated* effort."

CONCRETE

See **cement, concrete**.

CONFIDANT, CONFIDENT

Confidant: a trusted adviser.

Confident: certain, self-assured.

CONNIVE, CONSPIRE

One who *connives* pretends not to know while others are collaborating on something sneaky, wrong, or illegal.

To *conspire* is to work together on a secret scheme.

CONNOTE, DENOTE

Denote is used for descriptions that stick to the facts. The word "dog" *denotes* a domesticated animal.

Connote reveals additional meanings beyond what is clinical or objective. It is used when expressing what a word implies or reminds us of. The word "dog" *connotes* loyalty.

CONTINUAL, CONTINUOUS

The difference between *continual* and *continuous* is the subtle difference between *regular* and *nonstop*. If your car *continually* breaks down, it also runs some of the time.

A faucet that drips *continuously* never stops dripping, twenty-four hours a day. If a faucet drips *continually*, there are interludes when it's not dripping.

CONVINCE, PERSUADE

To many, these two are synonyms, but there are shades of difference. Someone might be persuaded, while at the same time, not convinced: *She persuaded me to do it, but I'm still not convinced it was right*. When something or someone *persuades* us to act, it might be by using reason or logic, but it could also be by using force, lies, or guilt.

Convince refers to an unforced change of mind and heart that precedes action. We consider the evidence, and if it is strong enough, it *convinces* us and changes our perspective.

In formal writing, *convince* never takes an infinitive, but *persuade* almost always does. You cannot be convinced *to do* something; you can only be convinced *that* something, or be convinced *of* something.

CORP., CORPS

Corp. (note the period) is an abbreviation for *corporation*.

Corps refers to a military unit or a body of people working together for a common cause.

CORAL

See **choral, coral**.

CORD

See **chord, cord**.

CORRAL

See **chorale, corral**.

COUNCIL, COUNSEL

Council: a group of people meeting for a purpose.

Counsel: advice (noun); an attorney (noun); to give advice or guidance (verb).

COUPLE

Savvy writers make *couple* plural (*The couple were late to their own wedding*) unless the sentence sounds absurd otherwise—and such sentences are rare. After all, what does *couple* mean if not "the two of them"? Keep *couple* plural, and you will avoid abominations like *Their friends say the couple looks alike* or *The couple was taking naps in adjoining rooms*.

COUPLE OF

The *of* stays. These days, even veteran communicators are saying and writing "couple miles from here" or "costs a couple bucks." That used to be the jargon of tough guys in gangster movies.

COURSE

See **coarse, course**.

CRASH

See **collide, crash**.

CRAVEN

To many people, a *craven scoundrel* is a flagrant or shameless rogue, not a spineless one. But *craven* means "cowardly," "weak."

CRITERIA

Criteria is the plural of *criterion*, a standard used for judging, deciding, or acting. The sentence *Honesty is our chief criteria* is ungrammatical; there can't be only one *criteria*. Make it *Honesty is our chief criterion* or *Honesty is one of our chief criteria*. Your criteria *are* your standards, plural.

Those who know that *criteria* is plural aren't out of the woods yet either: many believe the singular is "criterium." And there are some who will reveal to you their "criterias."

CUBICAL, CUBICLE

My office *cubicle* is *cubical* in shape.

CURRENTLY

Often unnecessary. What is the difference between *I'm currently writing a book* and *I'm writing a book*?

D

DAILY BASIS

I run five miles on a daily basis. In most cases, the windy and unwieldy *on a daily basis* can be replaced with *daily* or *every day*.

DATA

John B. Bremner, in *Words on Words*, states unequivocally, "The word is plural." This one is thorny, because the singular, *datum*, is virtually nonexistent in English. Many people see *data* as a synonym for "information," and to them, *These data are very interesting* sounds downright bizarre. Maybe, but it's also correct. Theodore M. Bernstein, in *The Careful Writer*, says, "Some respected and learned writers have used *data* as a singular. But a great many more have not."

DEFINITE, DEFINITIVE

Something *definite* is exact, clearly defined, with no ambiguity. But *definite* does not necessarily mean "correct": *George has a definite belief that two and two are five.*

Something *definitive* is authoritative, the best, the last word: *This is the definitive biography of Lincoln.*

DENOTE

See **connote, denote**.

DESERT, DESSERT

The noun *desert* refers to a desolate area. As a verb, it means "to abandon."

A *dessert* is the final course of a meal.

Many misspell the phrase *just deserts*, meaning "proper punishment." In that usage, *deserts* is derived from *deserve*.

DESPISE

"Syme despised him and slightly disliked him," wrote George Orwell in the novel *1984*. Orwell knew that, strictly speaking, *despise* means "to look down on" but not necessarily "to dislike," although that's usually part of the deal.

DEVICE, DEVISE

Device: an invention.

Devise: to invent.

DIFFERENT FROM, DIFFERENT THAN

Different from is the standard phrase. Traditionalists obstinately avoid *different than*, especially in simple comparisons, such as *You are different from me*.

More-liberal linguists point out that a sentence like *It is no different for men than it is for women* is clear and concise, and rewriting it with *different from* could result in a clumsy clunker like *It is no different for men from the way it is for women*.

From Bergen and Cornelia Evans's *Dictionary of Contemporary American Usage*: "No one has any grounds for condemning others who would rather say *different than*, since this construction is used by some of the most sensitive writers of English and is in keeping with the fundamental structure of the language."

This does not mean that you should now write *different than* every chance you get. There may be nothing grammatically wrong with *different than*, but it remains polarizing. *A is different than B* comes across as sloppy to a lot of literate readers. If you can replace *different than* with *different from* without having to rewrite the rest of the sentence, why not do so?

DILEMMA

Be careful when using *dilemma* as a synonym for *predicament*. Those who do so are guilty of SLIPSHOD EXTENSION. The *di* in *dilemma* (like *dichotomy* or *dioxide*) indicates *two*: if you have a dilemma, it means you're facing a tough choice between two things.

DISBURSE, DISPERSE

To *disburse* is to distribute or pay out money or other financial assets.

Use *disperse* when something other than money is being distributed: *The agency dispersed pamphlets after the meeting*.

Disperse also means "to scatter" or "make disappear": *The police dispersed the unruly mob*.

DISCOMFIT, DISCOMFORT

The two are often confused. *Discomfit* originally meant "to defeat utterly." It has come to mean "to fluster," "to embarrass."

Discomfort is usually used as a noun meaning "anxiety," "nervousness."

DISCREET, DISCRETE

Discreet: careful not to attract attention, tactful.

Discrete: separate, detached.

People often write *discrete* when they mean *discreet*. The situation is not helped by *discretion*, the noun form of *discreet*.

DISINTERESTED, UNINTERESTED

You can be both uninterested and disinterested, or one but not the other. *Disinterested* means "impartial"; *uninterested* means "unconcerned" or "apathetic."

Many would interpret *The judge was disinterested* to mean that the judge didn't care. But the sentence actually means that the judge was unbiased. Huge difference there. Would you rather have a judge who's fair or one who wants to go home?

DIVE

Dive, dived or dove, have dived

I dived off the high cliff. I dove off the high cliff. I have dived off the high cliff.

But not: *I have dove off the high cliff.*

DIVISIVE

The correct pronunciation is with a long *i* in the second syllable: di-VAI-sive. The short *i* pronunciation is nonstandard. Don't use it.

DOCK

What is often thought of as a *dock* is actually a *pier* or *wharf*. The book *Modern American Usage* (edited by Jacques Barzun, et al.) defines a *dock* as "the water-filled space in which the ship comes to rest. The *pier* is the structure on which the passengers stand or alight." Would Otis Redding's song still be a masterpiece if he'd called it *Sittin' on the Pier of the Bay?*

DREDGE, DRUDGE

It was backbreaking work to dredge the river, but we were able to drudge through it.

To *dredge* is to dig something up, often by using a *dredge*—a machine used to dig or scoop. As a verb, *drudge* means "to work at a monotonous task." As a noun, *drudge* refers to someone whose work is dull.

DRUG (DRAGGED)

She drug Joe out of his office at midnight. When did "drug" replace *dragged* as the past tense of *drag?* The answer is: It didn't, and it couldn't, and it better not.

DUAL, DUEL

Dual: double; having two parts.

Duel: a two-sided conflict (noun); to fight a duel (verb).

E

EAGER

See **anxious, eager**.

EFFECT

See **affect, effect**.

e.g., i.e.

These two helpful abbreviations are often used interchangeably, a sorry mistake that impoverishes the language.

The term *e.g.* means "for example."

The term *i.e.* means "that is" or "by which I mean" or "in other words."

To illustrate: *The so-called "method actors" (e.g., Marlon Brando and James Dean) electrified audiences in the 1950s.* Compare that sentence with *Artists like Marlon Brando and James Dean (i.e., the so-called "method actors") electrified audiences in the 1950s.*

Sometimes the right choice requires careful thought, as in this case: *Certain members of my family (i.e., Mom and Uncle Jake) are vegetarians.* In that sentence, the *i.e.* tells us that Mom and Uncle Jake are the only family members who don't eat meat. But what if we replaced *i.e.* with *e.g.*: *Certain members of my family (e.g., Mom and Uncle Jake) are vegetarians.* Now the sentence indicates that there are other vegetarians in the family besides Mom and Uncle Jake.

That is no small difference, and it highlights the dissimilarity of *i.e.* and *e.g.* Confusing one for the other can result in misunderstandings at best and nonsense at worst. So remember to use *i.e.* when further identifying a subject, and use *e.g.* when giving specific examples of a subject.

EKE OUT

It has come to mean "barely get by": *I eke out a living as a writer.* But its traditional meaning is either "to supplement": *I eke out my living as a writer by working a day job*, or "to make the most of": *We eked out the small amount of food we had left.*

ELICIT, ILLICIT

Elicit: to bring forth a reaction or response.
Illicit: illegal, forbidden.

ELUDE

See **allude, elude, refer**.

EMIGRATE, IMMIGRATE

Emigrate: to leave one country in order to live in another country. *Emigrate* takes the preposition *from*, as in *He emigrated from Russia to America.* It is incorrect to say. "He emigrated to America."

Immigrate: to enter a new country with the intention of living there. *Immigrate* takes the preposition *to*, as in *He immigrated to America from Russia.* It is incorrect to say, "He immigrated from Russia."

EMINENT, IMMINENT

Eminent: prominent; distinguished: *an eminent scholar.*

Imminent: about to happen: *in imminent danger.*

EMPATHY, SYMPATHY

When we have *empathy*, we are able to put ourselves in other people's place and even feel their pain, or think we do.

Sympathy is more removed than *empathy*. When we have *sympathy*, we may not suffer along with those who are hurting, but we have compassion and are often willing to help.

EMULATE, IMITATE

Emulate means "to try to be as good or successful as."

Imitate means "to copy or fashion oneself after."

A sentence like *He tried to emulate her* is repeating itself: He *tried to try* to be as good as she was. We don't "try to emulate." When we *emulate*, we're already trying.

ENERVATE

Many people think *enervate* is a fancy synonym for *energize*. The two words are near opposites. Someone who is *enervated* by work is weakened or exhausted by it, not invigorated.

ENORMITY

This word is frequently misused: the "enormity" of football linemen these days, or the "enormity" of the task. *Enormity* has nothing to do with something's size. For that, we have such words as *immensity*, *vastness*, *hugeness*, and *enormousness*.

Enormity is an ethical, judgmental word meaning "great wickedness," "a monstrous crime." *The enormity of Jonestown* doesn't mean Jonestown was a huge place, but rather that it was the site of a hugely outrageous tragedy.

ENSURE

See **assure, ensure, insure**.

ENTHUSE

Many writers, editors, scholars, and critics regard *enthuse* and *enthused* as unserious and unacceptable.

ENTITLED, TITLED

Either *entitled* or *titled* is an acceptable word in the sense of "give a title to." *Titled* is more commonly used today, but *entitled* was the preferred term until recently. We recommend avoiding *entitled* for this purpose to avoid any connection with the unfavorable sense of "believing oneself to be inherently deserving of privileges or special treatment."

EPITAPH, EPITHET

An *epitaph* is a tribute inscribed on a tombstone in honor of the person buried there.

An *epithet*, unlike an epitaph, is often an insult based on race, class, religion, politics, etc.: *The mob was shouting racial epithets.*

Otherwise, an epithet is a kind of nickname. It is a word or brief phrase that illustrates a defining trait of someone or something: *Alexander the Great, the wine-dark sea.*

EPITOME

The epitome of means "the essence of." It does not mean "the best," "the height of." *Sam is the epitome of humility* means that Sam is a perfect example of a humble person. It doesn't necessarily mean that he's one of the humblest men who ever lived.

ERSTWHILE

It's often confused with *worthwhile*. But *erstwhile* means "previous" or "one-time." *My erstwhile assistant* does not mean "my valuable assistant." It means "my former assistant" and nothing more.

etc., et al.

These abbreviations are a scholarly way of saying, "You get the point."

The term *etc.* means "and the rest," "and so on." It is usually placed at the end of a short list of things to save the writer (and reader) the trouble of going on needlessly.

When a list of people, rather than things, is involved, use *et al.* in place of *etc.*: *Joe Smith, Ray Jones, et al., led the team to victory.*

Both *etc.* and *et al.* require periods, even midsentence.

EVERY DAY, EVERYDAY

The two-word term *every day* is an adverbial phrase that answers the questions *when* or *how often*, as in *I learn something new every day.*

As one word, *everyday* is an adjective that means "ordinary" or "part of a daily routine": *These are my everyday clothes.*

EXACERBATE, EXAGGERATE

To *exacerbate* is to make a difficult situation worse or more intense: *The humidity exacerbated the intense heat.*

To *exaggerate* (note the double g) is to overstate, to stretch the truth: *He exaggerated when he said it was the hottest day on record.*

EXACT, EXTRACT

As verbs, these two words have subtle shades of meaning:

Exact: to obtain by force or demand, "exact revenge."

Extract: to remove or take out by force, "extract a confession."

EXALT, EXULT

Exalt: to praise; glorify.

Exult: to rejoice; be triumphant.

EXCEPT

See **accept, except**.

F

FACTIOUS, FRACTIOUS

Factious means "characterized by dissent and internal disputes." A factious group is liable to split off into *factions*.

Fractious means "irritable," "quarrelsome," "ill-tempered."

FAINT, FEINT

Faint: to go unconscious.

Feint: a distracting move meant to throw an opponent off guard (from *feign*).

FAIR, FARE, FARING

Fair: an exhibition (noun); just, impartial (adjectives).

Fare: payment for travel (noun); to have an experience (verb); to go through something (verb): *How did you fare on your test? How are you faring in your new job?*

FARTHER, FURTHER

The general rule: *farther* refers to real, physical distance: *Let's walk a little farther.*

Further deals with degree or extent: *Let's discuss this further.* May be used for physical distance, although *farther* is preferred.

FAZE, PHASE

When something or someone *fazes* you, you are disturbed or troubled: *Her behavior doesn't faze me*.

A *phase* is a period or chapter: *He's going through a difficult phase right now*.

FEASIBLE, POSSIBLE

Some use *feasible* as a synonym for *likely* or *reasonable*, as in *He gave a feasible explanation*, but this is SLIPSHOD EXTENSION. Others use it when they simply mean *possible*. While anything feasible is possible, not everything that is possible is feasible.

If a plan is *feasible*, it is not only possible but realistic and practical. It may be possible to build one's dream home on a bleak, stormy mountain with no roads, but who would call such a plan feasible?

FEAT, FEET

Feat: an extraordinary act or accomplishment.
Feet: twelve-inch increments; appendages below the ankles.

FEWER, LESS

Here's a seemingly innocent sentence: *I now have two less reasons for going*. Make it *two fewer reasons*. If you can count the commodity (two reasons), *less* will be wrong. You have *less justification*, but *fewer reasons*.

Exception: When the amount is *one*, such a sentence should read, "I now have *one* reason *fewer*" or "*one less* reason," but not "*one fewer* reason." Admittedly, this is a head-scratcher, but that's English for you.

Use *less* for specific measurements of money, distance, time, or weight: *It costs less than a million dollars. We walked less than fifty feet. Less than thirty minutes had passed. It weighs less than five pounds*. The book *Modern American Usage* explains why: "We take a *million dollars* as a sum of money, not as a number of units; *fifty feet* as a measure of distance, not as one foot added to forty-nine other feet; *thirty minutes* as a stretch of time, exactly like half an hour…and the quantitative *less* is therefore correct in comparisons; *fewer* would sound absurd."

FIR, FUR

Fir: a type of tree.
Fur: animal hair.

FIRSTLY

See **secondly, thirdly, fourthly**.

FLAIR, FLARE

Flair: style; talent.
Flare: to erupt; to blaze.

FLAMMABLE, INFLAMMABLE

Let's see: *flammable* means "combustible." *Inflammable* means "combustible." Any questions?

FLAUNT, FLOUT

He was a rebel who flaunted the rules. That sentence is incorrect. Make it *flouted the rules.* To *flout* is to ignore, disregard, defy.

To *flaunt* is to make a big display: *She flaunted her diamond necklace.*

FLEA, FLEE

Flea: a type of insect.
Flee: to run away.

FLOUNDER, FOUNDER

One way to avoid confusing these two verbs is to think of *flounder*, the fish. Something that is *floundering* is thrashing around helplessly, like a fish out of water.

Founder means "to fail." If a business is *floundering*, it is in distress but may yet be saved. If a business *founders*, nothing can revive it.

FLOUR, FLOWER

Flour: an edible powder prepared by grinding grains.
Flower: the bloom of a plant.

FOLKS

See **people, persons**.

FORBID, PROHIBIT

These verbs are near synonyms, but they take different prepositions. Use *to* rather than *from* with *forbid*, and *from* rather than *to* with *prohibit*. Take care to avoid sentences like *They were forbidden from using cameras* and *They were prohibited to use cameras.* Make it *forbidden to use* or *prohibited from using.*

FOREGO, FORGO

Many permissive editors allow *forego* in place of *forgo.* But *forego* with an *e* traditionally means "to go before," "precede": *A good stretching session should forego rigorous exercise.*

To *forgo* is to abstain from, do without: *If you forgo a good stretching session, you might pull a muscle.*

FOREWORD, FORWARD

A *foreword* is an introduction, usually to a book. It's sometimes confused with *forward*, meaning "ahead," "forth."

FORMER

See **latter**.

FORTE

Forte: a strength or talent. The traditionally preferred pronunciation is **fort**. American English has now tilted toward **for**-tay.

FORTH, FOURTH

Forth: onward.
Fourth: coming directly after whatever is third.

FORTUITOUS, FORTUNATE

Fortuitous is a chronically misunderstood word. To purists, it most emphatically does not mean "lucky" or "fortunate"; it simply means "by chance." You are *fortunate* if you win the lottery *fortuitously*, but you can also get flattened by a truck *fortuitously*.

FOUL, FOWL

Foul: tainted; sickening.
Fowl: edible bird or birds.

FRACTIOUS

See **factious, fractious**.

FREE GIFT

A curious term for *gift*.

FULSOME

Many people take *fulsome* to mean "abundant" or "lavish." But be wary of writing the likes of *He received a fulsome tribute* or *Please accept my fulsome apology*. The word actually means something darker: "excessive," "fawning," even "disgusting."

FUN

Fun is a noun, not an adjective. Sentences like *It was a fun time* or the ghastly *It was so fun* have no place in serious writing.

FUR

See **fir, fur**.

FURTHER

See **farther, further**.

G

GAIT, GATE

Gait: stride; the way a person or animal walks or runs.
Gate: a barrier.

GAMUT

Gamut originally referred to the entire range of musical notes that the ear can recognize. It has come to mean the range or extent of anything: *His speech ran a gamut of emotions.* Do not confuse *run the gamut* with *run the gantlet* (see **gantlet, gauntlet**).

GANTLET, GAUNTLET

These two words, despite their similarity, come from different roots. The distinction should be preserved.

The expression *run the gantlet* means "to undergo criticism or harassment from several sources in a concentrated period of time." It is often written *run the gauntlet*, which makes language nitpickers cry foul.

To *throw down the gauntlet* is to aggressively challenge someone. To *take up the gauntlet* is to accept such a challenge.

GEL, JELL

In popular usage, *jell* means "to come together": *Our team is starting to jell. Gel* refers to a jelly-like substance: *hair gel.*

GILT, GUILT

Gilt: gold coating.
Guilt: fault; blame; shame.

GLIB

A word with a split personality suitable for backhanded compliments and faint praise. *Glib* can mean "smooth," "urbane." But it can also mean "superficial," "too slick."

GOOGLE

Capitalized (*Google*) or not (*google*), the word has gained acceptance as a verb for searching the Internet using the Google search engine.

GOTTEN

"An uneasy idea persists that *gotten* is improper," says Roy H. Copperud in *A Dictionary of Usage and Style*. "Efforts to avoid *got* by substituting *obtained* or any other word the writer must strain after are misspent."

Gotten has been in continuous use for about seven hundred years, though it all but disappeared from England in the eighteenth century. "In Great Britain *got* is the only form of the participle used and the older form *gotten* is considered archaic," says Bergen and Cornelia Evans's *Dictionary of Contemporary American Usage*. "In the United States *gotten* is still the preferred form of the participle when it is used with *have* to express a completed action."

GRADUATE

He graduated high school last weekend. Make it *graduated from.* There are even some fussbudgets who'd insist he *was graduated from* high school. But *graduated from* is as correct as *was graduated from.*

GRAFFITI

Note the double *f* and single *t. Graffiti* is the plural of *graffito*, Italian for "little scratching." Therefore, some writers would change *There was graffiti all over the wall* to *There **were** graffiti all over the wall.*

GRILL, GRILLE

Grill: a grated metal cooking utensil (noun); to cook over direct heat (verb).
Grille: a network of metal, wooden, or plastic bars that acts as a barrier or screen.

GRISLY, GRISTLY, GRIZZLY

Grisly means "horrific," "gruesome." However, grisly bears are not necessarily *grizzly bears*, North American brown bears known for their fierceness.
Don't confuse *grisly* with *gristly*, which means "tough," "chewy."

GUERRILLA

Note the spelling: double *r*, double *l*. Some think "guerilla" with one *r* is a valid alternative, but the word derives from *guerra*, which means "war" in Spanish.

H

HAIR, HARE

Hair: what grows on the head and body.
Hare: a rabbit.

HALL, HAUL

Hall: a passageway; a large room.
Haul: to pull or drag.

HALVE, HAVE

Halve: to divide in two.
Have: to possess; to hold.

HANGAR, HANGER

Many think that a shed or shelter for housing airplanes is a "hanger," rather than a *hangar* (the correct spelling).

A *hanger* is something to hang a garment on, or someone who hangs things.

HANGED, HUNG

Speakers and writers who value precision know that the past tense of *hang*, when it means "to put to death using a rope," is *hanged*, not *hung*. This applies to both the active and passive voice: *They hanged the prisoner* and *The prisoner was hanged*.

For inanimate objects, use *hung*. Under unusual conditions, people also *hung* or *are hung*, e.g., *He hung from the tree with one hand* or *He found himself hung upside down*.

HARDY, HEARTY

Hardy: strong; able to withstand difficult or demanding situations.
Hearty: friendly or enthusiastic; healthful or good for you.

A *hardy* plant can survive the hardships of a cold winter. A *hearty* greeting from old friends can warm the heart.

HEAL, HEEL

Heal: to repair; to restore to health.
Heel: the back part of the foot; a scoundrel.

HEALTHFUL, HEALTHY

The difference between these two words is unquestionable, *healthful* meaning "something that promotes health" and *healthy* meaning "in good health." But in everyday speech, *healthful* has been nudged aside by *healthy* in phrases like *healthy food* or *a healthy diet*.

HEAR, HERE

There is an *ear* in *hear*, and *here* is 80 percent of *where*.

HEROIN, HEROINE

Heroin: a drug derived from morphine.
Heroine: a woman admired for courage or ability.

HISTORIC, HISTORICAL

A *historical* event occurred some time ago. A *historic* event is important, memorable, enduring. "A historical study concerns history; a historic one makes history," says editor Claire

Kehrwald Cook in *Line by Line*. "Often *historical* simply means 'actual' as opposed to 'literary,' 'mythic,' or 'figurative.'"

HOARD, HORDE

Hoard: to stockpile; to amass.
Horde: a large group; a crowd.

HOARSE, HORSE

Hoarse: raspy; sore-throated.
Horse: a type of animal.

HOLE, WHOLE

Hole: an opening.
Whole: entirety (noun); entire (adjective).

HOLY, WHOLLY

Holy: sacred.
Wholly: entirely.

HOMAGE

A critic called a film "a homage to motherhood." The critic wisely did not write "an homage," knowing full well that the *h* is sounded (see **an historic**). This word has spun out of control in the twenty-first century. Its traditional pronunciation is "HOMM-ij." Then "AHM-ij" gained a foothold, and it went downhill from there. Now, just about all one hears is the pseudo-sophisticated "oh-MAHZH," a pronunciation that was virtually nonexistent in English until the late twentieth century.

HONE IN

Make it *home in*. *Hone in* has achieved undeserved legitimacy for the worst of reasons: the similarity in sound and appearance of *n* and *m*. *Honing* is a technique used for sharpening cutting tools and the like.

To *home in*, like *zero in*, is to get something firmly in your sights, to get to the crux of a problem.

HOT WATER HEATER

A curious term for *water heater*.

HUNDRED AND TEN PERCENT

This widespread harebrained idiom has been traced back to a high school football coach of the 1950s. It certainly wasn't coined by a math teacher. The coach used it to exhort his players to do more than they thought they were capable of. To succeed, giving "just" one hundred percent would not suffice.

Inflation was bound to set in. Sure enough, today even a "hundred and ten percent" effort does not always get the job done. Now you must give "one hundred and twenty percent," "one hundred and fifty percent," "two hundred percent," and even "one thousand percent." Can "one thousand and ten percent" be far behind?

HUNG

See **hanged, hung**.

I

IDLE, IDOL, IDYLL

Idle: not active; unemployed.

Idol: an effigy; a beloved celebrity.

Idyll: a happy interlude; prose or poetry describing rural serenity.

i.e.

See **e.g., i.e.**

ILLICIT

See **elicit, illicit**.

ILLUSION

See **allusion, illusion**.

IMITATE

See **emulate, imitate**.

IMMIGRATE

See **emigrate, immigrate**.

IMMINENT

See **eminent, imminent**.

IMPACT

Impact has traditionally meant "to pack tightly together," as in *an impacted tooth*.

Traditionalists maintain that, as a verb, *impact* is constantly misused, and *affect* is almost always the better choice. Avoid such usages as *The proposition will impact property taxes* or *Greenhouse gas emissions negatively impact the environment*. Make it *affect* instead of *impact* in both sentences.

These more recent inflated substitutes for "affect significantly" are quickly becoming standard usage.

IMPEL

See **compel, impel.**

IMPLY, INFER

Infer is not a synonym for *imply*. *Imply* is done by a speaker or writer—specifically, one who is being indirect: *She implied that I'm a fool* means that she didn't come right out and say it, but she got her point across.

Infer is done by a perceptive listener or reader who "catches" your meaning: *I infer that you think I'm a fool.*

Imply is akin to *suggest* and *insinuate; infer* is akin to *deduce* and *conclude.*

IN, INTO

Use *in* for where something is: its location or position. *I am in my car.*

Use *into* for where something is going: its direction or destination. *I am driving into a tunnel.*

Idiomatic exception: *Go jump in the lake.* Strict grammar requires *into*, but that is a losing battle.

INCENTIVIZE

Many people who watch their language regard *incentivize* as a silly jargon word. It means simply "to offer incentives to or for." Some random examples found online: "We ought not to incentivize ignorance of the law." "Professor says legislature should incentivize utilities to improve efficiency." "If you are going to incentivize anyone, incentivize the buyer."

Those who scorn this usage believe *incentivize* is unnecessary because alternatives like *motivate, inspire, encourage,* and *persuade* are readily available.

INCIDENCES, INCIDENT

Incidences is technically a real word, but it is often misused and is rarely called for. Those who say "incidences" usually mean "incidents."

An *incident* is a single event or episode: *An incident of food poisoning was confirmed and investigated.*

Incidence is the rate at which something happens, usually something bad: *The incidence of diseases transmitted by food has decreased.*

Sometimes the words can overlap. When *incidents of crime* are occurring with some regularity, there is an *incidence of crime* in the vicinity.

INCITE, INSIGHT

Incite: to provoke; stir up.

Insight: understanding; comprehension.

INCLUDE

From a story about a rescue at sea: "The rescued pair included an American woman and a Danish man." This is a misuse of *include*, which means "to make someone or something part of a group." You can't be *included* unless others are involved. The sentence requires a rewrite, something like *The two people rescued were an American woman and a Danish man.*

A major-league baseball team doesn't *include* men; it *consists of* men, and only men. Compare: *Our office softball team includes women.* We realize immediately that it's a coed league and there are also men on the squad.

IN CONNECTION TO, IN CONNECTION WITH

In connection with is the standard idiom for expressing a relationship of one thing with another. For example, "Police questioned three senior citizens *in connection with* a spate of jay-walking violations downtown." For unknown reasons, local news announcers have begun using *in connection to* for this purpose. *Connected to* should be reserved for physical connection: "The gas pump is connected to the underground storage tank."

INCREDIBLE, INCREDULOUS

Something *incredible* is beyond belief, so when we experience it, we are *incredulous*.

Incredulous refers to a state of astonishment or disbelief. It is not a deft synonym for *incredible*.

INFER

See **imply, infer.**

INFLAMMABLE

See **flammable, inflammable.**

INGENIOUS, INGENUOUS

What a difference one letter makes. *Ingenious* refers to worldly brilliance; *ingenuous* refers to otherworldly innocence.

INITIALISM

See abbreviation, acronym, initialism

IN ORDER TO

Sometimes *in order to* is necessary, but it's often just a fussy way of saying *to: We should exercise in order to stay healthy.* Drop *in order* whenever possible.

IN REGARD(S) TO, WITH REGARD(S) TO

In regard to and *with regard to* are phrases that mean "regarding," "concerning," "on the subject of."

As regards—note the *s* on the end—means the same thing. Perhaps this is why people mindlessly pluralize *regard* and say *in regards to* and its partner in crime, *with regards to*.

Both of the following examples are correct: *With regard to your friend, let's hope she is well.* Compare that to *With regards to your friend. Let's hope she is well.*

In the first sentence, *With regard to* means "concerning." But in the second sentence, *regards* with an *s* is a plural noun meaning "best wishes."

INSURE

See **assure, ensure, insure**.

INTERNET

Internet, internet: Either capitalized or not is acceptable. Just be consistent.

INTO

See **in, into**.

IRONY, COINCIDENCE

When something is *ironic*, it has a grimly humorous or paradoxical twist, as if the universe were playing a wicked practical joke. Thus, it is *ironic* if a speeding car crashes into a "drive carefully" sign, or if someone named Joe Friendly turns out to be a serial killer.

Do not use *irony* or *ironic* to describe a simple coincidence: *It's so ironic that our birthdays fall on the same day.* No irony there; it's merely *coincidental*.

IRREGARDLESS

This nonsense word results from confusing and combining *regardless* and *irrespective*. If people would just think about it, what's that silly *ir* doing there?

In technical terms, *ir* is an **initial negative particle**. So if *irregardless* means anything, it means "not regardless" when the person using it is trying to say the exact opposite.

IS IS

*The thing is is that…The truth is is that…The problem is is that…*The airwaves are teeming with commentators afflicted with the *is is* hiccup, one of life's mysteries, even to those who say it. The most alarming case in point: *The fact of the matter is is that*, a bloated locution intoned by certain pundits, often right before they express an opinion.

ISLE

See **aisle, isle**.

IT'S, ITS

It's: a contraction for *it is* or *it has*.
Its: a possessive pronoun meaning "belonging to it."

J

JELL

See **gel, jell**.

JIBE, JIVE

The verb *jibe* means "to fit," "to be in harmony with": *His version did not jibe with hers.*

Many people say *jive* when they mean *jibe*, but *jive*, noun and verb, is African-American slang that originally referred to up-tempo, jazzy music. Then it became a term for hipster jargon. It has come to mean dishonesty, silliness, or inanity: *talking jive* is lying or talking nonsense. *Stop jiving* means "Stop fooling around."

JUST

Be careful where you put it. The meaning of *just* depends on its placement in a sentence, especially when it is accompanied by *not*, or by negative verbs such as *don't* or *wouldn't*.

Many people say *just not* when they mean *not just*, and this could lead to misunderstanding, embarrassment, even hurt feelings.

Not just means "not only," whereas *just not* means "simply not" or "definitely not."

He's a trusted adviser, not just a friend means "He's more than an adviser; he's a friend, too." But *He's a trusted adviser, just not a friend* means something quite different: "I trust his advice, but he's no friend of mine."

JUST DESERTS

See **desert, dessert**.

K

KARAT

See **carat, caret, karat**.

KINDERGARTNER

Note how the spelling differs from *kindergarten*.

KNEW, NEW

Knew: past tense of *know*.
New: up to date; original; unused.

KUDOS

To this great man, kudos are due. That sentence wouldn't raise many eyebrows, but *kudos* is not the plural of *kudo*. There's no such thing as "a kudo." *Kudos* is a Greek word (pronounced "KYOO-doss" or "KOO-doss") meaning "praise" or "glory," and you'd no more say "kudos are due" than you'd say "glory are due." Admittedly, *kudos is due* looks odd. Better to rewrite the sentence.

L

LASTLY

If you wouldn't say "firstly," why say "lastly"? Drop the *-ly*. (See also **secondly, thirdly, fourthly**.)

LATTER

He offered a trip to New York, Chicago, or Tarzana. She chose the latter. Oh no, she didn't. *Latter* can't be used when there are three (or more) options. It applies only to sentences like *He offered a trip to New York or Tarzana*, which makes New York the *former*, Tarzana the *latter*. When there are more than two people or things mentioned, use *last*.

LAXADAISICAL

The word doesn't exist, but that doesn't stop people from saying it. The word they're looking for is *lackadaisical*: "without energy or enthusiasm."

LAY, LIE

These may well be the two most confounding three-letter words in all the language. The use of *lay* where *lie* is indicated has been a major problem for generations. To *lay* is to put or place: *I will lay my cards on the table.* To *lie* is to rest or recline: *The cards lie on the table.* But *lie* also means "to tell an untruth." Maybe because of the word's negative double meaning, people shy away from saying *lie*.

All of the following are incorrect: *I'm going to lay on the couch. Your wallet is laying on the dresser. He wants to lay down.* Make it *lie, lying, lie*, respectively.

Lie: You *lie* down today; you *lay* down yesterday; you have *lain* down before.

Lay: Please *lay* the book down now; you *laid* the book down yesterday; you have *laid* that book down before.

- *Yesterday I lied/laid/lain/lay on the bed.*
  Most people would guess *laid on the bed*, but the correct answer is *lay*.

- *I have often lied/laid/lain/lay on the bed.*
  Again, most people would guess *laid*, but *lain* is correct.

- *I have often lied/laid/lain/lay my wallet on the dresser.*
  This time, *laid* is correct.

Lay vs. Lie Chart

	Present	**Past**
To recline	*lie; is/are lying*	*lay; has/have/had lain*
To put or place	*lay; is/are laying*	*laid; has/have/had laid*
To tell a falsehood	*lie; is/are lying*	*lied; has/have/had lied*

Examples in the present tense: *I like to lie down for a nap at 2 p.m.*
I am lying down for a nap today.
This is where my priorities lie.
Please lay the book down.
I am laying the book down.
I am tempted to lie about my age.
I am not lying about my age.

Examples in the past tense: *I lay down for a nap yesterday at 2 p.m.*
I laid the book down yesterday.
He lied on the witness stand.

Examples with a helping verb (has, have): *I have lain down for a nap every day this week.*
I have laid the book down for the last time.
He has lied each day on the witness stand.

LEACH, LEECH

Leach: to drain or seep: *The sludge leached into our water supply.*

Leech: literally, a parasite. Figuratively, a scrounger. As a verb, *leech* means "to exploit; take advantage of": *He leeches off his friends' generosity.*

LEAD, LED

Correct: *He led the parade.* Incorrect: *He lead the parade.* Budding writers are increasingly using *lead* instead of *led* as the past tense of the verb *to lead*.

There are three reasons for this confusion. First, the past tense of *read*, the other common *-ead* verb, is *read*. Second, the word *lead*, when it's a noun denoting a metal, is pronounced *led*, just like the past tense of the verb *to lead*. And third, they don't drill spelling in schools the way they used to.

LEAK, LEEK

Leak: an unintended discharge of liquid or gas.

Leek: a type of onion.

LECTERN

See **podium, lectern**

LEND, LOAN

Either word is acceptable in the sense "to give something temporarily."

Past tense: *lent, loaned.*

LESS

See **fewer, less**.

LESSEN, LESSON

Lessen: to decrease.

Lesson: something learned or studied.

LET HE WHO IS WITHOUT SIN…

One of the most notorious misquotations in the English language is "Let he who is without sin among you cast the first stone." This misuse of the pronoun *he* has been giving English sticklers nightmares for decades.

How could it be "Let he"? It couldn't. Here is the actual quotation from the Gospel of John: "He that is without sin among you, let him first cast a stone at her."

LIABLE, LIBEL, LIKELY

Liable has a negative connotation: *He's liable to have an accident if he doesn't slow down.*

Libel is a malicious attack on someone's character.

Likely refers to simple probability: *She is likely to be on time.*

LIE

See **lay, lie**.

LIGHTENING, LIGHTNING

That flash in an overcast sky is a bolt of *lightning*, which is sometimes misspelled *lightening*.

Lightening is the process of making something lighter in color or weight.

LIKE

Do it like she does. Sentences like that one have always been unacceptable to purists. Nowadays, however, such sentences go virtually unchallenged, even by many editors.

Traditionally, *like* can only be a preposition meaning "similar to" or "similarly to." So *Do it like her* (i.e., *similarly to her*) would be correct. But because no one would say, "Do it similarly to she does," there is no grammatical justification for *Do it like she does*.

In the mid-twentieth century, Theodore M. Bernstein said in *The Careful Writer*: "The usage of *like* as a conjunction … is not acceptable in better-grade writing."

The *American Heritage Dictionary's* panel of experts has noted that for more than a century, anyone who said *like she does* was considered illiterate. Yet today, the panel says, "*Like* is more acceptably used as a conjunction in informal style."

The traditional view is that if a verb follows the noun or pronoun, as in *like she does*, it means *like* is the wrong choice. Instead, use *as, as if, as though,* or *the way*.

- *Do it **the way** she does* (not *like she does*).
- *Say it **as if** or **as though** you mean it* (not *like you mean it*).
- *Go when the light is green, **as** it is now* (not *like it is now*).

LITERALLY

I was so amazed, I literally hit the ceiling. Someone who has *literally* hit the ceiling ought to move to a place with higher ceilings.

It was literally like being in Paris. Drop *literally.* Nothing is "literally like." Anyone who says "literally like" doesn't understand the word.

Literally is supposed to mean "100 percent fact"…period. But not today, when, as in the previous examples, *literally* is often used figuratively. This is classic SLIPSHOD EXTENSION.

In responsible usage, *literally* allows no room for poetry, analogy, hyperbole, frivolity, or any other flights of fancy. Any sentence containing *literally* should mean what it literally says. We are being asked to accept that sentence as fact and not interpret or infer. So if you say you were "literally stunned," we have no choice but to conclude that you were physically incapacitated.

A newspaper item told of a couple whose dreams "literally collapsed" when a fixer-upper they bought came down in a heap as they started working on it. Now, we know what the writer meant, but the house is what literally collapsed, not the dreams. How could a dream, the very essence of all that is beyond materiality, *literally* collapse?

One simple solution: Say "virtually": *I virtually hit the ceiling. Their dreams virtually collapsed.*

Virtually allows speakers and writers to enhance and embellish to their hearts' content, options they relinquish when using *literally*.

LOAN, LONE

Loan (noun): something given temporarily.

Lone (adjective): only; solitary.

LOATH, LOATHE

Loath: reluctant.

Loathe: to dislike intensely.

I am *loath* to work for anyone I *loathe*.

LOOSE, LOSE

Loose: opposite of *tight*.

Lose: to misplace; to be defeated.

M

MAIL, MALE

Mail: correspondence.

Male: masculine.

MAIZE, MAZE

Maize: corn.

Maze: a labyrinth.

MANNER, MANOR

Manner: a method; a behavior.

Manor: a palatial residence.

MARQUEE, MARQUIS

Marquee: a projection over a theater entrance.

Marquis: an aristocrat; a nobleman.

MARRY, MERRY

Marry: to wed.

Merry: cheerful.

MARSHAL, MARTIAL

Marshal: a law officer (noun). To assemble (verb). Note the spelling: one *l*.

Martial: warlike.

MASTERFUL, MASTERLY

Another pair of words whose distinct meanings have been blurred by carelessness. The problem centers on *masterful*, in such phrases as *a masterful artist* or *a masterful performance*. Make it *masterly*, which means "highly accomplished," "inspired," "demonstrating mastery."

Masterful has darker shadings. It's about being the alpha dog: dominant, supreme—almost ruthlessly so. A *masterful performance* should refer to a boxer or a victorious football team rather than a cello concert.

MATERIAL, MATERIEL

Material: whatever something is made from.

Materiel: military equipment and supplies.

MAY

See **can, may**.

MEDAL, MEDDLE, METAL, METTLE

Medal: a decoration; a badge.

Meddle: to interfere.

Metal: an earth element.

Mettle: boldness; grit.

MEDIA

Media is a plural noun; *medium* is the singular. A *medium* is a system of mass communication: *The medium of television is a prominent component of the mass media.*

Every day we hear and read statements like "The media is irresponsible," "The media has a hidden agenda." In those sentences, "media" should be followed by "are" and "have."

There are some who prefer and defend "the media is" and "the media has." To them, the various means of mass communication—newspapers, radio, TV, magazines, blogs, etc.—make up one "media."

The United States **is** *where I live* is correct, even though "States" is plural, so why not "the media is," even though *media* is plural? Nice try, but no sale.

Writers should insist on *the media are*. It's important that people think of *the media* as many voices, opinions, and perspectives rather than one monolithic entity.

MERETRICIOUS

A veteran newsman said, "His career is meretricious." He probably meant *meritorious*. Instead, the sentence as it stands is an insult.

When you hear it, the first two syllables echo *merit*, but the similarity to *meritorious* ends there. *Meretricious* means "flashy," "cheap," "tawdry": *The candidate made a meretricious display of piety.*

METAL, METTLE

See **medal, meddle, metal, mettle**.

MIC

Mic is a bogus and clueless abbreviation of *microphone*. For too many decades to count, the word was *mike*. "Ike is good on a mike" went a line from a popular early-1950s song about presidential candidate Dwight D. Eisenhower.

A bicycle is a *bike*, not a "bic." So how is a microphone a "mic"?

MINER, MINOR

Miner: one who works in a mine.

Minor: someone under the legal age of adulthood (noun); of less importance (adjective).

MINUSCULE

Be sure to note that first *u*. A lot of writers think the word is "miniscule." And it makes sense that a word for "tiny" would have a *mini* in it. Don't think *mini*, think *minus*.

MISNOMER

A *misnomer* is a mistake, but not all mistakes are misnomers. The word is wrongly used in this sentence: *It's a misnomer that elephants are afraid of mice.* A *misnomer* is not the same as a *misconception*. The *nome* in the middle is from the Latin *nomen*, meaning "name." A *misnomer* is a mistake in labeling: for instance, calling aluminum foil "tinfoil" or calling a koala a "bear" (it's a marsupial).

If "Lucky" Brown loses his fortune in the stock market and "Speedy" Green blows out his ankle, their respective nicknames become misnomers.

MORAL, MORALE

Moral: a lesson (noun); ethical (adjective).

Morale: spirit; level of enthusiasm.

MORE IMPORTANTLY, MOST IMPORTANTLY

At issue is the *ly*, which some find unnecessary (and somewhat snooty). Many sticklers do not accept *importantly* in the two sentences that follow: *I left my bed and, more importantly, I left the house. Most importantly, Churchill was a statesman.* Critics of those sentences would prefer "more important" (*what is more important, I left the house*) and "most important" (*what is most important, Churchill was a statesman*).

Other experts declare the phrases acceptable with or without *ly*. But since brevity is a virture, why not drop the *ly* and save yourself a superfluous syllable?

MORE THAN ONE

More than one person was involved. Why *was*? Doesn't *more* mean at least two? Yet even English scholars are wary of changing the verb to "*were* involved," even though we would say, "More *were involved* than one person."

Reference books do not offer much help with this conundrum, and the internet is no help at all. But John B. Bremner's *Words on Words* and Theodore M. Bernstein's *The Careful Writer* both address the topic. Bremner sees *more than* as an adverbial phrase modifying the adjective *one*, "which is singular and therefore qualifies a singular noun, which takes a singular verb." That explanation might fly in the rarefied air of academia, but to accept it we must ignore the inconvenient fact that *more than one person* means "two or more persons," and would seem to require the plural verb *were involved*.

Bernstein doesn't try to justify *More than one person was involved* as good grammar—just "good idiom." He says "*was* involved" is an example of *attraction*, a linguistic term that accounts for certain incorrect word choices: "The verb is singular 'by attraction' to the *one* and to the subsequent noun [*person*]."

All but one ship was sunk is another example of "good idiom." The principles that apply to *more than one* also apply to *all but one*. If we separate *all* from *but one*, the verb becomes plural: *Of the five ships, all **were** sunk but one.*

One is free to endorse elaborate justifications for the validity of *more than* (or *all but*) *one person **was** involved*. But it is just as reasonable to conclude that this oddity is nothing more than institutionalized error—people have been saying it wrong for so long that we've become used to it, and *more than one person **were** involved*, the logical construction, sounds wrong. We see institutionalized error on the march today in untraditional usages like "each of them were here," "neither of you are right," and "a person should do their best," all of which we suspect will eventually be standard English, despite the anguished screams of purists.

MORNING, MOURNING

Morning: the start of the day, between night and afternoon.

Mourning: sorrow over a tragedy.

MUSCLE, MUSSEL

Muscle: fibrous tissue; strength.

Mussel: an edible marine bivalve.

MYRIAD

In spite of objections from some purists, *myriad* may be an adjective or a noun, though some experts prefer its use as an adjective for economy.

adjective: *The restaurant has myriad vegetarian dishes to choose from.*

noun: *The restaurant has a myriad of vegetarian dishes to choose from.*

N

NAVAL, NAVEL

Naval: pertaining to ships; nautical.

Navel: belly button.

NEITHER … OR

As a conjunction, *neither* often teams with *nor*: "Neither a borrower nor a lender be." The rule many learned in fifth grade was, "Neither … nor, either … or, but never neither … or."

Neither ... or is another once-unthinkable faux pas gaining momentum among people who ought to know better. A political adviser's resignation letter read, "This position is not a fit for me, neither personally or professionally." (Make it "either.")

A big-city newspaper editor wrote, "I neither commissioned or approved it." Even editors need editors.

NEW

See **knew, new**.

NEW RECORD

See **all-time record**.

NONPLUSSED

Note the double *s*.

Nonplussed is widely misused as a synonym for *cool* or *unfazed: Despite his anxiety, he appeared nonplussed.* Clearly, the writer meant *nonchalant. Nonplussed* means the opposite: "confused," "thrown off." *His strange behavior left her nonplussed.*

NO ONE

Two words, no hyphen.

NOR

See **neither ... or**.

NOT JUST

See **just**.

NOTORIETY

A critic wrote: "Burgess gained notoriety with his wildly popular children's books." Another oft-abused word, *notoriety* has somehow become a good thing. But can't you hear the *notorious* in *notoriety*? There are all kinds of fame; *notoriety* is one of the bad kinds, just down the pike from *infamy*. This is a word best reserved for describing the world's scoundrels.

NUMBER

See **amount, number**.

O

OBTAIN

See **attain, obtain**.

OFF OF

"Hey! You! Get off of my cloud," sang the Rolling Stones, unnecessarily. Make it *off my cloud*. The *of* in "off of" adds nothing, so why not drop it?

OFTEN

All dictionaries list two pronunciations, OFF-en and OFF-tun, but the *t* should be silent, as it is in *soften* and many other English words (e.g., *listen, moisten, Christmas*).

ORAL

See **aural, oral**.

ORDINANCE, ORDNANCE

Ordinance: a law.
Ordnance: military weapons and ammunition.

OUT OF

The *of* is necessary; only careless speakers say *Get out my house*. Two notable exceptions: *door* and *window*—no *of* is needed in *We hurried out the door* or *I stared out the window*.

OUTSIDE OF

We stood outside of the building. Make it *outside the building*. In sentences indicating location, "*of* is superfluous with *outside*," says Roy H. Copperud. His fellow English scholar Theodore M. Bernstein calls *outside of* "a substandard casualism." With sentences where *outside of* is not literal, such as *Outside of you, I have no one*, there are better alternatives available, including *except for, other than, besides, apart from*, and *aside from*.

OVERDO, OVERDUE

Overdo: to go overboard with; behave excessively.
Overdue: behind time; payable.

OVER

According to a persistent superstition, *over* must be replaced with *more than* in sentences like *the package weighs over ten pounds*. This myth has been around a long time, but few if any language scholars take it seriously.

OVERLY

She is overly concerned about her job. Note that if the opposite were true, no one would say "underly concerned." Make it *too concerned* or *overconcerned*.

Many writers think *overly* is unnecessary and a bit precious. "Making *over* into *overly*," says *Bryson's Dictionary of Troublesome Words*, "is a little like turning *soon* into *soonly*. Adding *ly* does nothing for *over* that it could not already do."

P

PAIL, PALE

Pail: a bucket.

Pale: lacking color.

PAIN, PANE

Pain: physical or emotional suffering.

Pane: a glazed piece or section of a door, window, etc.

PALATE, PALETTE, PALLET

Palate: the roof of the mouth; taste.

Palette: a range of colors; a board to hold and mix paint colors.

Pallet: a low, portable platform.

PARISH, PERISH

Parish: a district with its own church and clergy.

Perish: to stop existing; to die.

PARODY, SATIRE

A *parody* is a humorous imitation of a book, film, song, poem, etc., meant to poke fun at the original's style or intentions.

A *satire* uses biting humor, hyperbole, sarcasm, irony, etc., to lay bare the toxic absurdity of civilization.

PASSED, PAST

Passed: gone ahead of; approved.

Past: a former time; beyond.

PAST HISTORY

A curious term for *history*.

PASTIME, PAST TIME

A *pastime* is a leisurely pursuit or hobby.

The phrase *past time* refers to something that should have happened or been done by now.

It's *past time* that people realized that *pastime* is one word.

PEACE, PIECE

Peace: tranquility.

Piece: a portion.

PEAK, PEEK, PIQUE

Peak: a summit.

Peek: a glance (noun); to steal a glance (verb).

Pique: ill humor (noun); to arouse or annoy (verb).

PEAL, PEEL

Peal: to ring.

Peel: to strip.

PEDAL, PEDDLE

Pedal: a foot-activated lever (noun); to operate something with pedals, such as a bicycle or organ (verb).

Peddle: to sell or publicize.

PEER, PIER

Peer: a person who is an equal (noun); to look attentively (verb).

Pier: a structure extending out over water.

PENULTIMATE

"He's the penultimate Washington insider," said the glib pundit, blissfully unaware that *penultimate* means "second to last."

PEOPLE, PERSONS

The noun *person* has two plurals: *persons* and *people*. Most people don't use *persons*, but the sticklers say there are times when we should. "When we say *persons*," says Wilson Follett's *Modern American Usage*, "we are thinking, or ought to be, of *ones*—individuals with identities; whereas when we say *people* we should mean a large group, an indefinite and anonymous mass."

The traditional rule is that *persons* is used for either an exact or a small number. So we might estimate that a hundred *people* were there. Or if we know the exact number, we'd say ninety-eight *persons* were there.

In *A Dictionary of Modern American Usage*, Bryan A. Garner calls the *persons-people* distinction "pedantic." To Garner, *twelve persons on the jury* "sounds stuffy." Roy H. Copperud agrees. In *A Dictionary of Usage and Style*, he dismisses the grammatical superiority of *persons* as "superstition," a law that "usage has in fact repealed."

Because *persons* sounds aloof and clinical, the word still thrives in legal, official, or formal usage. A hotel chain's website offers "options for three and more persons." Elevators carry signs saying, "Occupancy by more than eight persons is unlawful." The Department of Justice has a database called the National Missing and Unidentified Persons System.

A more timely debate these days would be *people* vs. *folks*. Traditionalists regard *folks* with suspicion and contempt. But judging by its growing popularity and acceptance in this informal age, *folks* will probably be synonymous with *people* in another ten years.

PEOPLES

The apostrophe in the following sentence is misplaced: *Mayor Sikes is the peoples' choice.* This blunder has become all too common in the print media. The sentence refers to *the people* rather than *the peoples*, so make it *the people's choice.*

The only need for *peoples'* would arise when collectively referring to two or more ethnic groups, tribes, or cultures of a particular region: *In that vast country, the indigenous peoples' rights were routinely violated.*

PERCENT

One word.

PERPETRATE, PERPETUATE

Perpetrate: to commit a crime.
Perpetuate: to prolong or sustain.

PERSECUTE, PROSECUTE

To *persecute* is to go after in an intimidating, bullying manner.
To *prosecute* is to go after in a legal manner.

PERSUADE

See **convince, persuade**.

PHASE

See **faze, phase**.

PHENOMENON

This troublemaker baffles even articulate speakers. And they know it. If you listen closely, you'll notice people trying to save face by fudging the last syllable.

Phenomenon is singular. "Management is a universal phenomenon," declares a business website. It helps to remember the *-on* on the end, which almost spells *one*.

The plural form is *phenomena*. A commentator on national television had it exactly backward. He spoke of "the phenomena of climate change" and later used *phenomenon* as a plural. Others say "phenomenas" when they mean *phenomena*.

PIECE

See **peace, piece**.

PIQUE

See **peak, peek, pique**.

PISTIL, PISTOL

Pistil: the female organ of a flower.

Pistol: a gun.

PLAIN, PLANE

Plain: a treeless area of land (noun); not fancy; evident (adjectives).

Plane: a flat or level surface; short form of *airplane*.

PLEADED, PLED

Traditionally, the past tense of *plead* is *pleaded*, not *pled*, and many sticklers reject *pled*. But it is gaining acceptance, and *pled* is listed as an alternative to *pleaded* in several dictionaries. However, both *The Chicago Manual of Style* and *The Associated Press Stylebook* avoid *pled*.

PLUM, PLUMB

Plum: a type of fruit.

Plumb: to examine (verb); upright; vertical (adjectives); totally; precisely (adverbs).

p.m.

See **a.m., p.m**.

PODIUM, LECTERN

Most people say "podium" when they mean "lectern." One stands *on* a podium; one stands *behind* a lectern.

A *podium* is a raised platform. A speaker or conductor or performer stands on the podium for increased visibility.

The words *lectern* and *lecture* are both from the Latin *legere*, meaning "to read." Speakers delivering a lecture place their notes on the slanted surface of the lectern.

POINT IN TIME

At that point in time is an exercise in empty pomposity, made (in)famous by the Watergate hearings of the early 1970s and still going strong. Why not just *at that point* or *at that time*?

POLE, POLL

Pole: a long, cylindrical piece of wood or metal.

Poll: a collection of opinions; a survey.

POOR, PORE, POUR

Poor: deprived.

Pore: a small opening (noun). To study carefully (verb).

Pour: to send liquid flowing.

Be careful not to say "pour over" if you mean *pore over*.

POST

See **blog, post.**

PRAY, PREY

Pray: to speak to a deity.

Prey: a victim (noun); to hunt, to exploit (verbs).

PRECIPITATE, PRECIPITOUS

Media pundits have errantly decided that *precipitous* means "immediate" or "swift," as when they discuss the advisability of "precipitous troop withdrawal." The correct adjective would be *precipitate*.

Precipitous means "steep," like a precipice.

PREDOMINATELY

Some mistakenly use it as an alternative to *predominantly*, as in "chiefly," "primarily." Funny thing about *predominately*: you might not see it for long stretches, and then, like some verbal swine flu, it crops up everywhere for a few weeks. Although *predominately* is technically a word, it's not easy to pinpoint what it means.

PREMIER, PREMIERE

Premier is generally an adjective meaning "the best," "of unsurpassed quality, skill, or importance." As a noun, it refers to a head of government.

A *premiere* is an opening night or first performance.

PRESENTLY

Careful speakers and writers might consider avoiding this word. If you tell hungry guests, "We're serving dinner presently," they might think you mean *now*. But *presently* means "in the near future." It's a stuffy word anyway; what's wrong with *soon*?

PRESUME

See **assume, presume**.

PRINCIPAL, PRINCIPLE

Principal: a major participant; the head of an institution (nouns); of first importance; chief (adjectives).

Principle: a fundamental belief; a fundamental fact.

PROFIT, PROPHET

Profit: gain.

Prophet: a predictor; a seer.

PROHIBIT

See **forbid, prohibit**

PRONE, SUPINE

The victim was found lying prone, her eyes gazing sightlessly at a full moon. Sorry, but this is a maneuver only the swivel-headed girl from *The Exorcist* could pull off, because when you're *prone*, you're lying on your stomach. Make that *supine*, which means "lying on one's back."

PROPHECY, PROPHESIZE, PROPHESY

A *prophecy* is a prediction.

When prophets make prophecies, they *prophesy*, not "prophesize."

It will be a crowning achievement, prophesized its chief engineer. Lose that *z* and make it *prophesied*. It is doubtful you could find any dictionary anywhere that lists "prophesize." Even the nonjudgmental *Webster's New World College Dictionary* shuns this common (mis)usage.

PROSECUTE

See **persecute, prosecute**.

PURPOSELY, PURPOSEFULLY

These words share much common ground, and they are sometimes interchangeable, but there are distinct differences. *Purposely* means "intentionally," but some acts are intentional, yet pointless: *Little Jimmy purposely threw Alice's lunch in the mud.*

Someone who does something *purposefully* is on a mission, with an important goal in mind: *The rescue team purposefully combed the woods for the missing child.*

Q-R

QUOTATION, QUOTE

To purists, *quote* is a verb only. When we *quote*, we repeat or reproduce someone's exact words.

The correct term for quoted material is a *quotation*. In casual usage, a quotation is often called a "quote," but *quote* as a noun is still not acceptable in formal writing.

RACK, WRACK

As a verb, *rack* means "to afflict," "oppress," "torment."

To *wrack* is to cause the ruin of.

A lot of people mistakenly write things like "nerve-wracking" and "I wracked my brains." Drop the *w* in both cases. Both expressions derive from that device in the torture hall of fame called the *rack*.

RAISE, RAZE

Raise: to lift up.

Raze: to take down.

RAP, WRAP

Rap: a sharp blow; a type of music (nouns); to strike sharply (verb).

Wrap: to enclose in a covering.

REAL, REEL

Real: actual, authentic.

Reel: a spool (noun); to stumble; falter (verbs).

REASON BEING IS

One hears this odd phrase frequently, in statements like *The economy is in trouble; the reason being is profligate spending*. Make it either *the reason being profligate spending* or *the reason is profligate spending*.

REASON IS BECAUSE

The reason is because we spend too much. Make it *The reason is that we spend too much*. Saying *the reason is* makes *because* unnecessary.

REEK, WREAK

Reek: to smell bad.

Wreak: to inflict.

REFER

See **allude, elude, refer**.

REGARDLESS

See **irregardless**.

REGRETFULLY, REGRETTABLY

Regretfully means "with sadness; apologetically": *Noah signed the eviction papers regretfully.*

However, this sentence is incorrect: *Regretfully, there was nothing that could be done.* Make it *regrettably*, which is close in meaning to *unfortunately*.

REIGN, REIN

Reign: period in power (noun); to be in power (verb).

Rein: a strap to control horses (noun); to control or guide (verb).

RELISH IN

Jones is relishing in his new role as financial adviser. The sentence mistakes *relish* for *revel*. Either Jones *relishes* his role or he *revels in* his role.

RENOWN

Ansel Adams is renown for his timeless photographs. Make that *renowned*. This widespread gaffe results from thinking *renown* is akin to *known*, probably because they share those last four letters.

REST, WREST

Rest: to relax.

Wrest: to take forcibly.

RESTAURATEUR

Note the spelling: no *n*.

RETCH, WRETCH

Retch: to heave.

Wretch: a lowly being; a scoundrel.

RETICENT

Reticent means "uncommunicative, reserved, silent." But many people wrongly use it to mean "reluctant": *I was reticent to spend so much on a football game.* No, you were *reticent* when you didn't protest the ticket price.

REVEREND

In formal writing, there's no such thing as "a reverend." The word is an honorific used before a pastor's name: *the Reverend Josiah Blank*. Important: *the* is mandatory. Also note the phrase must be followed by the person's full name—to say "Reverend Blank" is wrong twice.

REVIEW, REVUE

Review: an examination or criticism (noun); to assess, to analyze (verbs).

Revue: a variety show.

RIFF, RIFT

Riff: a brief musical phrase; pithy or flippant wordplay.

Rift: a crack; a disagreement.

RIGHT, RITE, WRITE

Right: an entitlement (noun); correct, opposite of *left*, opposite of *wrong* (adjectives).

Rite: a ritual; a ceremony.

Write: to compose letters or words.

RING, WRING

Ring: the sound of a bell; jewelry worn around a finger.

Wring: to twist.

ROAD, RODE, ROWED

Road: a street; a path; a highway.

Rode: past tense of *ride*.

Rowed: past tense of *row*.

ROAD TO HOE, ROW TO HOE

A lot of people say "a hard *road* to hoe" but what they mean is "a hard *row* to hoe" (i.e., a difficult task). "A hard road to hoe" almost seems acceptable, but it falls apart upon closer inspection.

A *road* handles a lot of foot traffic and takes a beating from bicycles and cars. No one but a lunatic would want to hoe a road.

The metaphorical row in *hard row to hoe* is a more or less straight line of growing plants. A farmer uses his hoe to cultivate the soil and keep it weed-free so the plants may thrive.

And yet *hard road to hoe* has its supporters. But those who defend it on the basis of "close enough" are doing a disservice not only to the language but to themselves. They should aim higher.

ROBBERY

See **burglary, robbery**.

ROLE, ROLL

Role: a position; a part in a play or film.

Roll: a baked food; a flowing movement (nouns); to rotate; to flow with a current (verbs).

RYE, WRY

Rye: a grain.

Wry: mocking; ironic; droll.

S

SATIRE

See **parody, satire**.

SAVER, SAVOR

Saver: someone or something that saves or conserves.

Savor: to appreciate.

SAY NO, SAY YES

When *say no* means "refuse" and *say yes* means "accept," they are often phrasal verbs with no need for quotation marks: *I said no to a second helping of pie, but I said yes to a cup of coffee.* However, if someone is actually being quoted, quotation marks make sense: *When he inquired if I'd lost my wallet, I said "No." When I asked if there was a store nearby, she said "Yes."*

SCENT, SENT

Scent: an aroma; a fragrance.

Sent: taken; moved.

SCHISM

The traditional pronunciation is "sizzum." However, "skizzum" is rapidly gaining ground.

SECONDLY, THIRDLY, FOURTHLY

As noted earlier, few people say "firstly," and fewer yet say "fifthly," "sixthly," "seventeenthly," etc. Many adverbs do not end in *ly*. It makes more sense to use *second, third*, and *fourth* rather than *secondly, thirdly*, and *fourthly*.

SEMIANNUAL

See **biannual, biennial, semiannual**.

SENSUAL, SENSUOUS

Sensual: relating to sexual pleasure.

Sensuous: relating to or affecting the physical senses.

SERF, SURF

Serf: a slave.

Surf: waves.

SERIAL

See **cereal, serial**.

SET, SIT

Set: to place something somewhere.

Sit: to take a seat.

SEW, SO, SOW

Sew: to stitch.

So: as a result; in the manner indicated.

Sow: to scatter or plant seed.

SHEAR, SHEER

Shear: to cut; to clip.

Sheer: pure; steep; translucent.

[*sic*]

This is found only in a direct quotation (note the brackets). An editor inserts [*sic*] directly after a word or sentence to notify readers that something is off or incorrect, but it is being reproduced exactly as it originally appeared.

SIERRA

Avoid "Sierras" when the topic is the vast California mountain range. An online camping guide says, "Translating from Spanish, *sierra* is plural in itself." A conservation organization elaborates: "The Sierra Nevada is a single, distinct unit, both geographically and topographically, and is well described by *una sierra nevada*. Strictly speaking, therefore, we should never pluralize the name—such as Sierras, or Sierra Nevadas, or even High Sierras."

SIGHT

See **cite, sight, site**.

SIMPLISTIC

It's not the same as *simple*. It means "oversimplified," as in *Your simplistic argument leaves out too many facts*.

At a memorial service, a well-meaning soul remembered a renowned artist as "a simplistic man." Some occasions are too solemn for foolish language lapses. Trying to express something commendable, the speaker instead said the dear departed had been a simpleton.

SINCE

See **because, since**.

SITE

See **cite, sight, site**.

SLASH

Despite its popularity, the slash (/), technically known as a **virgule**, is frowned on by purists. Other than to indicate dates (*9/11/2001*) or separate lines of poetry ("Celery, raw / Develops the jaw"), it has few defensible uses in formal writing.

Usually a hyphen, or in some cases the word *or*, will suffice. Instead of writing *the novelist/poet Eve Jones*, make it *the novelist-poet Eve Jones*. Rather than *available to any man/woman who is qualified*, make it *any man or woman*.

"The virgule is a mark that doesn't appear much in first-rate writing," says Bryan A. Garner in *A Dictionary of Modern American Usage*. "Use it as a last resort."

SLEIGHT, SLIGHT

Sleight: dexterity; skill.
Slight: slender; of little substance.

SLIPSHOD EXTENSION

This term, coined by the renowned lexicographer H.W. Fowler about a century ago, refers to the tendency of careless or ignorant speakers and writers to debase a word by overextending it beyond its proper meaning.

Several examples of this maddening phenomenon (e.g., **dilemma**, **literally**, **viable**) are scattered throughout the present chapter.

SNUCK

Many think *snuck* is the past tense of *sneak*, but it's not, at least not yet. The past tense of *sneak* is *sneaked*.

SO

See **sew, so, sow**.

SOAR, SORE

Soar: to fly high.
Sore: painful; in pain.

SOLE, SOUL

Sole: the bottom of a foot; a type of fish (nouns); single; solitary (adjectives).
Soul: essence; the spirit apart from the body.

SOME, SUM

Some: an unspecified number.
Sum: the total from adding numbers.

SON, SUN

Son: male offspring.
Sun: the star that is the central body of our solar system.

SOW

See **sew, so, sow**.

STAID, STAYED

Staid: solemn; serious.
Stayed: remained; waited.

STAIR, STARE

Stair: a step.
Stare: to gaze intently.

STAKE, STEAK

Stake: a wager; an investment; a pole.
Steak: a cut of meat.

STATIONARY, STATIONERY

Stationary: in one place; inactive.
Stationery: writing paper.

STEAL, STEEL

Steal: to rob.
Steel: an iron alloy (noun); to toughen (verb).

STEP, STEPPE

Step: a stair (noun); to move by lifting the foot (verb).
Steppe: vast grassland.

STOMPING GROUNDS

It started out as *stamping grounds*, which is still preferred by most dictionaries.

STRAIGHT, STRAIT

Words like *straitjacket* and *strait-laced* are frequently misspelled using *straight*, which is incorrect, but understandable. Wouldn't a "straightjacket" be just the thing to straighten you up and straighten you out? Doesn't "straight-laced" aptly describe a person of refinement (the *lace* part) who lives the "straight life"? This is why some authorities accept *straight-laced* as an alternative spelling. But a *strait* is a narrow channel, and it is that sense of "confinement with little room to maneuver" that generated these terms.

STRATEGY, STRATAGEM

Note the second *a* in *stratagem*.

Both words refer to plans of action. But *stratagem* denotes trickery. It is a scheme to deceive or outwit.

SUM

See **some, sum**.

SUN

See **son, sun**.

SUNDAE, SUNDAY

Sundae: ice cream with syrup.
Sunday: a day of the week.

SUPINE

See **prone, supine**.

SUPPOSE TO

Never "suppose to." Don't drop the *d* in usages like *You're supposed to be here.*

SURF

See **serf, surf**.

SYMPATHY

See **empathy, sympathy**.

T

TACK, TACT

Tack and *tact* are commonly confused when discussing strategy.

A *tack* is a course of action.

Tact is discretion.

We decided to try a new tack is correct, but "a new tact" is what a lot of people say, mistakenly thinking "tact" is short for *tactic*.

TAIL, TALE

Tail: the hindmost animal appendage.

Tale: a story.

TAKE

See **bring, take**.

TAKEN ABACK, TAKEN BACK

Taken back is a corruption of *taken aback*, a long-standing idiom meaning "taken by surprise." *Taken back* properly means "to be returned." These days, however, *taken back* is used in statements like, "I was taken back by his rudeness." The snarky online *Urban Dictionary* cautions that *taken back* is a "phrase used by semi-educated morons who mean to say 'taken aback' when describing an event that left them disconcerted or abashed."

TAUGHT, TAUT

Taught: trained; educated.

Taut: stiff; tightly stretched.

TEAM, TEEM

Team: a group with the same goal (noun); to form a squad (verb).

Teem: to swarm.

TEMBLOR

Although it produces tremors and makes the ground tremble, an earthquake is a *temblor*, not a "tremblor."

TENANT, TENET

A *tenant* is someone who pays rent to use or occupy a property. But "tenant" is often mistakenly used in place of *tenet*, a fundamental belief or principle held true by a group or organization.

THAN, THEN

Than is used for comparison.

Then means "next," "after that."

THANK-YOU

A hyphen is advisable when *thank-you* is used as a noun or adjective: *Some kind of thank-you seemed appropriate, so I sent a thank-you note.* However, avoid a hyphen with the expression *thank you* (as in *I thank you* or *we thank you*).

THAT

See **who, which, that**.

THEIR, THERE, THEY'RE

Their: belonging to them.

There: in that place.

They're: contraction of *they are*.

They're in *their* car over *there*.

THOUGH

See **although, though**

THOSE KIND OF

Instead of "those kind of things," say either *those kinds of things* or *things of that kind*. Better yet: *things like that*.

TILL, 'TIL

Always use *till*. You won't find a reference book anywhere that recommends *'til*. Writer John B. Bremner declares brusquely, "Either *till* or *until*, but not *'til*."

It's natural to assume that *'til* is a contraction of *until*. However, *till* predates *until* by several centuries.

TITLED

See **entitled, titled**

TO NOT

You see and hear *to not* everywhere: An editorial writer says he is "vowing to not become the next victim of this scam." A news item tells of a suspect's decision "to not waive his rights."

Some split infinitives are all right, but in most cases *to not* is just clumsy. The writers who chose it over "not to become" and "not to waive" in the above examples would strike many sticklers as either tone deaf or perverse.

TO, TOO, TWO

To: in the direction of; toward.

Too: also; excessively.

Two: the number after *one*.

TORT, TORTE

Tort: a wrongful act that can be redressed by awarding damages.

Torte: a rich cake made with little or no flour.

TORTUOUS, TORTUROUS

Tortuous: winding; twisting: *a tortuous trail*.

Torturous: painful; causing suffering: *held under torturous conditions*.

TOTALLY

Not to be used arbitrarily. How is *totally convinced* different from *convinced*?

TOWARD, TOWARDS

The *Associated Press Stylebook* insists on *toward*, but both are acceptable and mean the same thing.

TRANSPIRE

The celebrity issued a statement through his attorney that he was "sorry and saddened over what transpired." This usage of *transpire*, though common, is incorrect. The word doesn't mean "occur" or "happen." Something that transpires is revealed or becomes known over time. The Oxford online dictionary gives this example: "It transpired that millions of dollars of debt had been hidden in a complex web of transactions."

TREMBLOR

See **temblor**.

TROOP, TROUPE

Troop: a body of soldiers.

Troupe: a group of traveling performers.

Mike is a real trouper. Many would spell it "trooper." But a *trooper* is either a cop or a soldier in the cavalry, whereas a *trouper*, according to the *American Heritage Dictionary*, is "a reliable, uncomplaining, often hard-working person."

TRULY

Note the spelling: no *e*.

This word is often just window dressing. How is *I truly believe* different from *I believe*?

TURBID, TURGID

Turbid means "muddy," or "unclear," literally and figuratively. Both a river and a poem may properly be called turbid.

Turgid means "swollen," literally and figuratively. One may suffer physically from a turgid limb, or mentally from a turgid (i.e., pompous and bombastic) speech.

U

UNINTERESTED

See **disinterested, uninterested**.

UNIQUE

The Big Easy is one of America's most unique cities. Drop *most*. What's wrong with saying *one of America's unique cities*?

Unique is, on its own, a potent word, and it must never be accompanied by an intensifier, since modifying it saps its considerable power. When you use *unique*, put it out there alone—otherwise, say *unusual*.

Unique belongs to a group of words called **absolutes** or **incomparables**. Examples include *dead*, *equal*, *essential*, *eternal*, *opposite*, *supreme*. Such words resist being modified. Modifiers like *more*, *most*, *absolutely*, *rather*, and *very* either strip them of their strength or result in foolishness.

"Would you say 'very one-of-a-kind'?" asks Roy Blount Jr. in his book *Alphabet Juice*. Adding *very* or *absolutely* to *unique*, Blount says, "is like putting a propeller on a rabbit to make him hop better."

UTILIZE

All the way back in the 1940s, George Orwell blew the whistle on this pretentious word in his classic essay "Politics and the English Language." Orwell advised writers to get over themselves and go with *use*. But *use* is so humble, so mundane, whereas *utilize* really sounds like something. Bureaucrats in particular love to use *utilize*.

V

VAIN, VANE, VEIN

Vain: futile; narcissistic.
Vane: a blade moved by wind: *weather vane*.
Vein: a blood vessel; a mood.

VENAL, VENIAL

Venal: corrupt, able and willing to be bribed.

Venial: forgivable.

Any writer who inadvertently drops the *i* in a sentence like *Her lapse was venial* may want to think about getting a good lawyer.

VERSES, VERSUS

Verses: lines of poetry.

Versus: as compared to another choice; against.

VERY

Serious writers are wary of *very*. Very often, this very word is very unnecessary.

VIABLE

Viable means "able or fit to live": *viable cells, a viable fetus.*

Thanks to SLIPSHOD EXTENSION, *viable* has become synonymous with *possible, workable, feasible*. Many purists consider this unacceptable. Roy Copperud, in *American Usage and Style*, says "the word has had the edge hopelessly ground off it."

VIAL, VILE

Vial: a small container.

Vile: evil, depraved.

VICE, VISE

Vice: a bad habit; an immoral practice.

Vise: a device used to hold an object firmly.

VIRTUALLY

See **literally**.

W

WAIST, WASTE

Waist: the part of the human body between the ribs and hips.

Waste: garbage (noun); to squander (verb); to spend uselessly (verb).

WAIT, WEIGHT

Wait: to stay; to be available.

Weight: heaviness; significance.

WAIVER, WAVER

Waiver: relinquishment of a right.

Waver: to feel indecisive; to swing unsteadily.

WARN, WORN

Warn: to notify about trouble.

Worn: carried on the body; deteriorated.

WARRANTEE, WARRANTY

Warrantee: a person who is given a written guarantee or a warrant.

Warranty: a written guarantee.

WARY, WEARY

Wary: mistrustful; guarded.

Weary: exhausted; drained.

WAY, WEIGH

Way: a method; a direction; a manner.

Weigh: to measure mass; to mull over.

WAYS TO GO

A ways to go, meaning "a considerable distance," is best avoided in formal writing.

WEAK, WEEK

Weak: lacking strength.

Week: a period of seven days.

WEATHER, WHETHER

Weather: climatic conditions (noun); to withstand (verb).

Whether: if; in case.

WHETHER OR NOT

Often, the *or not* can be dropped, as in *I don't know whether or not you've heard this.*

WHICH

See **who, which, that**.

WHILE, WILE

While: during.

Wile: a ploy to fool, trap, or entice.

WHO, WHICH, THAT

Use *who* only when referring to humans. Avoid such usages as *a company who* or *a country who* or *a dog who*. For those, *that* or *which* is correct.

Contrary to superstition, *that* is perfectly acceptable when applied to people. *The Man That Got Away* and *The Girl That I Marry*, two hit ballads from the mid-twentieth century, were written at a time when the popular culture expected literacy from its songwriters. And don't forget the famous quotation from the Gospel of John which begins, "He that is without sin among you…"

Which as a pronoun should never refer to humans. (It's an adjective in sentences like *Which man do you mean?*)

WHOLE

See **hole, whole**.

WHOLLY

See **holy, wholly**.

WHO'S, WHOSE

Who's is a contraction of *who is* or *who has*.
Whose is the possessive case of *who*.
Who's the man whose wife called?

WITH REGARD(S) TO

See **in regard(s) to, with regard(s) to**.

WON'T, WONT

Won't: contraction of *will not*.
Wont: habit; custom (nouns); accustomed (adjective).

WORN

See **warn, worn**.

WRACK

See **rack, wrack**.

WRAP

See **rap, wrap**.

WREAK

See **reek, wreak**.

WREAK (WRECK) HAVOC

Because *wreak havoc* means "to cause destruction," some mistakenly think the first word of the phrase is *wreck*.

WREST

See **rest, wrest**.

WRETCH

See **retch, wretch**.

WRING

See **ring, wring**.

WRITE

See **right, rite, write**.

WRY

See **rye, wry**.

Y

YOKE, YOLK

Yoke: a harness for oxen.
Yolk: the yellow part of an egg.

YOU'RE, YOUR

You're: contraction of *you are*.
Your: belonging to you.

CHAPTER 6

QUIZZES

GRAMMAR *PRETEST*

Correct the **grammar** error in each sentence. Place a check mark in front of sentences that are correct. Answers are in Chapter Seven.

Example: *There is many ways to fix that trombone.*
Correction: *There are many ways to fix that trombone.*

1. That carload of clowns look a bit crowded.
2. If I was you, I would take the Yankees' offer to parachute into the stadium during Elvis Night.
3. Those are the things which we can discuss after Jerrod gets the job.
4. Vanessa responded indignant upon being told someone else had used her reward points.
5. Bill acts like Ted does when they start an excellent adventure.
6. There is too many things we'll need to do to fix that old sandbox.
7. If Jasmine is going to compete in the marathon, she'll need to train daily, maintain a proper diet, and sufficient sleep.
8. Darienne is a swimmer whom I think can qualify for the Olympics.
9. Between the two landscapers, Shangri-lawn is the best.
10. If Marietta doesn't start watering those plants, I fear they will parish.
11. If you ask me, Zed is as zany as him.

12. The goalie twisted her ankle, that had already been bothering her before the game.
13. Raja ran in to trouble when she tried to cook eggs in the microwave.
14. Before they went to sleep, they hanged the stockings by the chimney with care.
15. Whomever Thaddeus chooses will be the next baton-twirler to lead the parade.
16. The truth about who spilled the wine on the sofa is between she and I.
17. Much fuel, as well as many plastics, are made from petroleum.
18. Tell whoever you want that Abdul is organizing the hot air balloon race.
19. They are the soldiers which will bring the flag to the ceremony.
20. The court reporter's opinion appears to be much different than the judge's.
21. We've been hiking a long time. My legs are getting wary.
22. The majority of respondents has stated that shoelaces won't be necessary.
23. It is you who is misinformed about the research results.
24. The contents of the vault will be shared between Gunnar and myself.
25. Tasked with troubleshooting the problem, the technician purposely climbed the telephone pole.
26. Of all the cities tracked this year, Fairbanks, Alaska, is the colder.
27. Emily speaks of subjects that interest her.
28. Neither the silver medal nor the bronze are sufficient for Sandra; she wants the gold.
29. Just listen to Ozzy and sing like he asks.
30. The director should give raises to whomever deserves one.
31. Does anybody here know who ordered the jalapeño meat loaf?
32. Jermaine says he can't remember where the package was sent to.
33. Cheyenne is not uncertain about wanting to go to the blueberry festival.
34. Whom should I tell him inquired?
35. Because he is a well man, he always gives to charity whenever he can.
36. When you listen closely to the tape, you can hear it is her speaking.
37. The library is clearing the shelves of those titles, which will be available for purchase at the book sale on Saturday.
38. The commander lead the fleet that enforced the embargo.
39. Either the flag or the statue are sufficient for ceremonial purposes.
40. The decision to reopen the park was made by the committee.
41. The gym membership will be awarded to whomever wins the sit-up competition.
42. She responds intelligent when presented with highly challenging questions.
43. The dual between the light-saber experts is sure to attract media from throughout the galaxy.
44. I'd say that between Ruth and Rae, Rae is the most efficient at basket weaving.
45. Like most Martians do, I try not to include too much red in my house.

46. Each of the tree leaves make a fine resting place for caterpillars.
47. Everybody knows whom the book's "anonymous source" was; they just can't state it publicly.
48. A plane and a train is my way of getting there in less than a day.
49. In times of trouble, it means a lot to have friends that will be by your side.
50. While broadcasting the ball game, the swan flew into the booth and perched next to his microphone.

FINDING NOUNS, VERBS, AND SUBJECTS *QUIZ 1*

Underline all subjects once and all verbs twice. Correct the capitalization of nouns if needed. Answers are in Chapter Seven.

Example: *The Chicago Cubs won the World Series in 2016.*
Answer: *The Chicago <u>Cubs</u> <u>won</u> the World Series in 2016.*

1. The Brookfield zoo exhibit attracted thousands of visitors.
2. For months, she had been putting up with the squeaky wheel.
3. They will start cleaning as soon as the dance is over.
4. The meetings aim for much and achieve much too little.
5. I will stop at nothing to have those potato chips.
6. Your scooter looks new.
7. After weeks of preparation, the Kansas city company was ready for the unveiling.
8. Hurry, because the mall closes in an hour.
9. Jessie wants to see the London symphony orchestra, but Jake prefers we go to the pubs in Piccadilly circus.
10. All handbags appeal to Nanette, regardless of their color.

FINDING NOUNS, VERBS, AND SUBJECTS *QUIZ 2*

Underline the subjects once and the verbs twice. Correct the capitalization of nouns if needed. Answers are in Chapter Seven.

Example: *He arrived at heathrow airport on time.*
Answer: *<u>He</u> <u>arrived</u> at Heathrow Airport on time.*

1. The overturned truck blocked both lanes.
2. The Metropolitan Museum of Art is a New York city landmark.
3. She will fly part of the way and then drive fifty kilometers to get there.
4. I will just be watching the boston marathon, but my wife will be running in it.
5. Behind the door is a coat rack.
6. Watch your step.
7. He should have been more gracious.
8. On the table was her purse.
9. In the Newspaper, an interesting article appeared.
10. How long have you been living in new Delhi?
11. We are forced to inhale and exhale this smog-filled air.
12. From the bottom of the cave, the stalagmites rose ten feet high.

SUBJECT AND VERB AGREEMENT *QUIZ 1*

Underline the subjects once and the verbs twice. If the subjects and verbs do not agree, change the verbs to match the subjects. Place a check mark in front of sentences that are correct. Answers are in Chapter Seven.

Example: *The bank and the pharmacy is on either side of the dry cleaners.*
Correction: *The <u>bank</u> and the <u>pharmacy</u> <u>are</u> on either side of the dry cleaners.*

1. The jar of fruit is next to the can of tomato sauce.
2. There's many ways to catch a mouse.
3. It's one of those must-do chores that is easily forgotten.
4. If I was a billionaire, I'd buy a few ocean islands.
5. The audience are seated now.
6. The couple is planning to renew their wedding vows.
7. Here is my shoes.
8. The bed of roses were planted under the window.
9. A pen and paper are all I need.
10. Close to three-fourths of the earth's surface is covered by water.
11. The sack of treats belong to the boy.
12. The library, as well as the boutique shops, are affected by the new ordinance.
13. Either you or I am going to have to move this boulder.
14. All of my dollars is to be invested in that fund.

15. Do you know if every one of them like sugar cookies?
16. Jumping and shouting are prohibited in the arena.
17. "Rise and shine" are his mom's favorite greeting.
18. Three of the four candidates wields impressive technological insight.
19. The page of statistics confuse them.
20. Neither the Martians nor the Venusian want to vacation on Pluto.

SUBJECT AND VERB AGREEMENT *QUIZ 2*

Underline the subjects once and the verbs twice. If the subjects and verbs do not agree, change the verbs to match the subjects. Place a check mark in front of sentences that are correct. Answers are in Chapter Seven.

Example: *Harpreet and his sister is going for a long hike.*
Correction: <u>Harpreet</u> and his <u>sister</u> <u>are</u> <u>going</u> for a long hike.

1. That pack of lies are not going to cause me to change my mind.
2. Neither the rain nor the darkness are going to stop me.
3. My staff believes in providing high-quality service.
4. The conductor, as well as the musicians, are taking the stage.
5. My whole family are vacationing in Baja California this winter.
6. There's lots of people here.
7. If it was up to me, we would leave earlier in the morning.
8. One in three stressed Americans cope by shopping.
9. Four years are considered the normal amount of time to earn a bachelor's degree.
10. Law and order is the principle he based his campaign on.
11. Al and Eli go to the beach to surf with their friends.
12. There's three strawberries left.
13. Most of my savings is invested in real estate.
14. I wish it were summer and time for vacation.
15. Nervousness, not to mention lack of sleep, contribute to poor performance.
16. One-third of the city are experiencing a blackout tonight.
17. The next thing I heard were two shots.
18. Ladies and gentlemen, here's Wisin and Yandel.
19. Either the bikes or the lawn mower go in that space.
20. Her attitude is one of the things that's difficult.

IRREGULAR VERBS *QUIZ 1*

Circle the correct word in each sentence. Answers are in Chapter Seven.

1. We have chose/chosen/choosed a new topic.
2. They drug/drugged/dragged the heavy bag across the floor.
3. We should have done/have did/of done things differently.
4. I have drunk/drank/drinked the last soda.
5. I wish you had come/came/coming home sooner.
6. Things haven't went/go/gone the way we planned.
7. She seen/saw/seed us coming.
8. Yesterday he run/ran/runned a marathon.
9. When we arrived, the meeting had already began/begun/begin.
10. The eagle had already flew/flied/flown away.

IRREGULAR VERBS *QUIZ 2*

Circle the correct word in each sentence. Answers are in Chapter Seven.

1. We noticed that the sign had fell/falled/fallen.
2. Bobby sweared/swore/sworn he'd never do it again.
3. They have wrote/written/writed that they are coming in the spring.
4. They pretend they have forgot/forgotted/forgotten what they did.
5. My friends have ridden/ride/rode in that fancy car, but I never have.
6. André has brought/broughten/brung the beverages.
7. Cameron shown/showing/showed me the fastest way to get there.
8. We should have took/token/taken the other road.
9. The full moon has risen/rose/rised.
10. He got/has got/have got to try harder from now on.

PRONOUNS *QUIZ 1*

Circle the correct word(s) in each sentence. Answers are in Chapter Seven.

1. It's me/I who am/is on the phone.
2. Could it really be he/him?
3. Laquon is younger than I/me.

4. It is they/them who speak/speaks too much.
5. Is Barbara the only one of them who has/have read the book?
6. Paolo thinks well of she/her.
7. Either of us qualify/qualifies for the coaching position.
8. One must be ready to help one's self/oneself in order to succeed.
9. I prefer that you keep it between you and myself/me.
10. Him/He and his friends play/plays soccer each Tuesday.
11. Everyone on this committee have/has a point of view.
12. Is that confetti cannon mine or yours/your's/yours'?
13. Bernice of all people know/knows the answer.
14. He/Him and she/her will give the van a psychedelic paint job.
15. Today is just one of those days that seem/seems too short.
16. Agnes and I/myself ran five miles this morning.
17. But it's/its only fifty dollars!
18. The Venusians? The Martians are smarter than them/they.
19. The men all made his/their contribution.
20. It's/Its but one of the reasons that call/calls for an air conditioner.

PRONOUNS *QUIZ 2*

Fix any errors in the following sentences. Place a check mark in front of sentences that are correct. Answers are in Chapter Seven.

1. It is him who will be responsible for making all of the arrangements.
2. Julia is a faster runner than me.
3. She was one of those cruise passengers who is always complaining.
4. The sweater that we found at the church is your's.
5. The dog hurt it's paw while running through the empty field.
6. George and I finished staining the deck.
7. The honors committee nominated he and Ming.
8. Her and me are in charge of the sales presentation tomorrow.
9. Neither of the girls are planning a wedding in the near future.
10. It is we who will get the blame if things do not go well.
11. Each of the players get to make a speech before the parade.
12. He and I have been good friends since second grade.
13. It is I who am wrong.
14. Please talk to Daniela or myself next time you have a concern.

15. Who's hat is this?
16. It's obvious that the best team will prevail.
17. I weigh more than he.
18. You're friend told her friend that their's a party tonight.
19. The argument he gave had it's merits.
20. You more than anyone else knows what the risks are.

WHO, WHOM, WHOEVER, WHOMEVER *QUIZ 1*

Choose the correct word (*who*, *whom*, *whoever*, or *whomever*) to complete each sentence. Answers are in Chapter Seven.

1. They will choose _____ they please.
2. _____ finishes in second and third place will receive a consolation prize.
3. First we have to find out _____ is in charge.
4. _____ shall I say this is from?
5. Victor is a detective _____ leaves no details behind.
6. We will work with _____ they assign for the project.
7. The doctor prescribes the medicine to patients _____ she believes must have it.
8. Does the university know _____ will receive the scholarship funds?
9. _____ it turns out to be, we trust the new park commissioner will serve well.
10. Scientists developed the serum for _____ will benefit from it.
11. The actor _____ wins the award will be featured on the magazine cover.
12. My dad once said _____ is first to speak is often the last to listen.
13. That painting is for _____. Erica didn't have anyone specific in mind.
14. To _____ It May Concern: Your Shrimp Etouffee is outstanding. We want the recipe!
15. The lions are so well trained they respond to _____ they hear.
16. _____ identifies the cat burglar will receive the award money.
17. By _____ were they given the authority?
18. _____ has the papers Roger left by the air tunnel?
19. To _____ are you giving the discount?
20. The book is a great resource for those _____ need one.

WHO, WHOM, WHOEVER, WHOMEVER *QUIZ 2*

Choose the correct word (*who*, *whom*, *whoever*, or *whomever*) to complete each sentence. Answers are in Chapter Seven.

1. He is the doctor _____ took Jimmy's tonsils out.
2. _____ did you go to the movie with?
3. It does not matter to me _____ drives tomorrow.
4. I will ride with _____ is planning to stop at the store.
5. Please thank _____ brought in our mail while we were gone.
6. We will hire _____ you trust to do the work.
7. _____ used the grill last forgot to clean it.
8. The wedding florist _____ we wanted to hire is unavailable.
9. Fatima was the cashier _____ won the lottery.
10. Clare knows _____ the winner is already.
11. Kimiko donates her time to _____ she feels needs it most.
12. Kathy was not sure _____ she was voting for.
13. He is the man _____ Mr. O'Brian hired.
14. I will vote for _____ you think is best.
15. I will vote for _____ you suggest.
16. _____ shall I ask about this matter?
17. Give the information to _____ they prefer.
18. She is the woman _____ I believe was hired last year.
19. _____ are you mailing that letter to?
20. _____ do you suppose runs this show?

WHO, WHOM, THAT, WHICH *QUIZ 1*

Correct *who*, *whom*, *that*, or *which* in the following sentences. Place a check mark in front of sentences that are correct. Answers are in Chapter Seven.

1. I wish we had a teacher **that** let us out early.
2. Is that the man **who** found the divining rod **that** you had lost?
3. The funds **which** they said they don't have are all in an offshore account.
4. The lamp **which** is over there will not turn on.
5. Darsha would like to have a dog **who** becomes her best friend.

6. He no longer reads trade journals, **which** to him tend to favor certain advertisers.
7. Tayshawn appears to be a free agent **who** the team can afford.
8. The car, **that** costs what they'd expected, seats six and gets good mileage.
9. It could be one of those moments **which** lead to a lucky break.
10. Decide if it's a person **that** you trust and a mission **which** you believe in.

WHO, WHOM, THAT, WHICH *QUIZ 2*

Correct *who*, *whom*, *that*, or *which* in the following sentences. Place a check mark in front of sentences that are correct. Answers are in Chapter Seven.

1. Tina is looking for a pet **who** is small and easy to care for.
2. The mechanic **that** fixed my car did a great job.
3. The red vase, **that** she sold for $20, was worth $200.
4. Was he the only student in the class **who** applied for the scholarship?
5. Gandhi was a role model **who** millions admired.
6. I love hearing the owls **who** sit in the trees and hoot at dusk.
7. The game **which** intrigues Gretchen the most is dominoes.
8. That **that** doesn't kill you makes you stronger.
9. The tomatoes **which** grow in her garden are unlike those you buy in a store.
10. The tomatoes from her garden, **which** grew larger than those in the grocery store, were sweet and ripe.

ADJECTIVES AND ADVERBS *QUIZ 1*

Decide whether the sentences are written correctly. If not, change them. Place a check mark in front of the sentences that are correct. Answers are in Chapter Seven.

1. Si-woo prepares for tennis practice rather odd.
2. When you see Samantha, please let her know I hope she is good.
3. The inspector followed the evidence close.
4. If you spell poor, you probably won't get the writing job.
5. Okafor solves crossword puzzles more quick than Christophe.
6. Which of the two loans do the bankers like best?
7. The drink tastes bitterly to me.
8. Ask Miriam if she feels well about our latest donation.

9. Pedro has four dogs. The bigger of them weighs one hundred pounds.

10. The elves sounded merrily when they received the news about their fourth-quarter toy production.

11. If sleeping well is wise, then off to bed I go.

12. Teddy Roosevelt once said, "Speak soft and carry a big stick."

13. As usually, they ordered the shepherd's pie.

14. The sleepy fox wished the hyenas could be a little more quiet.

15. Those who want to be thoughtful will choose their words careful.

16. Dr. Azir is the more skilled of all the surgeons.

17. Bobby and Fiona are debating whether an ice cream headache is worser than the hiccups.

18. The twins are equal quickly witted.

19. This sentence demonstrates that the word *this* at the start is a pronoun.

20. The world seems so sanguine when viewed through rose-tinted glasses.

ADJECTIVES AND ADVERBS *QUIZ 2*

Decide whether the sentences are written correctly. If not, change them. Place a check mark in front of the sentences that are correct. Answers are in Chapter Seven.

1. I feel just as badly about this as you do.

2. I did good today on my final exam.

3. C.J. slept sound after running the marathon.

4. Despite her honest efforts, my grandmother's driving is worst than ever.

5. Of your three dogs, which is cuter?

6. His hearing is good for someone who's played in a rock band for twenty years.

7. He still hears good for someone who's played in a rock band for twenty years.

8. Our homemade fried rice was real tasty.

9. I think my left eye is my sharpest eye.

10. She looked suspiciously at the man in the trench coat.

11. Come quick or we will miss our bus.

12. Ella was the best of the two sisters at gymnastics.

13. Rochelle felt badly about forgetting Devlin's birthday.

14. To find her, we need to follow those set of tracks.

15. The new model of this chain saw operates much quieter than the old model.

16. She felt good about getting her puppy from the SPCA.

17. Which is the worst, a toothache or a headache?

18. She reacted swift, which made him feel badly about insulting her.
19. He swings the bat as good as anyone else in major-league baseball.
20. I have never been less surer of anything in my life.

PREPOSITIONS *QUIZ 1*

Correct the following sentences by adding, removing, or changing the prepositions. Place a check mark in front of sentences that are correct. Answers are in Chapter Seven.

1. Where are they traveling to this summer?
2. I should of been a millionaire, but I went swimming in the lake with the lottery ticket in the back pocket of my trunks.
3. The spy peered into the dimly lit corridor.
4. It looks like the plane will depart on time after all.
5. Imelda said it's different than anything she's ever read.
6. The panel just can't seem to get off of the subject of new taxes on domestic gardening.
7. Like any good acrobat, Pierre maintains his weight, strength, and flexibility.
8. The construction project was finished under budget and above expectations.
9. They will be treated as any other applicant.
10. The boys ran through the sprinkler and then in the mud.

PREPOSITIONS *QUIZ 2*

Correct the following sentences by adding, removing, or changing the prepositions. Place a check mark in front of sentences that are correct. Answers are in Chapter Seven.

1. We could of been there by now if we hadn't gotten lost.
2. Charles talks like his brother does.
3. He drove his car in the garage.
4. Did you take an envelope off of my desk?
5. Like the ranger said, this is an area with a lot of poison ivy.
6. Jacques acted like he never met your aunt.
7. Where did you get this from?
8. This problem is no different than many others I've dealt with.
9. You could of told me about the mistake earlier.
10. I'm going to turn this lost wallet into the police.

AFFECT VS. EFFECT *QUIZ 1*

Circle the correct word in each sentence. Answers are in Chapter Seven.

1. The managers believe the lasting affect/effect will be a steady market performance.
2. Martians avoid visiting Venus because the 800°F temperatures adversely affect/effect their antennae.
3. If we want to affect/effect better morale, we should find out what is important to our staff.
4. The infield's strategy of shifting left against the batter proved to be highly affective/effective.
5. Lena's yoga instruction seems to be affecting/effecting Hans in a good way.
6. Study harder and affect/effect better grades on your report card.
7. Not even high winds affect/effect Willy's command when he's riding in his hot air balloon.
8. Let's see if these seeds from Jack affect/effect our ability to grow some beans.
9. The approach is having an affect/effect on her affect/effect during therapy.
10. Calorie intake often affects/effects weight gain or loss.
11. What affect/effect are they hoping to achieve by raising the price?
12. The act of painting seems to improve her affect/effect.
13. Preparation affects/effects outcome.
14. They delivered the speech with great affect/effect.
15. Spending less on designer furniture will help affect/effect greater profitability.

AFFECT VS. EFFECT *QUIZ 2*

Circle the correct word in each sentence. Answers are in Chapter Seven.

1. Mark told Taneisha that cigarettes would negatively affect/effect her health.
2. The convict showed little affect/effect throughout her trial.
3. Do you think our campaign will be affective/effective?
4. Working overtime at the office negatively affected/effected Keeton's personal life.
5. One must be a powerful speaker to affect/effect social change.
6. Jojo found that meditation had therapeutic affects/effects.
7. The choices we make now will affect/effect society for generations to come.
8. The bike safety law currently in affect/effect should be improved.

9. The emergence of social networking websites affected/effected her productivity.
10. The affect/effect of the antibiotic on her infection was surprising.
11. I did not know that antibiotics could affect/effect people so quickly.
12. If the chemotherapy has no affect/effect, should she get surgery for the tumor?
13. When will we know if the chemotherapy has taken affect/effect?
14. The critics greatly affected/effected his thinking.
15. How were you able to affect/effect such radical changes?

LAY VS. LIE *QUIZ 1*

Make corrections to the words in **bold** where needed. Place a check mark in front of sentences that are correct. Answers are in Chapter Seven.

1. If you're tired, you can **lay** on the futon.
2. She has been **laying** in the hammock since this morning.
3. Malik said we should **lie** the tarp first.
4. The contractor said he has **laid** that type of brick many times.
5. So what happens if it **lays** in the sun too long?
6. Now I **lay** me down to sleep.
7. Of course nothing will get done if they keep **laying** around all day.
8. They might be **lyeing** about how much they spent on the office party.
9. Because of his business travel, Markus has **lain** his head on many hotel pillows.
10. When the golf tournament started, no one, including the experts, expected Noah to **lay** such an egg on the back nine of the course.
11. The ancient city has **laid** in the shadow of the tower since the fall of the empire.
12. Under the circumstances, if he **lyes,** he will only compound the case against him.

LAY VS. LIE *QUIZ 2*

Make corrections to the words in **bold** where needed. Place a check mark in front of sentences that are correct. Answers are in Chapter Seven.

1. Grandma is not feeling well and went to **lay** down.
2. The mail has **laid** on the table unopened for two days now.
3. The cat will probably be **lying** in the sun after she eats her lunch.

4. The chickens **layed** enough eggs for us to make three large omelets.
5. Omar **laid** on the air mattress and floated on the water for hours.
6. I am dizzy and need to **lay** down.
7. When I got dizzy yesterday, I **laid** down.
8. The lions have **laid** in wait for their prey.
9. I will **lie** my head on my pillow.
10. **Lay** out all the clothes you want to pack.
11. You should have **lain** out all the clothes you wanted to pack.
12. If you're **lieing** to me, I'll be very upset.

ADVICE VS. ADVISE *QUIZ 1*

Circle the correct word. Answers are in Chapter Seven.

1. If they want to improve, they must be willing to listen to advise/advice.
2. The consultant advised/adviced her client to focus on steel fabrication.
3. The electrician's advise/advice is to address the wiring before it is exposed.
4. It is possible to advise/advice without being wise.
5. The firm is willing to advise/advice if, of course, we pay the exorbitant fee.
6. Those who seek the advise/advice of others should be prepared for what it might be.
7. Wendy got a new job advising/advicing French bakers.
8. For customer service, their advise/advice is to under-promise and over-deliver.
9. The legal team is trying to advise/advice the defendant.
10. I advise/advice you to take my advise/advice.

ADVICE VS. ADVISE *QUIZ 2*

Circle the correct word. Answers are in Chapter Seven.

1. My doctor adviced/advised me to go to the gym more often.
2. My advice/advise is to talk to Georgia face-to-face, rather than by e-mail.
3. When giving advice/advise to a friend, I try to put myself in her shoes.
4. Teachers advice/advise parents to emphasize reading at home.
5. Sara always takes my advice/advise to heart.

6. I'd like to ask an engineer to advice/advise us on the design.
7. Lakeisha knows she can always go to her best friend for advice/advise.
8. The lawyer adviced/advised him to plead guilty.
9. Randall has a bad habit of offering unsolicited advice/advise.
10. I always ask my brother for advice/advise because he knows me best.

THEIR VS. THERE VS. THEY'RE *QUIZ 1*

Circle the correct word. Answers are in Chapter Seven.

1. I'm not sure why they have a NASCAR engine on their/there/they're patio.
2. The Aquinos said they will be their/there/they're when the fireworks start.
3. Ava and Elsie always sign their/there/they're names in purple ink.
4. Do you know if their/there/they're A's fans or Giants fans?
5. When you speak with the sales department, please find out their/there/they're preferred form of payment.
6. Their/There/They're are more ways to approach a solution.
7. If their/there/they're their/there/they're, Heidi will be their/there/they're too.
8. One has to wonder if the two sisters will ever get past their/there/they're differences.
9. They have to make a stop, and then their/there/they're off to see the wizard.
10. The rare edition of the book you're looking for is on the shelf over their/there/they're.

THEIR VS. THERE VS. THEY'RE *QUIZ 2*

Circle the correct word. Answers are in Chapter Seven.

1. The Garcias are having a costume party at their/there/they're house tonight.
2. Paul and Summer are in search of a tank for their/there/they're baby turtles.
3. On Thursday, their/there/they're going to take a paragliding lesson.
4. According to an old legend, their/there/there is buried treasure on that island.
5. Their/There/They're is a mouse in my closet!
6. I wonder if their/there/they're planning to go shopping with us.
7. It's their/there/they're decision, so I'll just stay out of it.

8. Their/There/They're are many ways to cut a cake.

9. To our surprise, Nick and Taylor just announced that their/there/they're getting married.

10. Juan and Pablo just called to let us know their/there/they're coming for dinner.

MORE CONFUSING WORDS AND HOMONYMS *QUIZ 1*

Choose the correct word from each pair in each sentence.

1. The lightning/lightening you saw in the sky was just an illusion/allusion.
2. When you come over for dinner tonight, don't forget to bring/take the desert/dessert.
3. Martin plans to canvas/canvass the neighborhood to promote his new band, the Martian Martinis.
4. The horde/hoard gathered to hear her teaching.
5. If it looks like I'm wracking/racking my brain, the <u>reason is because</u>/<u>reason is</u>/<u>reason is that</u> I have an advanced physics exam tomorrow.
6. The critics censored/censured our performance, but the audiences loved it.
7. According to calculations, the change in planetary alignment is imminent/eminent.
8. By the way his tail is wagging, it's clear that Fido has been eager/anxious to see you.
9. Penny is loath/loathe to peel/peal the wrapping from the tort/torte box because she knows no one can have just one piece.
10. The former magician used sleight/slight of hand to convince/persuade the doubtful customers that the coins were genuine.

MORE CONFUSING WORDS AND HOMONYMS *QUIZ 2*

Correct all usage errors as listed in Chapter Five. Beware: There may be more than one error per quiz question. Answers are in Chapter Seven.

1. It takes awhile to adopt to this hot weather when you're from Anchorage.
2. You don't need fancy stationary to thank someone–that's besides the point.
3. I explained my principle reasons for quitting to a couple guys from work.
4. You have to be more discrete or you'll literally drive your husband up the wall.
5. It's not everyday that I get to spend several hours on my favorite past time.

6. He wore a gold metal when he lead the parade yesterday.
7. It won't phase me in the least if you just sit your drink on the chair next to you.
8. It was not just a great day; it was an historic occasion, and I was feeling alright.
9. He's one of the premiere actors of our generation, irregardless of his messy personal life.
10. I have no flare for geography: I thought Buffalo was the capitol of New York, but it's Albany.

EFFECTIVE WRITING *QUIZ 1*

Rewrite these sentences to make them more effective. Your sentences may be different from the answers given in Chapter Seven.

1. The shoes were black, shiny, and had cushioned soles.
2. Veronica is not unsure of herself when there is a sale to be made.
3. The statue will be finished by the sculptor in time for the unveiling.
4. The children need to pick up their toys, books, and their clothes.
5. Her glory days behind her, Chuck defeated Farrah in the competition for best pianist.
6. I have a guitar that Eric played in my locker.
7. The accounts were mismanaged by the company.
8. The story you're telling is not unclear.
9. It was two years ago that Krystal learned to play the flute.
10. Behind the curtain. Under the shelf. Hide the cashews.

EFFECTIVE WRITING *QUIZ 2*

Rewrite these sentences to make them more effective. Your sentences may be different from the answers given in Chapter Seven.

1. While I am in town. Let's visit Golden Gate Park.
2. Good employees are prompt, courteous, and they help you when you need it.
3. It is expected that you will report for work by no later than nine o'clock.
4. The patient is not unresponsive.
5. The boy was hit in the face by the pie as it left the girl's hand.

6. We washed the dishes, swept the floor, and the tables were dusted.
7. On a hike with my wife, a bear climbed a tree.
8. Jordan did not believe that Serena had embarrassed him unintentionally.
9. Lying on a stretcher, they carried him out.
10. I was wearing the sweater that Amy knitted at the concert.
11. The weather had adverse impacts on our boat, resulting in the necessity of rescuing us from the water.
12. Walking aimlessly down the street, a bus almost clipped me.
13. The cars were worn down by the taxi drivers.
14. Maria encountered a stranger clad in her parka and blue jeans.
15. Looking back, the dog was following us.

GRAMMAR *MASTERY TEST*

In the following sentences, underline the correct choice from those given or treat the sentence as directed. Answers are in Chapter Seven.

Example: *Giuseppe couldn't recall who/whom he'd spoken to first.*
Correction: *Giuseppe couldn't recall who/<u>whom</u> he'd spoken to first.*

1. The box of handmade chocolates *is/are* a gift from *she/her* and *I/me*.
2. You speak *like/as if* I am the one *who/whom* they said is the next great Frisbee player.
3. Instead of *hording/hoarding* the old paintings in the basement, they *hung/hanged* them throughout the house.
4. Either of us *is/are* capable of fixing the fence, but between the two of us, he is probably the *quickest/quicker*.
5. (*Rewrite as needed.*) Hakeem wants to learn how to play drums, the piano, and to study the guitar.
6. Ninety percent of the orders *is/are* for the German chocolate cake? I *should of/should have* known not to make so much of the pistachio.
7. I want to speak with *whoever/whomever* was in charge of the wood-carving contest, because *whoever/whomever* they chose did the job *good/well*.
8. The Midwest is having unusually pleasant weather, and *there are those who/some* say it could last for months.
9. She is the one *who/that* told them the article was written about *whoever/whomever* swam the English Channel wearing a shark fin.

10. Grover needs to stop broadcasting from pirate radio on Saturday nights—it's starting to *mettle/meddle* with Bert and Ernie's walkie-talkie chats.

11. Neither the tin-foil gizmo nor the rabbit-ears antenna *is/are* going to help much with the reception, I'm afraid.

12. *Whoever/Whomever* you want to be the team captain will wear the special cape.

13. Zachary does not read books *that/which* have highlighter marks in them.

14. Rodrigo may not be as strong as *he/him*, but I'll bet he can still lift those weights.

15. They are no different *than/from* all of the other players *who/that/which* want a fair set of rules for pick-up basketball games at the park.

16. For my birthday, Shaynee got me a case of my favorite locally brewed strawberry ale, *that/which* I enjoy because it always tastes so perfectly *sweetly/sweet*.

17. *Who/Whom* should we say is calling?

18. The elaborate presentation *persuaded/convinced* Paolo to buy the ear-cleaning wand even though he wasn't sure he really needed it.

19. The panel will award the ribbon to *whoever/whomever* completes the obstacle course first.

20. It will be *they/them who/whom* are first to enter *in to/into* an agreement.

21. Alberto is *sure/totally sure* that the moon and the sun will switch places by the year 2072.

22. (*Rewrite as needed.*) Luckily, when writing her new story, the computer saved Anita's file before the power went out.

23. *There's/There are* still five more tests to run before the vaccine is approved.

24. (*Underline the sentence subjects.*) The needles and pins are in the tray, and the tacks are in the little jar.

25. You're looking *good/well* after your cold—your medication must have worked.

26. Rose thinks *whoever/whomever* is involved in the project-planning phase will also have a big say in *who/whom* gets the labor contracts.

27. Where should Mason send *this/this to*?

28. The Venusians believe it is you who *is/are* responsible for the false astrology report.

29. (*Underline the dependent clause.*) The playoffs will continue even though the league did not complete a full season.

30. Jed appears to be aging *slower/more slowly* than Jeremiah.

31. Either the magician or I *am/are* going to find your missing rabbit after the show.

32. That *that/which* one survives can become wisdom passed on to others.

33. Just like all other stars in the galaxy, three-fourths of the new star just discovered *consist/consists* of helium.

34. If the cruise ship voyages any longer, the kitchen's supply of cocktail sauce will go no *farther/further*.

35. *Whoever/Whomever* left the garden faucet running while we were on vacation owes me a lot of money.

36. Simone acts just *as/like* her sister whenever she hears something funny.

37. (*Underline the four phrases.*) I can't wait to see my old neighbor at the farm when I return to my hometown in ten days.

38. (*Rewrite as needed.*) Shoveling the walk after a heavy snow. It's important.

39. The couple *think/thinks* that two hundred dollars *is/are* too much to pay for the ceramic bowl.

40. The custom sailboat was built by Ahab and *me/myself*.

41. (*Rewrite as needed.*) Fletcher is looking fit these days—he must be adjusting his diet, started exercising, and getting more sleep.

42. (*Underline all* main *verb parts.*) Ilyana has been studying Danish for six years now, and she will eventually put it into practice when she travels to Denmark to visit her relatives.

43. You don't smell too *bad/badly* for someone who worked outside all day.

44. The recording engineers have often asked themselves *who/whom* the true source of that tinkling sound was.

45. Uncle Saul wants us to *get off of/get off* the porch because he says we're *reeking/wreaking* havoc up here.

46. The decision is and always will be *her's/hers*.

47. Controlling *one's self/oneself* when faced with disagreement is a mark of maturity. *Its/It's* something I always try to remember.

48. Rae is one of those people who always <u>look</u>/<u>looks like</u>/<u>as if</u> they are ready to have fun.

49. The new arts center, as well as the adjoining Japanese garden, *add/adds* a welcome touch of cultural beauty near the downtown riverwalk.

50. The smell from the pile has gone from bad to *worse/worst*.

PUNCTUATION, CAPITALIZATION, AND WRITING NUMBERS *PRETEST*

Correct any errors in punctuation, capitalization, and writing numbers. Place a check mark in front of sentences that are correct. Answers are in Chapter Seven.

1. Was that delivery on the porch your's?
2. Daniel has never been good at Spelling.

3. Fifty two people became ill on the ship that day.
4. November 4, 2006 was the date of their wedding.
5. One of her dog's is in our yard.
6. His house is just East of the high school.
7. Sara's and Darnell's house was damaged by the hail storm.
8. Aiden wondered if you had listened to his podcast?
9. Samir likes all of these outdoor activities: Fishing, camping, boating, and snorkeling.
10. If you plan to do any online shopping today please let me know.
11. "Why," she asked, "have you been streaming movies all day?"
12. Mom tried making your new chicken recipe and it was a huge success.
13. Please complete all the paperwork, it is due by tomorrow.
14. "Would you like to go to a baseball game Thursday," asked Grayson?
15. They recently visited Key West, Florida and are anxious to go back.
16. Would you Jordyn, please run an errand for me?
17. Have you ever met her Grandma?
18. 40 trees were planted at the Earth Day celebration.
19. The Town of Plainfield was recently featured in a magazine.
20. I never received my order, therefore, I am going to call customer service.
21. The speaker at the seminar was Sushama Patel, Ph.D..
22. Oliver responded, "Thank you for the gift".
23. He referred to his cousin as his 'frenemy.'
24. They enjoyed a fun relaxing vacation in Jamaica.
25. The store was not well-stocked, they had no milk or eggs.
26. We wanted guacamole not queso.
27. Uncle Joe doesnt' have any interest in hiking with us.
28. There are no off-road vehicles allowed here.
29. We held the last meeting on June the 30th, 2020.
30. Julio's food truck is two-years-old already.
31. Julio already has to repair his two-year-old food truck.
32. The treasurer reported there was $18257 in the account.
33. It was time to bring there [sic] boat in for the night.
34. Watch out for that nail sticking up!.
35. Make sure all the chairs, cushions, towels, etc. are put away before it rains.
36. The giraffes tongue was able to reach all the leaves.
37. One half of the money was donated by one board member.
38. Annika speaks fluent japanese and english.

39. That was a nicely written note.
40. We need: plates, cups, and silverware.
41. Yolanda got up at 4:00 a.m. in the morning to catch her plane.
42. You enjoy watching football don't you?
43. The three sisters went on a pub crawl for their girl's night out.
44. I am only available one day next week (Monday).
45. Geoffrey our tour guide joined us for dinner.
46. The childrens' school bus was late.
47. Mason put sausage olives jalapenos and bacon on the pizza.
48. Brody said, "make sure you don't forget the ice cream!"
49. Mirna Garcia M.D. is the owner of this office building.
50. There are many things to do there, for instance swimming and surfing.

COMMAS AND PERIODS *QUIZ 1*

Correct any comma or period errors. Place a check mark in front of sentences that are correct. Answers are in Chapter Seven.

1. Is it just me or does the sun look twice its normal size?
2. Umar said he's going to study mathematics chemistry, art history and political science.
3. If you're hungry, you can look in the cupboard for crackers, peanut butter and jelly and raisins.
4. Jakob has written an unlikely, dramatic scene in the script. The director wants him to revise it.
5. The computer predicts that on May 7 2032 all of Earth's surface water will stop moving for exactly one-eighth of a second.
6. Yes my friend, I will gladly drive you to the kosher deli.
7. The new chief operating officer thinks Landeski, Ohio is the best place to open a new store branch but the CEO doesn't agree.
8. Corrine is after all the better conditioned of the two climbers.
9. Well you don't say—that old nickel is now worth a dollar?
10. "Those mountains look menacing" Reiki said "when the sun no longer shines on them."
11. Aida would have been an only child if her brother Edward hadn't been born.

12. Because he is so kind, he will probably be easy to trust.
13. Zara seriously thinks that's a pearl not a golf ball?
14. The speakers, which they just purchased, are too big for their stands.
15. You can buy bracelets, earrings, necklaces, etc. at the jeweler's booth here at the fair.
16. Rocco turned the key, the rocket engine ignited.
17. After Thea finishes the master's program she will pursue her Ph.D..
18. Bip Crandall, Jr. hits the ball as far as his father once did.
19. The paper was published in October, 1967.
20. Knowing she had little time to spare her mom Mila began to move much faster.

COMMAS AND PERIODS *QUIZ 2*

Correct any comma or period errors. Place a check mark in front of sentences that are correct. Answers are in Chapter Seven.

1. "Yes," Ting said "I did see the baby panda at the zoo today."
2. Yes, Mother I did remember to place the bakery order.
3. Jackson's white cat was born in June, 2013, at his farm.
4. Jackson's white cat was born on June 28 2013 at his farm.
5. Pencils, pens, paper, calculators, etc., will be provided.
6. I would be hesitant however, to take the trip alone.
7. He hosted a cowboy-themed party in the big, red barn.
8. My oldest cousin who lives in Detroit used to be a policeman.
9. The keynote speaker at the conference will be Jonathan Green, M.D..
10. Well do you think we'll see the sun today?
11. I want to go now not later.
12. I really enjoyed the show, the acting was superb.
13. She left Albany, New York on January 18 of that year.
14. I am typing a letter and she is talking on the phone.
15. You said that I could go, didn't you?
16. To apply for this job you must have a Social Security card.
17. He seems to be such a lonely quiet man doesn't he?
18. Although my wife hates anchovies. I like them on my pizza.
19. She finished her work, and then took a long lunch.
20. I need sugar, butter, and eggs, from the grocery store.

SEMICOLONS AND COLONS *QUIZ 1*

Correct any punctuation errors. Some sentences may require removing punctuation. Place a check mark in front of sentences that are correct. Answers are in Chapter Seven.

Example: *On my sundae I want: bananas, strawberries, and blueberries, chopped nuts and crushed graham crackers, and plenty of chocolate sauce.*

Correction: *On my sundae I want bananas, strawberries, and blueberries; chopped nuts and crushed graham crackers; and plenty of chocolate sauce.*

1. The things you need to bring are: hiking boots; a backpack; a compass; and water.
2. The walls will be green and yellow; the floor will be brown; and the paintings will be pink, purple, and red.
3. Helene understands the relationship between scientific theory and scientific method: therefore, she qualifies to participate in the panel discussion.
4. Irene wants a finished patio, Stan wants a finished basement.
5. Logan has visited several European cities, such as: Paris, Rome, Vienna, and Budapest.
6. The board wants a new proposal with updated numbers; including, among everything else, the most current budget.
7. They made the announcement: It's a baby girl.
8. It's what Jessa always wanted; a Stradivarius violin.
9. Felix has expressed his wishes; start early, stay late, and bring a stress ball to squeeze.
10. Zelda has always wanted to be one of three things: a dentist, an accountant, or a sports agent.
11. I like the essay: however, the writer could use further study at grammarbook.com.
12. Our road trip south will include Nashville, Tennessee, Atlanta, Georgia, and Miami, Florida.
13. If Freya finishes skating before 9:00 p.m., and I think she will, she will join us at the lobby and we'll discuss tomorrow's training schedule there.
14. This recipe needs more: cumin, garlic, and lemon juice.
15. The truth is out: the Martians' chief diplomat is actually a Venusian spy.
16. The band's lead singer, Rikk Vikktor, wants to revise the contract rider for the tour, namely: he wants his own mat and instructor for pre-show yoga and, in the green room; a fully stocked sushi bar.

17. They are a property-management company; not a land developer.

18. Raphael made all of his field-goal attempts: no surprise.

19. The characters who appeared in The Three Stooges were: Moe, Larry, Curly; Shemp, Joe, and Curly Joe.

20. Seek to find; ask to receive; listen to understand.

SEMICOLONS AND COLONS *QUIZ 2*

Focus on using semicolons or colons to correct any punctuation errors. Some sentences may require removing punctuation. Place a check mark in front of sentences that are correct. Answers are in Chapter Seven.

1. Denise prefers to eat chicken or fish: I'm a vegetarian.

2. The centerpieces had her favorite flowers; roses, carnations, and daisies.

3. While visiting the beach, we saw: pelicans, stingrays, and iguanas.

4. On our last trip we stayed in Nashville, Tennessee, Atlanta, Georgia, and Orlando, Florida.

5. Estella landed her dream summer job: She'll be an intern in a senator's office.

6. Roberto can't decide among three careers: dentist; veterinarian; or physical therapist.

7. I need to buy: shampoo, toothpaste, soap, and contact lens solution.

8. Give her a break, she just started working here two days ago!

9. Max and Sue have been to the Caribbean many times, however; they have not visited St. Lucia.

10. You asked for forgiveness, he granted it to you.

11. The order was requested six weeks ago, therefore I expected the shipment to have arrived by now.

12. I answered the phone, no one seemed to be on the other end of the line.

13. We have set this restriction, do your homework before watching television.

14. If you can possibly arrange it, please visit us but if you cannot, let us know.

15. Nature lovers will appreciate seeing whales, sea lions, and pelicans.

QUESTION MARKS AND QUOTATION MARKS *QUIZ 1*

Correct the punctuation errors in the following sentences. Place a check mark in front of sentences that are correct. Answers are in Chapter Seven.

Example: *"Well, I really don't know" she said.*
Correction: *"Well, I really don't know," she said.*

1. Is the answer "yay" or "nay?"
2. Jaden likes to pass off rearranging items on shelves as "working."
3. My so-called advisor forgot to advise me about the opt-out clause in the agreement.
4. Jake said, "Simone shouted, 'That's it! No more driving with the windows open in winter!'"
5. Darren tried climbing the clock tower again. I wonder what else is new?
6. That couldn't be the missing diamond, could it.
7. Might the ship have changed course, he said, "or is that just wishful thinking?".
8. "Are you really going to drink that whole carton of cream," she asked?
9. The last thing anyone heard him say was, "I'll be back".
10. "I'll think it over," he said. Then she said, "And may we not grow old while you do."

QUESTION MARKS AND QUOTATION MARKS *QUIZ 2*

Correct the punctuation errors in the following sentences. Place a check mark in front of sentences that are correct. Answers are in Chapter Seven.

1. "Have you already completed our survey," the cashier asked?
2. I wonder why Allen left so early this morning?
3. Do you know the words to 'The Star-Spangled Banner'?
4. She said, "T.J. shouted, "We are not staying at that hotel."
5. "Well," she said, "you certainly didn't waste any time".
6. The song asks, "Would you like to swing on a star?"
7. There was no agreed-upon 'rule' among the club members.
8. "I've had it up to here!", she screamed.

9. Do you believe the saying, "It is better to vote for what you want and not get it than to vote for what you don't want and get it?"

10. Betty is the one who found out first, isn't she?

PARENTHESES AND BRACKETS *QUIZ 1*

Correct the punctuation errors in the following sentences. Place a check mark in front of sentences that are correct. Answers are in Chapter Seven.

1. If they had wanted to speak with a manager [or somebody similar], they could have spoken with Ray.

2. If all that was left was five dollars, they should have used it on video games instead of the box of cookies. (At least, that's how I see it).

3. Supposably (sic), the mayor was a trapeze artist before she got into politics.

4. Jackhammer Joe (and, of course, his trusted rusty wrench) fixes people's plumbing all the time.

5. The reward ($500) seems a little light considering finding the fugitive would require searching the forest with a penlight at night.

6. Ahmet has requested a second meeting with committee chairman [and local bamboozler] Sid Mackaberry.

7. In 1962, *The Sporting News* reported, "The Yankees' Mickey Mantle and the Giants' Willie Mays are the highest-paid players in major league baseball at $90,000 each (today's highest-paid players make over $30 million)."

8. When Oscar stepped on the scale, (he'd already lost nine pounds) he noted he was only six pounds away from his goal.

9. Everyone loves that movie (except me.)

10. Autumn (as well as her ever-present gypsy caravan are) traveling from city to city to offer food and clothing to the homeless.

PARENTHESES AND BRACKETS *QUIZ 2*

Correct the punctuation errors in the following sentences. Place a check mark in front of sentences that are correct. Answers are in Chapter Seven.

1. My cousin wrote, "I herd (*sic*) a rumor that Jack and Jennifer are getting engaged."

2. Our first meeting will be held at First Central Bank's community room. [Main Street branch].

3. We all decided to go out for pizza after the meeting (except for Dan).
4. I overheard her say, "Our favorite cousin (she meant Dale) will be accompanying us on our trip."
5. Gerard (and his friend Bertrand) want to have lunch with you tomorrow.
6. After his family came to the United States, (settling in Washington state) they became farmers.
7. In the movie, Vanessa exclaims, "Whatever shall I do if he (the sheriff) comes looking for you tomorrow?"
8. Joe called today. (He's been sick.) and said he felt better.
9. Luigi moved to this country shortly after he was born (about 1925).
10. The first line of his letter said, "My freinds [*sic*], I never thought we would all be together again like this."

APOSTROPHES *QUIZ 1*

Correct any apostrophe errors. Answers are in Chapter Seven.

1. The mens' locker room is down the hall and up the ramp.
2. I'd really like to go for a ride on the Thomas' new boat.
3. It sounds like Linnea is planning a girl's weekend with her friends.
4. In the summer of '69' I built my first guitar.
5. If it had'nt been for Helena's attention to the Spider Man Chia Pet, it would'nt look half as good as it does now.
6. Penelope was excited when she learned her United States visa had been approved.
7. The ladies greatest wish is that her son be able to pursue his dream to be a policeman.
8. Jack's and Jill's pail of water could really use a refill.
9. The Kellys send greeting cards to everyone for everything, including for their sister-in-laws' anniversaries.
10. Do you know if the Chapman's have arrived yet?
11. I don't think I've ever seen a mens hat like that one before.
12. Jimmys CD collection is almost all music from the '80's.
13. Why did you give that man your last token? The million-dollar jackpot should have been ours'!
14. The department manager gave the staff the rest of the week off with three days' pay.
15. Illinois's changes of season prepare a person to live just about anywhere.

APOSTROPHES *QUIZ 2*

Correct any apostrophe errors. Answers are in Chapter Seven.

1. The movie had it's desired effect.
2. Both of my brother-in-law's live near Durango.
3. Those actress's costumes look beautiful on them.
4. She always let me stay up past the other childrens' bedtime.
5. Would that companies health plan give you peace of mind?
6. Does'nt it seem strange that I didn't see that friend of your's anywhere?
7. If it isn't her's then who's is it?
8. The five injured sailor's relatives are waiting outside.
9. Joe Wilson said, "I may be biased, but the Wilson's holiday meals are the best."
10. In some peoples' opinion, Faulkner is too difficult.
11. The two little bird's feather's were ruffled.
12. I really felt that I got my monies worth.
13. Jackson's and Janet's home was damaged by a tornado.
14. We looked at some old yearbook photos from '99.
15. Our group had a good time at Sam's '80's party.

HYPHENS BETWEEN WORDS *QUIZ 1*

Add, remove, or fix hyphens as necessary. Place a check mark in front of sentences that are correct. Answers are in Chapter Seven.

1. Is that custom made sandbox really thirty feet wide?
2. Herberto has been school principal since he was twenty nine years old.
3. That vocal sounds off-key to me.
4. The Muldoons have a two hundred year old oak tree in their backyard.
5. The party planner figures that 200 - 225 people will attend the gala.
6. The sales team is following a carefully-calculated strategy to gain more share in the main competitor's market.

7. When all else failed, Bryan tried to super glue the door handle back onto the car.
8. Has anyone seen my high-school yearbook?
9. If anyone is still unsure, I believe Marek has some more certain ideas.
10. Jake spoke with Hambone, and Hambone said that the frat party on top of the police station was a no go. Apparently somebody disapproved.
11. I give him about a two-percent chance of lifting that eighty pound box.
12. Would you rather it be served in a chalice or in a 12-oz. cup?
13. It was the number-one play in box-office receipts 2001-2006.
14. After Josefina married Jonathan Martin, she changed her last name to Sanchez Martin.
15. The park district activated additional crowd control personnel when attendance at the festival exceeded three fourths capacity.

HYPHENS BETWEEN WORDS *QUIZ 2*

Add, remove, or fix hyphens as necessary. Place a check mark in front of sentences that are correct. Answers are in Chapter Seven.

1. The storm blew down a seventy foot tall tree last night.
2. The tree that blew down last night was seventy feet tall.
3. We offer around the clock coverage.
4. The badly injured fireman was taken to a hospital.
5. That two year old is adorable.
6. That child is two years old.
7. The summer camp was designed for gymnasts 16-18 years old.
8. The left handed pitcher threw fastballs at almost 100 miles per hour.
9. You certainly have a go get it nature.
10. It's a two hour meeting, 2:30 - 4:30.
11. My sister is moving from her home next to the heavily-congested highway.
12. She jumped from a two story building.
13. If we split the bill evenly, we each owe thirty four dollars.
14. If we split the bill evenly, we'll each owe one fourth of the total.
15. No parking rules make little sense on Sundays.

HYPHENS WITH PREFIXES AND SUFFIXES *QUIZ 1*

Add or remove hyphens as necessary. Place a check mark in front of sentences that are correct. Answers are in Chapter Seven.

1. The Griswalds will be returning to Wally World in mid August.
2. If you want to know more about sparring, you could ask the exprofessional boxer who works across the street.
3. Beatrice is always ultra-active when she sets her mind to something.
4. Maybe we should deemphasize the part about having thirty hot dogs but only twenty-five hot dog buns.
5. It takes a while for the crosswalk signal to change, so you don't need to repress the button so much.
6. Governor elect B. Arthur Fife will give his acceptance speech at six-thirty p.m.
7. The park is so pleasant that they revisited it the following day.
8. The delegates of anti-Bears and anti-Packers are meeting for beers and brats to discuss burying the pigskin once and for all.
9. David sure looks self confident for somebody who's got just a sling and a few stones, don't you think?
10. The recreation of the pirate ship is an exact replica of the original vessel.

HYPHENS WITH PREFIXES AND SUFFIXES *QUIZ 2*

Insert hyphens or close up the space where appropriate. Answers are in Chapter Seven.

1. ex mayor
2. de emphasized
3. do able
4. non Jewish
5. self styled
6. re establish
7. anti inflammatory
8. error free
9. semi illiterate
10. absentee ism

CAPITALIZATION *QUIZ 1*

Correct the following sentences where capitalization errors appear. Place a check mark in front of sentences that are correct. Answers are in Chapter Seven.

1. Most of my relatives still live in the U.S. northwest.
2. If I could, I would lasso the moon and give it to you.
3. Randall Rickbob, Team President, said that pitcher Tom Gunner will be signed to a new four-year deal.
4. Denzel is a Junior in college.
5. Sarah handed the book to her Grandpa.
6. This Summer they want to head South.
7. Chester's favorite band is The Cure.
8. This semester Fatima plans to study English, Biology, Political Science, and Speech Communications. She also plans to take Psychology 102.
9. Claude Monet was an impressionist painter.
10. Director Martin Scorsese has made several films with Writer Paul Schrader, as well as with Actors Robert De Niro and Joe Pesci.
11. Here's what she said she needs: Paper, scissors, markers, tape, and balloons.
12. The constitution refers to a balance and separation of power including an executive branch (led by a president), a legislative branch (congress), and a judiciary branch (supreme court).

CAPITALIZATION *QUIZ 2*

Correct the following sentences where capitalization errors appear. Place a check mark in front of sentences that are correct. Answers are in Chapter Seven.

1. My Grandmother lives on Fillmore street.
2. Have you ever visited New England in the Fall?
3. I will be excited to listen to our Chief Executive Officer, Nancy Williamson, speak today in the auditorium.
4. Uncle Walter said, "please use left or right, not North, South, East, or West."
5. "You must understand," he pleaded, "That I need more time to pay you."
6. We saw Director George Lucas walking down the street.

7. Have you read *Harry Potter And The Order Of The Phoenix*?

8. We all stood for the National Anthem before watching The New York Mets play The Chicago Cubs.

9. The supreme court unanimously struck down the proposed Constitutional Amendment today.

10. The West, especially California, is famous for its cutting-edge technology.

11. Adriana is dreading Spring Quarter because she has to take Organic Chemistry and Physics 105.

12. I plead not guilty, your honor.

WRITING NUMBERS *QUIZ 1*

Correct, simplify, or improve consistency regarding how numbers are expressed in the following sentences. Answers are in Chapter Seven.

1. I have seen *Star Wars* one hundred thirty seven times.

2. You need money? Okay, here's my $0.75.

3. The latest census shows that the town's population is two thousand and four hundred sixty nine.

4. Kristie was born on June 17th, 1986.

5. The quarterback will probably earn between twenty million and 30 million dollars.

6. 1999 was the first year I bought a cell phone.

7. The Eighties was a golden age of stand-up comedy.

8. Do you ever miss the music from the 1990's?

9. I get up early for work, so I'm usually in bed by 9 o'clock.

10. Todd says he'd rather have one third of the gate revenue from the concert than one half of the merchandise sales.

11. Sabrina is one point two inches taller than she was nine months ago.

12. The astronomer says the comet will be visible just before or soon after 12:00 AM.

WRITING NUMBERS *QUIZ 2*

Correct, simplify, or improve consistency regarding how numbers are expressed in the following sentences. Answers are in Chapter Seven.

1. Next week's lottery jackpot is expected to reach between four million and 5 million dollars.
2. The new stadium will hold 43520 fans.
3. The next meeting of the holiday planning committee will be held on the 31st of October at 12 Noon.
4. A two thirds majority is needed to pass the measure.
5. The tree grew only .5 inches because of the drought.
6. We all agreed. $2,500 is a lot of money.
7. 1/5 of the inventory was ruined in the fire.
8. I will be twenty - one years old on December 9.
9. We have only received point five four inches of rain this year.
10. The tree grew two and one-half feet after all the rain we had last year.
11. Some people now refer to the Forties and Fifties as "mid-century."
12. Including tax, my new car cost thirty two thousand, six hundred seventy two dollars, fifty seven cents.

PUNCTUATION, CAPITALIZATION, AND WRITING NUMBERS *MASTERY TEST*

Correct any errors in punctuation, capitalization, and writing numbers. Place a check mark in front of sentences that are correct. Answers are in Chapter Seven.

1. No Johnny I don't think they sell ice cream at this hardware store.
2. Our Mom sent us a funny video from her goat yoga class today.
3. Mateo wont' be able to join us on our annual camping trip this year.
4. We must supply them with the following; Soap, hand sanitizer, bandages, and bottled water.
5. You have been playing video games all afternoon haven't you?
6. We had no idea we would owe additional money, that was not in the original contract.
7. Madison asked, "can we please stop and see the waterfall after lunch?"
8. She was asking if the winery is going to be open tomorrow?
9. January 1, 2024 is the date Grandpa plans to retire from his job at the hospital.
10. 20 vehicles participated in the birthday celebration parade for Kaito.
11. When Mike referred to you as a 'slacker,' what was he talking about?
12. That stray pit bull running at the baseball field is not our's.

13. Buddy and Coco her two dogs were looking for plenty of attention.
14. Anton is interested in learning how to cook french cuisine.
15. Thirty two volunteers helped out at the food bank on Saturday.
16. Ava was quick to reply, "We had no idea you just got back from London".
17. If you would like to meet with a personal trainer you may sign up at the front desk.
18. Mario's and Amber's yard has twelve bird feeders and a koi pond.
19. The used car Kai is buying is a very well-maintained vehicle.
20. The car Kai is trading in has not been well-maintained.
21. One half of the pie was already eaten before the appetizers were served.
22. Teagan wants to be a lifeguard this summer and she is already certified in CPR and first aid.
23. The chefs special for today is chili lime salmon with Spanish rice.
24. Dad knows nothing about investments, therefore, he wants to hire a financial planner.
25. Omar is interested in taking online classes in African history and geography in the fall.
26. "Can you believe it has been ten years since we graduated," asked Phoenix?
27. Jocelyn and Lina are cousins not sisters.
28. Diego received a check for $9349 from the insurance company to cover the damage.
29. Leon wrote to the homeowners' association complaining they "… had to [sic] many restrictions."
30. The womens' volleyball league plays here on Tuesday nights.
31. The witnesses to the accident included a law student, an advertising intern, a teacher and a retired minister.
32. Mrs. Drake is so proud of her beautifully-decorated garden shed.
33. The baby always takes a nap at 1:00 p.m. in the afternoon.
34. Drive North on Oak St. past the firehouse to get to the zoo.
35. Mei Lee CPA is currently working from home instead of her office.
36. We invited the Silverman's and the Brown's to join us this evening.
37. We are invited to the Brown's lakeside cabin in July.
38. We need: dog treats, cat litter, rabbit food, and mealworms.
39. Aunt Helen was born in Dodgeville, Wisconsin and still lives there.
40. That eighty year old oak is the oldest tree in Cottersville.
41. Sanjay's aunt will be eighty-years-old this Sunday.
42. She has fond memories of growing up on the farm in the 1970s.
43. The funds for the children's wing were donated by Dr. Andre Wilson, M.D..
44. The furniture she purchased at the estate sale was fairly inexpensive ($300).

45. They offer all kinds of children's camp themes, for instance nature, science, and creative arts.
46. Sharon said, "Delilah shouted, "I didn't ask for any help!"
47. We will need to clean, paint, make repairs, etc. before we can move in.
48. Please make sure you are back home before dark!.
49. The twins were born on July 30th, 2019.
50. This isn't at all what I expected, this place is such a mess!

CHAPTER 7

ANSWERS TO QUIZZES

GRAMMAR *PRETEST ANSWERS*

1. That carload of clowns **looks** a bit crowded.
2. If I **were** you, I would take the Yankees' offer to parachute into the stadium during Elvis Night.
3. Those are the things **that** we can discuss after Jerrod gets the job.
4. Vanessa responded **indignantly** upon being told someone else had used her reward points.
5. Bill acts **like Ted** when they start an excellent adventure.
6. There **are** too many things we'll need to do to fix that old sandbox.
7. If Jasmine is going to compete in the marathon, she'll need to train daily, maintain a proper diet, and **sleep sufficiently (OR get sufficient sleep)**.
8. Darienne is a swimmer **who** I think can qualify for the Olympics.
9. Between the two landscapers, Shangri-lawn is the **better**.
10. If Marietta doesn't start watering those plants, I fear they will **perish**.
11. If you ask me, Zed is as zany as **he**.
12. The goalie twisted her ankle, **which** had already been bothering her before the game.
13. Raja ran **into** trouble when she tried to cook eggs in the microwave.
14. Before they went to sleep, they **hung** the stockings by the chimney with care.
15. Whomever Thaddeus chooses will be the next baton-twirler to lead the parade. (CORRECT)

16. The truth about who spilled the wine on the sofa is between **me and her** (**OR her and me**).

17. Much fuel, as well as many plastics, **is** made from petroleum.

18. Tell **whomever** you want that Abdul is organizing the hot air balloon race.

19. They are the soldiers **who** (**OR that**) will bring the flag to the ceremony.

20. The court reporter's opinion appears to be much different **from** the judge's.

21. We've been hiking a long time. My legs are getting **weary**.

22. The majority of respondents **have** stated that shoelaces won't be necessary.

23. It is you who **are** misinformed about the research results.

24. The contents of the vault will be shared between Gunnar and **me**.

25. Tasked with troubleshooting the problem, the technician **purposefully** climbed the telephone pole.

26. Of all the cities tracked this year, Fairbanks, Alaska, is the **coldest**.

27. Emily speaks of subjects that interest her. (CORRECT)

28. Neither the silver medal nor the bronze **is** sufficient for Sandra; she wants the gold.

29. Just listen to Ozzy and sing **as** he asks.

30. The director should give raises to **whoever** deserves one.

31. Does anybody here know who ordered the jalapeño meat loaf? (CORRECT)

32. Jermaine says he can't remember where the package **was sent.**

33. Cheyenne is **certain** about wanting to go to the blueberry festival.

34. **Who** should I tell him inquired?

35. Because he is a **good** man, he always gives to charity whenever he can.

36. When you listen closely to the tape, you can hear it is **she** speaking.

37. The library is clearing the shelves of those titles, which will be available for purchase at the book sale on Saturday. (CORRECT)

38. The commander **led** the fleet that enforced the embargo.

39. Either the flag or the statue **is** sufficient for ceremonial purposes.

40. The committee decided to reopen the park. (*"The decision to reopen the park was made by the committee," is grammatically acceptable. However, extra credit to students improving this sentence using active voice instead of passive voice.*)

41. The gym membership will be awarded to **whoever** wins the sit-up competition.

42. She responds **intelligently** when presented with highly challenging questions.

43. The **duel** between the light-saber experts is sure to attract media from throughout the galaxy.

44. I'd say that between Ruth and Rae, Rae is the **more** efficient at basket weaving.

45. **Like most Martians** (**OR As most Martians do**), I try not to include too much red in my house.

46. Each of the tree leaves **makes** a fine resting place for caterpillars.

47. Everybody knows **who** the book's "anonymous source" was; they just can't state it publicly.

48. A plane and a train **are** my **ways** of getting there in less than a day.

49. In times of trouble, it means a lot to have friends that will be by your side. (CORRECT **OR** "… **friends who** …")

50. While **he was** broadcasting the ball game, the swan flew into the booth and perched next to his microphone.

FINDING NOUNS, VERBS, AND SUBJECTS
QUIZ 1 ANSWERS

1. The Brookfield **Z**oo <u>exhibit</u> <u>attracted</u> thousands of visitors.
2. For months, <u>she</u> <u>had been putting up with</u> the squeaky wheel.
3. <u>They</u> <u>will start cleaning</u> as soon as the <u>dance</u> <u>is</u> over.
4. The <u>meetings</u> <u>aim</u> for much and <u>achieve</u> much too little.
5. <u>I</u> <u>will stop</u> at nothing to have those potato chips.
6. Your <u>scooter</u> <u>looks</u> new.
7. After weeks of preparation, the Kansas City <u>company</u> <u>was</u> ready for the unveiling.
8. (<u>You</u>) <u>Hurry</u>, because the <u>mall</u> <u>closes</u> in an hour.
9. <u>Jessie</u> <u>wants</u> to see the London Symphony Orchestra, but <u>Jake</u> <u>prefers</u> we go to the pubs in Piccadilly Circus.
10. All <u>handbags</u> <u>appeal</u> to Nanette, regardless of their color.

FINDING NOUNS, VERBS, AND SUBJECTS
QUIZ 2 ANSWERS

1. The overturned <u>truck</u> <u>blocked</u> both lanes.
2. The <u>Metropolitan Museum of Art</u> <u>is</u> a New York City landmark.
3. <u>She</u> <u>will fly</u> part of the way and then <u>drive</u> fifty kilometers to get there.
4. <u>I</u> <u>will</u> just <u>be watching</u> the **B**oston **M**arathon, but my <u>wife</u> <u>will be running</u> in it.
5. Behind the door <u>is</u> a coat <u>rack</u>.
6. (<u>You</u>) <u>Watch</u> your step.

7. <u>He</u> <u>should have been</u> more gracious.
8. On the table <u>was</u> her <u>purse</u>.
9. In the **n**ewspaper, an interesting <u>article</u> <u>appeared</u>.
10. How long <u>have</u> <u>you</u> <u>been living</u> in New Delhi?
11. <u>We</u> <u>are forced</u> to inhale and exhale this smog-filled air. (OR <u>are</u>)
12. From the bottom of the cave, the <u>stalagmites</u> <u>rose</u> ten feet high.

SUBJECT AND VERB AGREEMENT *QUIZ 1 ANSWERS*

1. The <u>jar</u> of fruit <u>is</u> next to the can of tomato sauce. (CORRECT)
2. There <u>are</u> many <u>ways</u> to catch a mouse.
3. <u>It's</u> one of those must-do <u>chores</u> that <u>are</u> easily <u>forgotten</u>.
4. If <u>I</u> <u>were</u> a billionaire, <u>I'd buy</u> a few ocean islands.
5. The <u>audience</u> <u>is</u> seated now.
6. The <u>couple</u> <u>are</u> planning to renew their wedding vows.
7. Here <u>are</u> my <u>shoes</u>.
8. The <u>bed</u> of roses <u>was planted</u> under the window.
9. A <u>pen</u> and <u>paper</u> <u>are</u> all I need. (CORRECT)
10. <u>Close to three-fourths</u> of the earth's surface <u>is covered</u> by water. (CORRECT)
11. The <u>sack</u> of treats <u>belongs</u> to the boy.
12. The <u>library</u>, as well as the boutique shops, <u>is affected</u> by the new ordinance.
13. Either <u>you</u> or <u>I</u> <u>am going</u> to have to move this boulder. (Awkward but CORRECT)
14. <u>All</u> of my dollars <u>are</u> to be invested in that fund.
15. Do <u>you</u> <u>know</u> if every <u>one</u> of them <u>likes</u> sugar cookies?
16. <u>Jumping</u> and <u>shouting</u> <u>are</u> prohibited in the arena. (CORRECT)
17. "<u>Rise and shine</u>" <u>is</u> his mom's favorite greeting.
18. <u>Three</u> of the four candidates <u>wield</u> impressive technological insight.
19. The <u>page</u> of statistics <u>confuses</u> them.
20. Neither the <u>Martians</u> nor the <u>Venusian</u> <u>wants</u> to vacation on Pluto.

SUBJECT AND VERB AGREEMENT *QUIZ 2 ANSWERS*

1. That <u>pack</u> of lies <u>is</u> not <u>going</u> to change my mind.
2. Neither the <u>rain</u> nor the <u>darkness</u> <u>is going</u> to stop me.
3. My <u>staff</u> <u>believes</u> in providing high-quality service. (CORRECT)

4. The <u>conductor</u>, as well as the musicians, <u>is taking</u> the stage.
5. My whole <u>family</u> <u>is vacationing</u> in Baja California this winter.
6. There <u>are</u> <u>lots</u> of people here.
7. If <u>it</u> <u>were</u> up to me, <u>we</u> <u>would leave</u> earlier in the morning.
8. <u>One</u> in three stressed Americans <u>copes</u> by shopping.
9. <u>Four years</u> <u>is</u> considered the normal amount of time to earn a bachelor's degree.
10. <u>Law and order</u> <u>is</u> the principle <u>he</u> <u>based</u> his campaign on. (CORRECT)
11. <u>Al</u> and <u>Eli</u> <u>go</u> to the beach to surf with their friends. (CORRECT)
12. There <u>are</u> three <u>strawberries</u> left.
13. <u>Most</u> of my savings <u>are invested</u> in real estate.
14. <u>I</u> <u>wish</u> <u>it</u> <u>were</u> summer and time for vacation. (CORRECT)
15. <u>Nervousness,</u> not to mention lack of sleep, <u>contributes</u> to poor performance.
16. <u>One-third</u> of the city <u>is experiencing</u> a blackout tonight.
17. The next <u>thing</u> <u>I</u> <u>heard</u> <u>was</u> two shots.
18. Ladies and gentlemen, here <u>are</u> <u>Wisin</u> and <u>Yandel</u>.
19. Either the <u>bikes</u> or the <u>lawn mower</u> <u>goes</u> in that space.
20. Her <u>attitude</u> <u>is</u> one of the <u>things</u> that <u>are</u> difficult.

IRREGULAR VERBS *QUIZ 1 ANSWERS*

1. We have **chosen** a new topic.
2. They **dragged** the heavy bag across the floor.
3. We should **have done** things differently.
4. I have **drunk** the last soda.
5. I wish you had **come** home sooner.
6. Things haven't **gone** the way we planned.
7. She **saw** us coming.
8. Yesterday he **ran** a marathon.
9. When we arrived, the meeting had already **begun**.
10. The eagle had already **flown** away.

IRREGULAR VERBS *QUIZ 2 ANSWERS*

1. We noticed that the sign had **fallen**.
2. Bobby **swore** he'd never do it again.

3. They have **written** that they are coming in the spring.
4. They pretend they have **forgotten** what they did.
5. My friends have **ridden** in that fancy car, but I never have.
6. André has **brought** the beverages.
7. Cameron **showed** me the fastest way to get there.
8. We should have **taken** the other road.
9. The full moon has **risen**.
10. He **has got** to try harder from now on.

PRONOUNS QUIZ 1 ANSWERS

1. It's **I** who **am** on the phone.
2. Could it really be **he?**
3. Laquon is younger than **I**.
4. It is **they** who **speak** too much.
5. Is Barbara the only one of them who **has** read the book?
6. Paolo thinks well of **her**.
7. Either of us **qualifies** for the coaching position.
8. One must be ready to help **oneself** in order to succeed.
9. I prefer that you keep it between you and **me**.
10. **He** and his friends **play** soccer each Tuesday.
11. Everyone on this committee **has** a point of view.
12. Is that confetti cannon mine or **yours?**
13. Bernice of all people **knows** the answer.
14. **He** and **she** will give the van a psychedelic paint job.
15. Today is just one of those days that **seem** too short.
16. Agnes and **I** ran five miles this morning.
17. But **it's** only fifty dollars!
18. The Venusians? The Martians are smarter than **they**.
19. The men all made **their** contribution.
20. **It's** but one of the reasons that call for an air conditioner.

PRONOUNS *QUIZ 2 ANSWERS*

1. It is **he** who will be responsible for making all of the arrangements.
2. Julia is a faster runner than **I**.
3. She was one of those cruise passengers who **are** always complaining.
4. The sweater that we found at the church is **yours**.
5. The dog hurt **its** paw while running through the empty field.
6. George and I finished staining the deck. (CORRECT)
7. The honors committee nominated **him** and Ming.
8. **She** and **I** are in charge of the sales presentation tomorrow.
9. Neither of the girls **is** planning a wedding in the near future.
10. It is we who will get the blame if things do not go well. (CORRECT)
11. Each of the players **gets** to make a speech before the parade.
12. He and I have been good friends since second grade. (CORRECT)
13. It is I who am wrong. (CORRECT)
14. Please talk to Daniela or **me** next time you have a concern.
15. **Whose** hat is this?
16. It's obvious that the best team will prevail. (CORRECT)
17. I weigh more than he. (CORRECT)
18. **Your** friend told her friend that **there's** a party tonight.
19. The argument he gave had **its** merits.
20. You more than anyone else **know** what the risks are.

WHO, WHOM, WHOEVER, WHOMEVER *QUIZ 1 ANSWERS*

1. They will choose **whom** (OR **whomever**) they please.
2. **Whoever** finishes in second and third place will receive a consolation prize.
3. First we have to find out **who** is in charge.
4. **Whom** shall I say this is from?

5. Victor is a detective **who** leaves no details behind.
6. We will work with **whomever** they assign for the project.
7. The doctor prescribes the medicine to patients **who** she believes must have it.
8. Does the university know **who** will receive the scholarship funds?
9. **Whoever** it turns out to be, we trust the new park commissioner will serve well.
10. Scientists developed the serum for **whoever** will benefit from it.
11. The actor **who** wins the award will be featured on the magazine cover.
12. My dad once said **whoever** is first to speak is often the last to listen.
13. That painting is for **whomever**. Erica didn't have anyone specific in mind.
14. To **Whom** It May Concern: Your Shrimp Etouffee is outstanding. We want the recipe!
15. The lions are so well trained they respond to **whomever** they hear.
16. **Whoever** identifies the cat burglar will receive the award money.
17. By **whom** were they given the authority?
18. **Who** has the papers Roger left by the air tunnel?
19. To **whom** are you giving the discount?
20. The book is a great resource for those **who** need one.

WHO, WHOM, WHOEVER, WHOMEVER *QUIZ 2 ANSWERS*

1. He is the doctor **who** took Jimmy's tonsils out.
2. **Whom** did you go to the movie with?
3. It does not matter to me **who** drives tomorrow.
4. I will ride with **whoever** is planning to stop at the store.
5. Please thank **whoever** brought in our mail while we were gone.
6. We will hire **whomeve**r you trust to do the work.
7. **Whoever** used the grill last forgot to clean it.
8. The wedding florist **whom** we wanted to hire is unavailable.
9. Fatima was the cashier **who** won the lottery.
10. Clare knows **who** the winner is already.
11. Kimiko donates her time to **whoever** she feels needs it most.
12. Kathy was not sure **whom** she was voting for.
13. He is the man **whom** Mr. O'Brian hired.
14. I will vote for **whoever** you think is best.
15. I will vote for **whomever** you suggest.
16. **Whom** shall I ask about this matter?

17. Give the information to **whomever** they prefer.
18. She is the woman **who** I believe was hired last year.
19. **Whom** are you mailing that letter to?
20. **Who** do you suppose runs this show?

WHO, WHOM, THAT, WHICH *QUIZ 1 ANSWERS*

1. I wish we had a teacher **that** let us out early. (CORRECT) **OR** I wish we had a teacher **who** let us out early.
2. Is that the man **who** found the divining rod **that** you had lost? (CORRECT)
3. The funds **that** they said they don't have are all in an offshore account.
4. The lamp **that** is over there will not turn on.
5. Darsha would like to have a dog **that** becomes her best friend.
6. He no longer reads trade journals, **which** to him tend to favor certain advertisers. (CORRECT)
7. Tayshawn appears to be a free agent **whom** the team can afford.
8. The car, **which** costs what they'd expected, seats six and gets good mileage.
9. It could be one of those moments **that** lead to a lucky break.
10. Decide if it's a person **whom** you trust and a mission **that** you believe in.

WHO, WHOM, THAT, WHICH *QUIZ 2 ANSWERS*

1. Tina is looking for a pet **that** is small and easy to care for.
2. The mechanic **that** fixed my car did a great job. (CORRECT) **OR** The mechanic **who** fixed my car did a great job.
3. The red vase, **which** she sold for $20, was worth $200.
4. Was he the only student in the class **who** applied for the scholarship? (CORRECT)
5. Gandhi was a role model **whom** millions admired.
6. I love hearing the owls **that** sit in the trees and hoot at dusk.
7. The game **that** intrigues Gretchen the most is dominoes.
8. That **which** doesn't kill you makes you stronger.
9. The tomatoes **that** grow in her garden are unlike those you buy in a store.
10. The tomatoes from her garden, **which** grew larger than those in the grocery store, were sweet and ripe. (CORRECT)

ADJECTIVES AND ADVERBS *QUIZ 1 ANSWERS*

1. Si-woo prepares for tennis practice rather **oddly**.
2. When you see Samantha, please let her know I hope she is **well**.
3. The inspector followed the evidence **closely**.
4. If you spell **poorly**, you probably won't get the writing job.
5. Okafor solves crossword puzzles more **quickly** than Christophe.
6. Which of the two loans do the bankers like **better**?
7. The drink tastes **bitter** to me.
8. Ask Miriam if she feels **good** about our latest donation.
9. Pedro has four dogs. The **biggest** of them weighs one hundred pounds.
10. The elves sounded **merry** when they received the news about their fourth-quarter toy production.
11. If sleeping well is wise, then off to bed I go. (CORRECT)
12. Teddy Roosevelt once said, "Speak **softly** and carry a big stick."
13. As **usual**, they ordered the shepherd's pie.
14. The sleepy fox wished the hyenas could be a little more quiet. (CORRECT)
15. Those who want to be thoughtful will choose their words **carefully**.
16. Dr. Azir is the **most** skilled of all the surgeons.
17. Bobby and Fiona are debating whether an ice cream headache is **worse** than the hiccups.
18. The twins are **equally quick-witted**.
19. This sentence demonstrates that the word *this* at the start is **an adjective**.
20. The world seems so sanguine when viewed through rose-tinted glasses. (CORRECT)

ADJECTIVES AND ADVERBS *QUIZ 2 ANSWERS*

1. I feel just as **bad** about this as you do.
2. I did **well** today on my final exam.
3. C.J. slept **soundly** after running the marathon.
4. Despite her honest efforts, my grandmother's driving is **worse** than ever.

5. Of your three dogs, which is **cutest**?
6. His hearing is **good** for someone who's played in a rock band for twenty years. (CORRECT)
7. He still hears **well** for someone who's played in a rock band for twenty years.
8. Our homemade fried rice was **really** tasty.
9. I think my left eye is my **sharper** eye.
10. She looked **suspiciously** at the man in the trench coat. (CORRECT)
11. Come **quickly** or we will miss our bus.
12. Ella was the **better** of the two sisters at gymnastics.
13. Rochelle felt **bad** about forgetting Devlin's birthday.
14. To find her, we need to follow **this** set of tracks. (OR **that**)
15. The new model of this chain saw operates **more quietly** than the old model.
16. She felt **good** about getting her puppy from the SPCA. (CORRECT)
17. Which is **worse**, a toothache or a headache?
18. She reacted **swiftly**, which made him feel **bad** about insulting her.
19. He swings the bat as **well** as anyone else in major-league baseball.
20. I have never been less **sure** of anything in my life.

PREPOSITIONS *QUIZ 1 ANSWERS*

1. Where are they traveling this summer?
2. I should **have** been a millionaire, but I went swimming in the lake with the lottery ticket in the back pocket of my trunks.
3. The spy peered into the dimly lit corridor. (CORRECT)
4. It looks **as if** the plane will depart on time after all.
5. Imelda said it's different **from** anything she's ever read.
6. The panel just can't seem to get off the subject of new taxes on domestic gardening.
7. Like any good acrobat, Pierre maintains his weight, strength, and flexibility. (CORRECT)
8. The construction project was finished under budget and above expectations. (CORRECT)
9. They will be treated **like** any other applicant.
10. The boys ran through the sprinkler and then **into** the mud.

PREPOSITIONS *QUIZ 2 ANSWERS*

1. We could **have** been there by now if we hadn't gotten lost.
2. Charles talks **the way** his brother does.
3. He drove his car **into** the garage.
4. Did you take an envelope **off** my desk?
5. **As** the ranger said, this is an area with a lot of poison ivy.
6. Jacques acted **as if** he never met your aunt.
7. Where did you get this?
8. This problem is no different **from** many others I've dealt with.
9. You could **have** told me about the mistake earlier.
10. I'm going to turn this lost wallet **in to** the police.

AFFECT VS. EFFECT *QUIZ 1 ANSWERS*

1. The managers believe the lasting **effect** will be a steady market performance.
2. Martians avoid visiting Venus because the 800°F temperatures adversely **affect** their antennae.
3. If we want to **effect** better morale, we need to find out what matters to our employees.
4. The infield's strategy of shifting left against the batter proved to be highly **effective**.
5. Lena's yoga instruction seems to be **affecting** Hans in a good way.
6. Study harder and **effect** better grades on your report card.
7. Not even high winds **affect** Willy's command when he's riding in his hot air balloon.
8. Let's see if these seeds from Jack **affect** our ability to grow some beans.
9. The approach is having an **effect** on her **affect** during therapy.
10. Calorie intake often **affects** weight gain or loss.
11. What **effect** are they hoping to achieve by raising the price?
12. The act of painting seems to improve her **affect**.
13. Preparation **affects** outcome.
14. They delivered the speech with great **effect**.
15. Spending less on designer furniture will help **effect** greater profitability.

AFFECT VS. EFFECT *QUIZ 2 ANSWERS*

1. Mark told Taneisha that cigarettes would negatively **affect** her health.
2. The convict showed little **affect** throughout her trial.
3. Do you think our campaign will be **effective**?
4. Working overtime at the office negatively **affected** Keeton's personal life.
5. One must be a powerful speaker to **effect** social change.
6. Jojo found that meditation had therapeutic **effects**.
7. The choices we make now will **affect** society for generations to come.
8. The bike safety law currently in **effect** should be improved.
9. The emergence of social networking websites **affected** her productivity.
10. The **effect** of the antibiotic on her infection was surprising.
11. I did not know that antibiotics could **affect** people so quickly.
12. If the chemotherapy has no **effect**, should she get surgery for the tumor?
13. When will we know if the chemotherapy has taken **effect**?
14. The critics greatly **affected** his thinking.
15. How were you able to **effect** such radical changes?

LAY VS. LIE *QUIZ 1 ANSWERS*

1. If you're tired, you can **lie** on the futon.
2. She has been **lying** in the hammock since this morning.
3. Malik said we should **lay** the tarp first.
4. The contractor said he has **laid** that type of brick many times. (CORRECT)
5. So what happens if it **lies** in the sun too long?
6. Now I **lay** me down to sleep. (CORRECT)
7. Of course nothing will get done if they keep **lying** around all day.
8. They might be **lying** about how much they spent on the office party.
9. Because of his business travel, Markus has **laid** his head on many hotel pillows.
10. When the golf tournament started, no one, including the experts, expected Noah to **lay** such an egg on the back nine of the course. (CORRECT)
11. The ancient city has **lain** in the shadow of the tower since the fall of the empire.
12. Under the circumstances, if he **lies**, he will only compound the case against him.

LAY VS. LIE *QUIZ 2 ANSWERS*

1. Grandma is not feeling well and went to **lie** down.
2. The mail has **lain** on the table unopened for two days now.
3. The cat will probably be **lying** in the sun after she eats her lunch. (CORRECT)
4. The chickens **laid** enough eggs for us to make three large omelets.
5. Omar **lay** on the air mattress and floated on the water for hours.
6. I am dizzy and need to **lie** down.
7. When I got dizzy yesterday, I **lay** down.
8. The lions have **lain** in wait for their prey.
9. I will **lay** my head on my pillow.
10. **Lay** out all the clothes you want to pack. (CORRECT)
11. You should have **laid** out all the clothes you wanted to pack.
12. If you're **lying** to me, I'll be very upset.

ADVICE VS. ADVISE *QUIZ 1 ANSWERS*

1. If they want to improve, they must be willing to listen to **advice**.
2. The consultant **advised** her client to focus on steel fabrication.
3. The electrician's **advice** is to address the wiring before it is exposed.
4. It is possible to **advise** without being wise.
5. The firm is willing to **advise** if, of course, we pay the exorbitant fee.
6. Those who seek the **advice** of others should be prepared for what it might be.
7. Wendy got a new job **advising** French bakers.
8. For customer service, their **advice** is to under-promise and over-deliver.
9. The legal team is trying to **advise** the defendant.
10. I **advise** you to take my **advice**.

ADVICE VS. ADVISE *QUIZ 2 ANSWERS*

1. My doctor **advised** me to go to the gym more often.
2. My **advice** is to talk to Georgia face-to-face, rather than by e-mail.

3. When giving **advice** to a friend, I try to put myself in her shoes.
4. Teachers **advise** parents to emphasize reading at home.
5. Sara always takes my **advice** to heart.
6. I'd like to ask an engineer to **advise** us on the design.
7. Lakeisha knows she can always go to her best friend for **advice**.
8. The lawyer **advised** him to plead guilty.
9. Randall has a bad habit of offering unsolicited **advice**.
10. I always ask my brother for **advice** because he knows me best.

THEIR VS. THERE VS. THEY'RE *QUIZ 1 ANSWERS*

1. I'm not sure why they have a NASCAR engine on **their** patio.
2. The Aquinos said they will be **there** when the fireworks start.
3. Ava and Elsie always sign **their** names in purple ink.
4. Do you know if **they're** A's fans or Giants fans?
5. When you speak with the sales department, please find out **their** preferred form of payment.
6. **There** are more ways to approach a solution.
7. If **they're there**, Heidi will be **there** too.
8. One has to wonder if the two sisters will ever get past **their** differences.
9. They have to make a stop, and then **they're** off to see the wizard.
10. The rare edition of the book you're looking for is on the shelf over **there**.

THEIR VS. THERE VS. THEY'RE *QUIZ 2 ANSWERS*

1. The Garcias are having a costume party at **their** house tonight.
2. Paul and Summer are in search of a tank for **their** baby turtles.
3. On Thursday, **they're** going to take a paragliding lesson.
4. According to an old legend, **there** is buried treasure on that island.
5. **There** is a mouse in my closet!
6. I wonder if **they're** planning to go shopping with us.
7. It's **their** decision, so I'll just stay out of it.

8. **There** are many ways to cut a cake.
9. To our surprise, Nick and Taylor just announced that **they're** getting married.
10. Juan and Pablo just called to let us know **they're** coming for dinner.

MORE CONFUSING WORDS AND HOMONYMS
QUIZ 1 ANSWERS

1. The **lightning** you saw in the sky was just an **illusion**.
2. When you come over for dinner tonight, don't forget to **bring** the **dessert**.
3. Martin plans to **canvass** the neighborhood to promote his new band, the Martian Martinis.
4. The **horde** gathered to hear her teaching.
5. If it looks like I'm **racking** my brain, the **reason is** (**OR reason is that**) I have an advanced physics exam tomorrow.
6. The critics **censured** our performance, but the audiences loved it.
7. According to calculations, the change in planetary alignment is **imminent**.
8. By the way his tail is wagging, it's clear that Fido has been **eager** to see you.
9. Penny is **loath** to **peel** the wrapping from the **torte** box because she knows no one can have just one piece.
10. The former magician used **sleight** of hand to **persuade** the doubtful customers that the coins were genuine.

MORE CONFUSING WORDS AND HOMONYMS
QUIZ 2 ANSWERS

1. It takes **a while** to **adapt** to this hot weather when you're from Anchorage.
2. You don't need fancy **stationery** to thank someone—that's **beside** the point.
3. I explained my **principal** reasons for quitting to a **couple of** guys from work.
4. You have to be more **discreet** or you'll **virtually** drive your husband up the wall.
5. It's not **every day** that I get to spend several hours on my favorite **pastime**.
6. He wore a gold **medal** when he **led** the parade yesterday.
7. It won't **faze** me in the least if you just **set** your drink on the chair next to you.

8. It was not just a great day; it was **a historic** occasion, and I was feeling **all right.**

9. He's one of the **premier** actors of our generation, **regardless** of his messy personal life.

10. I have no **flair** for geography: I thought Buffalo was the **capital** of New York, but it's Albany.

EFFECTIVE WRITING *QUIZ 1 ANSWERS*

1. The shoes were black, shiny, and had cushioned soles.
   Use parallel construction: *The shoes were black, shiny, and cushioned.*

2. Veronica is not unsure of herself when there is a sale to be made.
   Be careful with multiple negatives (*not unsure*) and avoid wordiness: *Veronica is sure of herself when making a sale.*

3. The statue will be finished by the sculptor in time for the unveiling.
   Use active verbs: *The sculptor will finish the statue in time for the unveiling.*

4. The children need to pick up their toys, books, and their clothes.
   Use parallel construction: *The children need to pick up their toys, books, and clothes.*

5. Her glory days behind her, Chuck defeated Farrah in the competition for best pianist.
   Correct the dangling modifier (misplaced in describing Farrah) and adjust the verb: *Her glory days behind her, Farrah lost to Chuck in the competition for best pianist.*

6. I have a guitar that Eric played in my locker.
   Descriptive words and phrases should be close to the words they describe: *I have in my locker a guitar that Eric played.* (**OR** *In my locker I have a guitar that Eric played.* **OR** *Eric played the guitar that I have in my locker.*)

7. The accounts were mismanaged by the company.
   Use active verbs: *The company mismanaged the accounts.*

8. The story you're telling is not unclear.
   Be careful with double negatives (*not unclear*): *The story you're telling is clear.* (**OR,** if conveying not being clear more subtly, *The story you're telling could be more clear.*)

9. It was two years ago that Krystal learned to play the flute.
   Avoid wordiness and be direct: *Krystal learned to play the flute two years ago.*

10. Behind the curtain. Under the shelf. Hide the cashews.

    Make sentence fragments part of a full sentence: *Hide the cashews under the shelf that is behind the curtain.* (OR *Hide the cashews behind the curtain and under the shelf.*)

EFFECTIVE WRITING *QUIZ 2 ANSWERS*

1. While I am in town. Let's visit Golden Gate Park.

   Make a sentence fragment a full sentence: *While I am in town, let's visit Golden Gate Park.*

2. Good employees are prompt, courteous, and they help you when you need it.

   Use parallel construction: *Good employees are prompt, courteous, and helpful.*

3. It is expected that you will report for work by no later than nine o'clock.

   Use active verbs: *I expect you to report for work by nine o'clock.*

4. The patient is not unresponsive.

   Be careful with multiple negatives (*not unresponsive*): *The patient is responsive.*

5. The boy was hit in the face by the pie as it left the girl's hand.

   Use active verbs to avoid dull writing: *The girl flung the pie, and it exploded in the boy's face.*

6. We washed the dishes, swept the floor, and the tables were dusted.

   Use parallel construction: *We washed the dishes, swept the floor, and dusted the tables.*

7. On a hike with my wife, a bear climbed a tree.

   Correct the dangler (the bear was not hiking with "my wife"): *On a hike with my wife, I saw a bear climb a tree.*

8. Jordan did not believe that Serena had embarrassed him unintentionally.

   Avoid pretentious multiple negatives (*not … unintentionally*): *Jordan believed that Serena had embarrassed him intentionally.*

9. Lying on a stretcher, they carried him out.

   Correct the dangler ("they" were not lying on a stretcher): *They carried him out lying on a stretcher.*

10. I was wearing the sweater that Amy knitted at the concert.

    Descriptive words and phrases should be close to the words they describe: *At the concert, I was wearing the sweater that Amy knitted.*

11. The weather had adverse impacts on our boat, resulting in the necessity of rescuing us from the water.

    Avoid wordiness: *Our boat capsized in the storm, so we needed rescuing.*

12. Walking aimlessly down the street, a bus almost clipped me.
    Correct the dangler (the sentence as written says the bus was walking down the street): *As I was walking aimlessly down the street, a bus almost clipped me.* **OR** *Walking aimlessly down the street, I was almost clipped by a bus.*

13. The cars were worn down by the taxi drivers.
    Use active verbs: *The taxi drivers wore down their cars.*

14. Maria encountered a stranger clad in her parka and blue jeans.
    Descriptive words and phrases should be close to the words they describe: *Maria, clad in her parka and blue jeans, encountered a stranger.*

15. Looking back, the dog was following us.
    Correct the dangler (the sentence as written says the dog was looking back): *Looking back, we saw the dog following us.*

GRAMMAR *MASTERY TEST ANSWERS*

1. The box of handmade chocolates **is** a gift from **her** and **me**.

2. You speak **as if** I am the one **who** they said is the next great Frisbee player.

3. Instead of **hoarding** the old paintings in the basement, they **hung** them throughout the house.

4. Either of us **is** capable of fixing the fence, but between the two of us, he is probably the **quicker**.

5. Hakeem wants to learn how to play the drums, the piano, and the guitar.

6. Ninety percent of the orders **are** for the German chocolate cake? I **should have** known not to make so much of the pistachio.

7. I want to speak with **whoever** was in charge of the wood-carving contest, because **whomever** they chose did the job **well**.

8. The Midwest is having unusually pleasant weather, and **some** say it could last for months.

9. She is the one **who** [or **that**] told them the article was written about **whoever** swam the English Channel wearing a shark fin.

10. Grover needs to stop broadcasting from pirate radio on Saturday nights—it's starting to **meddle** with Bert and Ernie's walkie-talkie chats.

11. Neither the tin-foil gizmo nor the rabbit-ears antenna **is** going to help much with the reception, I'm afraid.

12. **Whomever** you want to be the team captain will wear the special cape.

13. Zachary does not read books **that** have highlighter marks in them.

14. Rodrigo may not be as strong as **he,** but I'll bet he can still lift those weights.

15. They are no different **from** all of the other players **who (OR that)** want a fair set of rules for pick-up basketball games at the park.

16. For my birthday, Shaynee got me a case of my favorite locally brewed strawberry ale, **which** I enjoy because it always tastes so perfectly **sweet.**

17. **Who** should we say is calling?

18. The elaborate presentation **persuaded** Paolo to buy the ear-cleaning wand even though he wasn't sure he really needed it.

19. The panel will award the ribbon to **whoever** completes the obstacle course first.

20. It will be **they who** are first to enter **into** an agreement.

21. Alberto is **sure** that the moon and the sun will switch places by the year 2072.

22. Luckily, when writing her new story, Anita saved her file before the power went out.

23. **There are** still five more tests to run before the vaccine is approved.

24. The <u>needles</u> and <u>pins</u> are in the tray, and the <u>tacks</u> are in the little jar.

25. You're looking **well** after your cold—your medication must have worked.

26. Rose thinks **whoever** is involved in the project-planning phase will also have a big say in **who** gets the labor contracts.

27. Where should Mason send **this**?

28. The Venusians believe it is you who **are** responsible for the false astrology report.

29. The playoffs will continue <u>even though the league did not complete a full season</u>.

30. Jed appears to be aging **more slowly** than Jeremiah.

31. Either the magician or I **am** going to find your missing rabbit after the show.

32. That **which** one survives can become wisdom passed on to others.

33. Just like all other stars in the galaxy, three-fourths of the new star just discovered **consists** of helium.

34. If the cruise ship voyages any longer, the kitchen's supply of cocktail sauce will go no **further**.

35. **Whoever** left the garden faucet running while we were on vacation owes me a lot of money.

36. Simone acts just **like** her sister whenever she hears something funny.

37. I can't wait to see <u>my old neighbor</u> at the farm when I return <u>to my hometown in ten days</u>.

38. Shoveling the walk after a heavy snow is important. (**OR** After a heavy snow, shoveling the walk is important.)

39. The couple **thinks** that two hundred dollars **is** too much to pay for the ceramic bowl.

40. The custom sailboat was built by Ahab and **me.**

41. Fletcher is looking fit these days—he must be adjusting his diet, exercising, and getting more sleep.

42. Ilyana <u>has been studying</u> Danish for six years now, and she <u>will</u> eventually <u>put</u> it into practice when she <u>travels</u> to Denmark to visit her relatives.

43. You don't smell too **bad** for someone who worked outside all day.

44. The recording engineers have often asked themselves **who** the true source of that tinkling sound was.

45. Uncle Saul wants us to **get off** the porch because he says we're **wreaking** havoc up here.

46. The decision is and always will be **hers.**

47. Controlling **oneself** when faced with disagreement is a mark of maturity. **It's** something I always try to remember.

48. Rae is one of those people who always **look as if** they are ready to have fun.

49. The new arts center, as well as the adjoining Japanese garden, **adds** a welcome touch of cultural beauty near the downtown riverwalk.

50. The smell from the pile has gone from bad to **worse.**

PUNCTUATION, CAPITALIZATION, AND WRITING NUMBERS *PRETEST ANSWERS*

1. Was that delivery on the porch **yours**?

2. Daniel has never been good at **spelling**.

3. **Fifty-two** people became ill on the ship that day.

4. November 4, 2006, was the date of their wedding.

5. One of her **dogs** is in our yard.

6. His house is just **east** of the high school.

7. **Sara** and Darnell's house was damaged by the hail storm.

8. Aiden wondered if you had listened to his podcast.

9. Samir likes all of these outdoor activities: **fishing**, camping, boating, and snorkeling.

10. If you plan to do any online shopping today, please let me know.

11. "Why," she asked, "have you been streaming movies all day?" CORRECT

12. Mom tried making your new chicken recipe, and it was a huge success.

13. Please complete all the paperwork; it is due by tomorrow.

14. "Would you like to go to a baseball game Thursday?" asked Grayson.

15. They recently visited Key West, Florida, and are anxious to go back.

16. Would you, Jordyn, please run an errand for me?

17. Have you ever met her **grandma**?

18. **Forty** trees were planted at the Earth Day celebration.

19. The **town** of Plainfield was recently featured in a magazine.

20. I never received my order; therefore, I am going to call customer service.

21. The speaker at the seminar was Sushama Patel, Ph.D.

22. Oliver responded, "Thank you for the gift."

23. He referred to his cousin as his "frenemy."

24. They enjoyed a fun, relaxing vacation in Jamaica.

25. The store was not well-stocked. They had no milk or eggs. **OR** The store was not well-stocked; they had no milk or eggs. **OR** The store was not well-stocked, and they had no milk or eggs.

26. We wanted guacamole, not queso.

27. Uncle Joe **doesn't** have any interest in hiking with us.

28. There are no off-road vehicles allowed here. CORRECT

29. We held the last meeting on June 30, 2020. **OR** We held the last meeting on the 30th of June, 2020.

30. Julio's food truck is two years old already.

31. Julio already has to repair his two-year-old food truck. CORRECT

32. The treasurer reported there was $18,257 in the account.

33. It was time to bring there [*sic*] boat in for the night. CORRECT

34. Watch out for that nail sticking up!

35. Make sure all the chairs, cushions, towels, **etc.,** are put away before it rains.

36. The **giraffe's** tongue was able to reach all the leaves.

37. **One-half** of the money was donated by one board member.

38. Annika speaks fluent **Japanese** and **English**.

39. That was a nicely written note. CORRECT

40. We need plates, cups, and silverware.

41. Yolanda got up at 4:00 a.m. to catch her plane.

42. You enjoy watching football, don't you?

43. The three sisters went on a pub crawl for their **girls'** night out.

44. I am only available one day next week (Monday). CORRECT

45. Geoffrey, our tour guide, joined us for dinner.

46. The **children's** school bus was late.
47. Mason put sausage, olives, jalapenos, and bacon on the pizza.
48. Brody said, "**Make** sure you don't forget the ice cream!"
49. Mirna Garcia, M.D., is the owner of this office building.
50. There are many things to do there, for instance, swimming and surfing.

COMMAS AND PERIODS *QUIZ 1 ANSWERS*

1. Is it just me, or does the sun look twice its normal size?
2. Umar said he's going to study mathematics, chemistry, art history, and political science.
3. If you're hungry, you can look in the cupboard for crackers, peanut butter and jelly, and raisins.
4. Jakob has written an unlikely dramatic scene in the script. The director wants him to revise it.
5. The computer predicts that on May 7, 2032, all of Earth's surface water will stop moving for exactly one-eighth of a second.
6. Yes, my friend, I will gladly drive you to the kosher deli.
7. The new chief operating officer thinks Landeski, Ohio, is the best place to open a new store branch, but the CEO doesn't agree.
8. Corrine is, after all, the better conditioned of the two climbers.
9. Well, you don't say— that old nickel is now worth a dollar?
10. "Those mountains look menacing," Reiki said, "when the sun no longer shines on them."
11. Aida would have been an only child if her brother, Edward, hadn't been born.
12. Because he is so kind, he will probably be easy to trust. (CORRECT)
13. Zara seriously thinks that's a pearl, not a golf ball?
14. The speakers, which they just purchased, are too big for their stands. (CORRECT)
15. You can buy bracelets, earrings, necklaces, etc., at the jeweler's booth here at the fair.
16. Rocco turned the key. The rocket engine ignited. (**OR** Rocco turned the key, and the rocket engine ignited. **OR** Rocco turned the key; the rocket engine ignited.)
17. After Thea finishes the master's program, she will pursue her Ph.D.

18. Bip Crandall, Jr., hits the ball as far as his father once did.
19. The paper was published in October 1967.
20. Knowing she had little time to spare, her mom, Mila, began to move much faster.

COMMAS AND PERIODS *QUIZ 2 ANSWERS*

1. "Yes," Ting said, "I did see the baby panda at the zoo today."
2. Yes, Mother, I did remember to place the bakery order.
3. Jackson's white cat was born in June 2013 at his farm.
4. Jackson's white cat was born on June 28, 2013, at his farm.
5. Pencils, pens, paper, calculators, etc., will be provided. (CORRECT)
6. I would be hesitant, however, to take the trip alone.
7. He hosted a cowboy-themed party in the big red barn.
8. My oldest cousin, who lives in Detroit, used to be a policeman.
9. The keynote speaker at the conference will be Jonathan Green, M.D.
10. Well, do you think we'll see the sun today?
11. I want to go now, not later.
12. I really enjoyed the show. **T**he acting was superb. **OR** I really enjoyed the show, **and** the acting was superb. **OR** I really enjoyed the show; the acting was superb.
13. She left Albany, New York, on January 18 of that year.
14. I am typing a letter, and she is talking on the phone.
15. You said that I could go, didn't you? (CORRECT)
16. To apply for this job, you must have a Social Security card.
17. He seems to be such a lonely, quiet man, doesn't he?
18. Although my wife hates anchovies, I like them on my pizza.
19. She finished her work and then took a long lunch.
20. I need sugar, butter, and eggs from the grocery store.

SEMICOLONS AND COLONS *QUIZ 1 ANSWERS*

1. The things you need to bring are hiking boots, a backpack, a compass, and water.
2. The walls will be green and yellow; the floor will be brown; and the paintings will be pink, purple, and red. (CORRECT)

3. Helene understands the relationship between scientific theory and scientific method; therefore, she qualifies to participate in the panel discussion.

4. Irene wants a finished patio; Stan wants a finished basement.

5. Logan has visited several European cities, such as Paris, Rome, Vienna, and Budapest.

6. The board wants a new proposal with updated numbers, including, among everything else, the most current budget.

7. They made the announcement: It's a baby girl. (CORRECT **OR** … it's a baby girl.)

8. It's what Jessa always wanted: a Stradivarius violin.

9. Felix has expressed his wishes: start early, stay late, and bring a stress ball to squeeze.

10. Zelda has always wanted to be one of three things: a dentist, an accountant, or a sports agent. (CORRECT)

11. I like the essay; however, the writer could use further study at grammarbook.com.

12. Our road trip south will include Nashville, Tennessee; Atlanta, Georgia; and Miami, Florida.

13. If Freya finishes skating before 9:00 p.m., and I think she will, she will join us at the lobby; and we'll discuss tomorrow's training schedule there.

14. This recipe needs more cumin, garlic, and lemon juice.

15. The truth is out: the Martians' chief diplomat is actually a Venusian spy. (CORRECT **OR** The Martians' …)

16. The band's lead singer, Rikk Vikktor, wants to revise the contract rider for the tour; namely, he wants his own mat and instructor for pre-show yoga and, in the green room, a fully stocked sushi bar.

17. They are a property-management company, not a land developer.

18. Raphael made all of his field-goal attempts: no surprise. (CORRECT)

19. The characters who appeared in The Three Stooges were Moe, Larry, Curly, Shemp, Joe, and Curly Joe.

20. Seek to find; ask to receive; listen to understand. (CORRECT: three independent clauses with understood You/you)

SEMICOLONS AND COLONS *QUIZ 2 ANSWERS*

1. Denise prefers to eat chicken or fish; I'm a vegetarian.

2. The centerpieces had her favorite flowers: roses, carnations, and daisies.

3. While visiting the beach, we saw pelicans, stingrays, and iguanas.

4. On our last trip we stayed in Nashville, Tennessee; Atlanta, Georgia; and Orlando, Florida.

5. Estella landed her dream summer job: She'll be an intern in a senator's office. (CORRECT **OR** she'll)

6. Roberto can't decide among three careers: dentist, veterinarian, or physical therapist.

7. I need to buy shampoo, toothpaste, soap, and contact lens solution.

8. Give her a break; she just started working here two days ago!

9. Max and Sue have been to the Caribbean many times; however, they have not visited St. Lucia.

10. You asked for forgiveness; he granted it to you.

11. The order was requested six weeks ago; therefore, I expected the shipment to have arrived by now.

12. I answered the phone; no one seemed to be on the other end of the line.

13. We have set this restriction: do your homework before watching television.

14. If you can possibly arrange it, please visit us, but if you cannot, let us know.

15. Nature lovers will appreciate seeing whales, sea lions, and pelicans. (CORRECT)

QUESTION MARKS AND QUOTATION MARKS
QUIZ 1 ANSWERS

1. Is the answer "yay" or "nay"**?**

2. "I'll think it over," he said. Then she said, "And may we not grow old while you do." (CORRECT)

3. My so-called **"advisor"** forgot to advise me about the opt-out clause in the agreement.

4. Jake said, "Simone shouted, 'That's it! No more driving with the windows open in winter!' " (CORRECT)

5. Darren tried climbing the clock tower again. I wonder what else is new.

6. That couldn't be the missing diamond, could **it?**

7. "Might the ship have changed course," he said, "or is that just wishful thinking?"

8. "Are you really going to drink that whole carton of cream?" she asked.
9. Jaden likes to pass off rearranging items on shelves as "working." (CORRECT)
10. The last thing anyone heard him say was "I'll be back."

QUESTION MARKS AND QUOTATION MARKS
QUIZ 2 ANSWERS

1. "Have you already completed our survey?" the cashier asked.
2. I wonder why Allen left so early this morning.
3. Do you know the words to "The Star-Spangled Banner"?
4. She said, "T.J. shouted, 'We are not staying at that hotel.' "
5. "Well," she said, "you certainly didn't waste any time."
6. The song asks, "Would you like to swing on a star?" (CORRECT)
7. There was no agreed-upon "rule" among the club members.
8. "I've had it up to here!" she screamed.
9. Do you believe the saying, "It is better to vote for what you want and not get it than to vote for what you don't want and get it"?
10. Betty is the one who found out first, isn't she? (CORRECT)

PARENTHESES AND BRACKETS *QUIZ 1 ANSWERS*

1. If they had wanted to speak with a manager (or somebody similar), they could have spoken with Ray.
2. If all that was left was five dollars, they should have used it on video games instead of the box of cookies. (At least, that's how I see it.)
3. Supposably [sic], the mayor was a trapeze artist before she got into politics.
4. Jackhammer Joe (and, of course, his trusted rusty wrench) fixes people's plumbing all the time. (CORRECT)
5. The reward ($500) seems a little light considering finding the fugitive would require searching the forest with a penlight at night. (CORRECT)

6. Ahmet has requested a second meeting with committee chairman (and local bamboozler) Sid Mackaberry.

7. In 1962, *The Sporting News* reported, "The Yankees' Mickey Mantle and the Giants' Willie Mays are the highest-paid players in major league baseball at $90,000 each [today's highest-paid players make over $30 million]."

8. When Oscar stepped on the scale (he'd already lost nine pounds), he noted he was only six pounds away from his goal.

9. Everyone loves that movie (except me**)**.

10. Autumn (as well as her ever-present gypsy caravan) **is** traveling from city to city to offer food and clothing to the homeless.

PARENTHESES AND BRACKETS *QUIZ 2 ANSWERS*

1. My cousin wrote, "I herd [*sic*] a rumor that Jack and Jennifer are getting engaged."

2. Our first meeting will be held at First Central Bank's community room (Main Street branch).

3. We all decided to go out for pizza after the meeting (except for Dan). (CORRECT)

4. I overheard her say, "Our favorite cousin [she meant Dale] will be accompanying us on our trip."

5. Gerard (and his friend Bertrand) **wants** to have lunch with you tomorrow.

6. After his family came to the United States (settling in Washington state), they became farmers.

7. In the movie, Vanessa exclaims, "Whatever shall I do if he [the sheriff] comes looking for you tomorrow?"

8. Joe called today (**he's** been sick) and said he felt better.

9. Luigi moved to this country shortly after he was born (about 1925). (CORRECT)

10. The first line of his letter said, "My freinds [*sic*], I never thought we would all be together again like this." (CORRECT)

APOSTROPHES *QUIZ 1 ANSWERS*

1. The **men's** locker room is down the hall and up the ramp.

2. I'd really like to go for a ride on the **Thomases'** new boat.

3. It sounds like Linnea is planning a **girls'** weekend with her friends.
4. In the summer of **'69**, I built my first guitar.
5. If it **hadn't** been for Helena's attention to the Spider Man Chia Pet, it **wouldn't** look half as good as it does now.
6. Penelope was excited when she learned her United States visa had been approved. (CORRECT)
7. The **lady's** greatest wish is that her son be able to pursue his dream to be a policeman.
8. **Jack and Jill's** pail of water could really use a refill.
9. The Kellys send greeting cards to everyone for everything, including for their **sisters-in-law's** anniversaries.
10. Do you know if the **Chapmans** have arrived yet?
11. I don't think I've ever seen a me**n's** hat like that one before.
12. **Jimmy's** CD collection is almost all music from the **'80s**.
13. Why did you give that man your last token? The million-dollar jackpot should have been our**s**!
14. The department manager gave the staff the rest of the week off with three days' pay. (CORRECT)
15. Illinoi**s'** changes of season prepare a person to live just about anywhere.

APOSTROPHES *QUIZ 2 ANSWERS*

1. The movie had **its** desired effect.
2. Both of my **brothers-in-law** live near Durango.
3. Those **actresses'** costumes look beautiful on them.
4. She always let me stay up past the other **children's** bedtime.
5. Would that **company's** health plan give you peace of mind?
6. **Doesn't** it seem strange that I didn't see that friend of **yours** anywhere?
7. If it isn't **hers** then **whose** is it?
8. The five injured **sailors'** relatives are waiting outside.
9. Joe Wilson said, "I may be biased, but the **Wilsons'** holiday meals are the best."
10. In some **people's** opinion, Faulkner is too difficult.
11. The two little **birds' feathers** were ruffled.
12. I really felt that I got my **money's** worth.
13. **Jackson** and Janet's home was damaged by a tornado.

14. We looked at some old yearbook photos from '99.
15. Our group had a good time at Sam's **'80s** party. **OR 80's**

HYPHENS BETWEEN WORDS *QUIZ 1 ANSWERS*

1. Is that **custom-made** sandbox really thirty feet wide?
2. Herberto has been school principal since he was **twenty-nine** years old.
3. That vocal sounds **off key** to me.
4. The Muldoons have a **two-hundred-year-old** oak tree in their backyard.
5. The party planner figures that **200-225** people will attend the gala.
6. The sales team is following a **carefully calculated** strategy to gain more share in the main competitor's market.
7. When all else failed, Bryan tried to **super-glue** the door handle back onto the car.
8. Has anyone seen my **high school** yearbook?
9. If anyone is still unsure, I believe Marek has some **more-certain** ideas.
10. Jake spoke with Hambone, and Hambone said that the frat party on top of the police station was a **no-go.** Apparently somebody disapproved.
11. I give him about a **two percent** chance of lifting that **eighty-pound** box.
12. Would you rather it be served in a chalice or in a **12 oz.** cup?
13. It was the number-one play in box-office receipts 2001-2006. (CORRECT)
14. After Josefina married Jonathan Martin, she changed her last name to **Sanchez-Martin.**
15. The park district activated additional crowd-control personnel when attendance at the festival exceeded **three-fourths** capacity.

HYPHENS BETWEEN WORDS *QUIZ 2 ANSWERS*

1. The storm blew down a **seventy-foot-tall** tree last night.
2. The tree that blew down last night was seventy feet tall. (CORRECT)
3. We offer **around-the-clock** coverage.
4. The badly injured fireman was taken to a hospital. (CORRECT)
5. That **two-year-old** is adorable.
6. That child is two years old. (CORRECT)
7. The summer camp was designed for gymnasts 16-18 years old. (CORRECT)

8. The **left-handed** pitcher threw fastballs at almost 100 miles per hour.
9. You certainly have a **go-get-it** nature.
10. It's a **two-hour** meeting, 2:30-4:30 p.m. (Remember: no spaces around hyphens.)
11. My sister is moving from her home next to the **heavily congested** highway.
12. She jumped from a **two-story** building.
13. If we split the bill evenly, we each owe **thirty-four** dollars.
14. If we split the bill evenly, we'll each owe **one-fourth** of the total.
15. **No-parking** rules make little sense on Sundays.

HYPHENS WITH PREFIXES AND SUFFIXES
QUIZ 1 ANSWERS

1. The Griswalds will be returning to Wally World in **mid-August.**
2. If you want to know more about sparring, you could ask the **ex-professional** boxer who works across the street.
3. Beatrice is always ultra-active when she sets her mind to something. (CORRECT)
4. Maybe we should **de-emphasize** the part about having thirty hot dogs but only twenty-five hot dog buns.
5. It takes a while for the crosswalk signal to change, so you don't need to **re-press** the button so much.
6. **Governor-elect** B. Arthur Fife will give his acceptance speech at six-thirty p.m.
7. The park is so pleasant that they revisited it the following day. (CORRECT)
8. The delegates of anti-Bears and anti-Packers are meeting for beers and brats to discuss burying the pigskin once and for all. (CORRECT)
9. David sure looks **self-confident** for somebody who's got just a sling and a few stones, don't you think?
10. The **re-creation** of the pirate ship is an exact replica of the original vessel.

HYPHENS WITH PREFIXES AND SUFFIXES
QUIZ 2 ANSWERS

1. ex-mayor
2. de-emphasized

3. doable
4. non-Jewish
5. self-styled
6. reestablish
7. anti-inflammatory
8. error-free
9. semi-illiterate
10. absenteeism

CAPITALIZATION *QUIZ 1 ANSWERS*

1. Most of my relatives still live in the U.S. **Northwest.**
2. If I could, I would lasso the moon and give it to you. (CORRECT)
3. Randall Rickbob, **team president,** said that pitcher Tom Gunner will be signed to a new four-year deal.
4. Denzel is a **junior** in college.
5. Sarah handed the book to her **grandpa.**
6. This **summer** they want to head **south.**
7. Chester's favorite band is **the** Cure.
8. This semester Fatima plans to study English, **biology, political science,** and **speech communications.** She also plans to take Psychology 102.
9. Claude Monet was an **Impressionist** painter.
10. Director Martin Scorsese has made several films with **writer** Paul Schrader, as well as with **actors** Robert De Niro and Joe Pesci.
11. Here's what she said she needs: **paper,** scissors, markers, tape, and balloons.
12. The **Constitution** refers to a balance and separation of power including an executive branch (led by a president), a legislative branch (**Congress**), and a judiciary branch (**Supreme Court**).

CAPITALIZATION *QUIZ 2 ANSWERS*

1. My **grandmother** lives on Fillmore **Street.**
2. Have you ever visited New England in the **fall**?

3. I will be excited to listen to our **chief executive officer**, Nancy Williamson, speak today in the auditorium.
4. Uncle Walter said, "**Please** use left or right, not **north, south, east**, or **west**."
5. "You must understand," he pleaded, "**that** I need more time to pay you."
6. We saw **director** George Lucas walking down the street.
7. Have you read *Harry Potter* **and the** *Order* **of the** *Phoenix*?
8. We all stood for the **national anthem** before watching **the** New York Mets play **the** Chicago Cubs.
9. The **Supreme Court** unanimously struck down the proposed **constitutional amendment** today.
10. The West, especially California, is famous for its cutting-edge technology. (CORRECT)
11. Adriana is dreading **spring quarter** because she has to take **organic chemistry** and Physics 105.
12. I plead not guilty, **Your Honor**.

WRITING NUMBERS *QUIZ 1 ANSWERS*

1. I have seen *Star Wars* one hundred **thirty-seven** times.
2. You need money? Okay, here's my **seventy-five cents**.
3. The latest census shows that the town's population is **two thousand four hundred sixty-nine**.
4. Kristie was born on June **17**, 1986.
5. The quarterback will probably earn between twenty million and **thirty** million dollars. (OR **20** million and 30 million dollars)
6. 1999 was the first year I bought a cell phone. (CORRECT OR **Nineteen ninety-nine** …)
7. The **eighties** was a golden age of stand-up comedy.
8. Do you ever miss the music from the **1990s**?
9. I get up early for work, so I'm usually in bed by **nine** o'clock.
10. Todd says he'd rather have **one-third** of the gate revenue from the concert than **one-half** of the merchandise sales.
11. Sabrina is **1.2** inches taller than she was nine months ago.
12. The astronomer says the comet will be visible just before or soon after **midnight**.

WRITING NUMBERS *QUIZ 2 ANSWERS*

1. Next week's lottery jackpot is expected to reach between four million and **five million dollars. OR** Next week's lottery jackpot is expected to reach between **4** million and **5** million dollars.
2. The new stadium will hold **43,520** fans.
3. The next meeting of the holiday planning committee will be held on the 31ˢᵗ of October at **noon.**
4. A **two-thirds** majority is needed to pass the measure.
5. The tree grew only **0.5** inches because of the drought.
6. We all agreed. **Twenty-five hundred dollars** is a lot of money.
7. **One-fifth** of the inventory was ruined in the fire.
8. I will be **twenty-one** years old on December 9.
9. We have only received **0.54** inches of rain this year.
10. The tree grew **2 ½** feet after all the rain we had last year.
11. Some people now refer to the **forties** and **fifties** as "mid-century." (**OR** midcentury)
12. Including tax, my new car cost **thirty-two** thousand, six hundred **seventy-two** dollars, **and fifty-seven** cents.

PUNCTUATION, CAPITALIZATION, AND WRITING NUMBERS *MASTERY TEST ANSWERS*

1. No, Johnny, I don't think they sell ice cream at this hardware store.
2. Our **mom** sent us a funny video from her goat yoga class today.
3. Mateo **won't** be able to join us on our annual camping trip this year.
4. We must supply them with the following: **s**oap, hand sanitizer, bandages, and bottled water.
5. You have been playing video games all afternoon, haven't you?
6. We had no idea we would owe additional money; that was not in the original contract.
7. Madison asked, "**Can** we please stop and see the waterfall after lunch?"
8. She was asking if the winery is going to be open tomorrow.

9. January 1, 2024, is the date Grandpa plans to retire from his job at the hospital.

10. **Twenty** vehicles participated in the birthday celebration parade for Kaito.

11. When Mike referred to you as a "slacker," what was he talking about?

12. That stray pit bull running at the baseball field is not **ours**.

13. Buddy and Coco, her two dogs, were looking for plenty of attention.

14. Anton is interested in learning how to cook **French** cuisine.

15. **Thirty-two** volunteers helped out at the food bank on Saturday.

16. Ava was quick to reply, "We had no idea you just got back from London."

17. If you would like to meet with a personal trainer, you may sign up at the front desk.

18. **Mario** and Amber's yard has twelve bird feeders and a koi pond.

19. The used car Kai is buying is a very well-maintained vehicle. (CORRECT)

20. The car Kai is trading in has not been **well maintained**.

21. **One-half** of the pie was already eaten before the appetizers were served.

22. Teagan wants to be a lifeguard this summer, and she is already certified in CPR and first aid.

23. The **chef's** special for today is chili lime salmon with Spanish rice.

24. Dad knows nothing about investment**s**; therefore, he wants to hire a financial planner.

25. Omar is interested in taking online classes in African history and geography in the fall. (CORRECT)

26. "Can you believe it has been ten years since we graduated?" asked Phoenix.

27. Jocelyn and Lina are cousins, not sisters.

28. Diego received a check for **$9,349** from the insurance company to cover the damage.

29. Leon wrote to the homeowners' association complaining they "…had to [*sic*] many restrictions." (CORRECT)

30. The **women's** volleyball league plays here on Tuesday nights.

31. The witnesses to the accident included a law student, an advertising intern, a teacher, and a retired minister.

32. Mrs. Drake is so proud of her **beautifully decorated** garden shed.

33. The baby always takes a nap at 1:00 p.m. **OR** The baby always takes a nap at one o'clock in the afternoon.

34. Drive **north** on Oak St. past the firehouse to get to the zoo.

35. Mei Lee, CPA, is currently working from home instead of her office.

36. We invited the **Silvermans** and the **Browns** to join us this evening.

37. We are invited to the **Browns'** lakeside cabin in July.

38. We **need dog** treats, cat litter, rabbit food, and mealworms.

39. Aunt Helen was born in Dodgeville, Wisconsin, and still lives there.
40. That **eighty-year-old** oak is the oldest tree in Cottersville.
41. Sanjay's aunt will be **eighty years old** this Sunday.
42. She has fond memories of growing up on the farm in the 1970s. (CORRECT; *1970's* is acceptable to some, but the apostrophe is unnecessary.)
43. The funds for the children's wing were donated by Dr. Andre Wilson, **M.D.**
44. The furniture she purchased at the estate sale was fairly inexpensive ($300). (CORRECT)
45. They offer all kinds of children's camp themes, for instance, nature, science, and creative arts.
46. Sharon said, "Delilah shouted, 'I didn't ask for any help!' "
47. We will need to clean, paint, make repairs, etc., before we can move in.
48. Please make sure you are back home before dark!
49. The twins were born on July 30, 2019. **OR** The twins were born on the 30th of July, 2019.
50. This isn't at all what I expected. This place is such a mess! **OR** This isn't at all what I expected; this place is such a mess!

INDEX

GrammarBook.com is your site for helpful rules, real-world examples, and fun quizzes.

Free Online English Usage Rules

Grammar, Punctuation, and Other English Rule Info

- ✓ Finding Subjects and Verbs
- ✓ Subject and Verb Agreement
- ✓ Commas and Semicolons
- ✓ Vocabulary, Spelling, Capitalization, and Commonly Confused Words

Quizzes on Each Topic Covered in the Book

- ✓ Get scored instantly.
- ✓ Explanations for each quiz question.
- ✓ Take interactively or download and reproduce the quizzes.

Premium Subscription Levels!

For Instructors and Employers

- ✓ Unlimited number of student and employee logins.
- ✓ Quiz results tallied and organized in account automatically.
- ✓ Makes grading quizzes and explaining answers a thing of the past.

For Grammar Enthusiasts

- ✓ One subscription works for an entire family, classroom, or office.
- ✓ Take the quizzes online or download and copy them.

www.GrammarBook.com